THE THEATRE OF

GARCIA LORCA

ROBERT LIMA

THE THEATRE OF
GARCIA LORCA

LAS AMERICAS PUBLISHING COMPANY
NEW YORK   1963

Published and Distributed by:
LAS AMERICAS PUBLISHING COMPANY
152 East 23rd Street
New York 10, New York

Printed in the United States of America
by
CHARLES PRESS, INC.

TO MY PARENTS

with all the thoughts
a dedication implies.

PREFACE

Although the poet may be thought of as literature's ostrich because of his primary concern with subjective writing, as opposed to the objective brand, he, so it usually occurs, has chosen to keep his head in the ground of subjectivism to preserve unimpaired his vision—to him far greater and more worthwhile than the apparent loveliness of that which surrounds his world. He has, nonetheless, often tried to present himself to the world in other guises; the most sought after "other life" has been that of the dramatist. The list of such transference is extensive, including the names of many outstanding poets: Eliot, Yeats, Hoffsmanthal, Browning, Claudel, McLeish, Fry, Auden, Cummings, Apollinaire, Gil Vicente, William Carlos Williams, Pound and many others.

Generally, the poet has approached the theatre as a poet and not as a dramatist. He has seldom realized the intricacies that characterize good drama, and therefore has undertaken to invent a drama by placing poetic dialogue within a framework of action. The results have been, for the most part, unsatisfactory as drama though their value as dramatic poetry can seldom be questioned. In seeking to approach the theatre, the poet has lost sight of the art of the form he strives to employ. He fails to realize that for poetry to enter the realm of the theatre successfully, and not become merely dramatic poetry, it must be blended carefully with the theatre's techniques. In short, it must become theatrical. Rather than dramatic poetry or poetry in the theatre, the poet's creation must become *poetic drama*. Then the word *poetic* attains the standing of an adjective, becoming a contributor rather than the principal agency.

In the case of Federico Garcia Lorca's drama the affiliation is most effectively achieved. But this only occurs after his drama has gone beyond that point where most others terminate. It was necessary that Lorca's theatre first entertain the dramatic weaknesses of *El maleficio de la mariposa* and *Mariana Pineda;* these served as the first important outlets for his dramatic imagination and allowed him to experiment with poetry in the dramatic medium. The lessons he learned were not in vain. His dramatic writing began to attain a fuller maturity with his vivid *La Zapatera Prodigiosa* and *El amor de don Perlimplin*, which resulted from the earlier puppet farces. *Asi que pasen cinco años* and *Doña Rosita* attest to an even greater understanding of theatricality, while the tragic trilogy *Bodas de sangre, Yerma,* and *La casa de Bernarda Alba* reveals fully the heights to which poetic drama could rise.

This book has as its object the presentation of what was previously unavailable in English—a complete study of Garcia Lorca's theatre. Unlike other works which deal with the entire scope of his productivity and thereby tend to minimize his theatre, this study will concentrate only on the plays, analyzing each under several critical, historical and biographical microscopes. All of Lorca's known theatrical writings—lectures, interviews, letters—have been called upon to substantiate the views his plays disclose, as have the pertinent observations of his many companions and co-workers. The study, then, serves also as a compendium of critical opinion and personal reminiscences.

The book has been sectionalized for convenience. Its three main parts are supplemented by an extensive bibliography dedicated solely to Lorca's theatre. It contains pertinent materials, such as adaptations of texts for operas and ballets, not formerly included in any such compilation, acquired with the assistance of Townsend Brewster.

While the biographical section is not intended to be an elaborate re-telling of the events in Lorca's life, it does consider the major moments of his creative career and the influence of people, places and things on the impressionable playwright. Wherever appropriate, these factors are related to the plays he produced. The matter of biography is not intended to be complete, except where it concerns Lorca as a playwright, nor can it be until much of the conjecture on his life is replaced by fact.

All translations, textual and otherwise, are mine unless indicated. The originals of these can be found in the book or article cited in the pertinent footnote. As these Spanish sources are generally available through libraries or specialized book shops, it is unnecessary to include the originals here.

It is one of the aims of this study to better acquaint the public with Garcia Lorca's theatre. Since much of his dramatic production has yet to appear in print in English or, if it has appeared, is no longer available, I have chosen to translate large segments of his plays. This, it is hoped, will serve to create a better understanding and, therefore, appreciation of the playwright.

In acknowledgment, I would like to thank Francisco Garcia Lorca of Columbia University for our conversations which clarified several points; Eugenio Florit of Barnard College; Walter Starkie, author and lecturer; Gonzalo Sobejano of the University of Cologne; Julio Garcia Morejon of the University of Assis, Brazil; and Robert M. MacGregor of New Directions for their attentive correspondence when this work was first begun. To Richard A. Duprey, Professor of Drama, and to Dr. B. J. Bedard, Professor of English, both of Villanova University, goes my gratitude for the reading of the manuscript and the many helpful suggestions, as well as for their enthusiasm and encouragement.

Robert Lima

New York, N.Y.
1962

CONTENTS

BIOGRAPHY
I
The Life of Federico Garcia Lorca
(1)

THEATRE
II
"El maleficio de la mariposa"
("The Spell of the Butterfly")
(55)

III
"Los titeres de Cachiporra"
("Three Puppet Plays")
(67)

IV
"Mariana Pineda"
(96)

V
"La Zapatera Prodigiosa"
("The Marvellous Shoewife")
(120)

VI
"El amor de don Perlimplin"
("The Love of Don Perlimplin")
(141)

VII
"Asi que pasen cinco años"
("When Five Years Pass")
(157)

xi

VIII
"Bodas de sangre"
("Blood Wedding")
(188)

IX
"Yerma"
(217)

X
"Doña Rosita la soltera"
("Doña Rosita, the Spinster")
(241)

XI
"La casa de Bernarda Alba"
("The House of Bernarda Alba")
(263)

CONCLUSION
XII
A Summation of Garcia Lorca's Theatre
(289)

BIBLIOGRAPHY
"Federico Garcia Lorca—A Bibliography of His Theatre"
(301)

INDEX
(333)

BIOGRAPHY

I. THE LIFE OF FEDERICO GARCIA LORCA

THE SHORT LIFE of Federico Garcia Lorca, renowned dramatist and poet of Spain, is fraught with many inconsistencies and errors as to factual matters. Many of these are attributable to well-meaning friends whose memories are not as consistent as biography demands. Then, too, there is a regrettable wealth of "folklore" which had its first publication in the days and months following Lorca's death and which grew with each so-called disclosure. Even the subject is chargeable for he was always reluctant to speak of his personal life and to assert or deny statements about it. Consequently, even a basic fact like his date of birth has become controversial with at least five prominent contenders.

The most impressive of these is that espoused by Francisco Garcia Lorca, the playwright's brother. The date—June 5, 1898—is likewise accepted by the editors of the definitive edition of Lorca's complete works, *Obras Completas*.[1] On the other hand, it is curious to note the variety of dates proposed by other writers. F. Vazquez Ocaña, for example, who is the most recent biographer of the playwright, cites June 11, 1898, on the basis that:

> ...in the parish register of "Nuestra Señora de la Anunciacion" in Fuentevaqueros, where he was baptized by Rev. Gabriel Lopez Barranco, the date of his birth is June 11, 1898.[2]

Arturo Barea, an outstanding Lorca critic, gives another variation when he proposes June 15, 1899 as the date. Roy Campbell, a poet in his own right, has entered the lists with January 5, 1899. The last, Edwin Honig, another notable critic, seems to bridge the main camps when he estimates

---

1. Federico Garcia Lorca, *Obras Completas* (Madrid, Aguilar, 1957).
2. Fernando Vazquez Ocaña, *Garcia Lorca* (Mexico, D. F., Editorial Grijalbo, 1957), p. 32.

1

that June 5, 1899 is the correct date. But Lorca's secrecy—whether intended or sincere—remains the only positive factor:

Lorca was a man of curious shynesses (he was rather evasive about the date of his birth, for example).[3]

It is unusual, too, that the man whose birth was somewhat obscured by his own doing should have died in circumstances to which, to say the least, a great aura of mystery has attached.

The other facts of Lorca's early life are not tinged by the same vagueness characteristic of his birth and death. The only problems arise when facts are conspicuously missing from what would otherwise be the ideal pattern of biography. He was born in the small village of Fuentevaqueros, not far from the city of Granada—the very city which was to be his glory and his downfall. Both his father and mother were well-read and well-to-do people, typical of the Spanish Catholic tradition, and parents of four children—Isabel, Concha, Francisco and Federico. Lorca's father, Don Federico Garcia Rodriguez, was a landowner of stature in the community, and his holdings were of considerable size as evidenced by the family's lands in the country as well as in the city. Doña Vicenta Lorca, his mother, had been a schoolteacher until the time of her marriage to the widowed Don Federico. It was at her hands that the young Federico Garcia Lorca[4] received his early education.

His growing years are important in more than the usual way. When he was two months old, Federico was taken very ill. The exact nature of the illness is not reported but it is known that this primary contact with the evil of the world retarded the boy's normal growth so that it was not until he was three that he began to speak. He did not walk

---

3. A. L. Lloyd, *Lament for the Death of a Bullfighter* (London, Heinneman Ltd., 1937), p. xiii.
4. Lorca is properly the mother's maiden name. Spanish custom necessitates using the mother's maiden name after that of the father.

until he was about four. Curiously enough, the boy did hum the songs that he heard around the house. As his life went on he recovered, to all appearances, fully and if in later life he was to have any marks from this bout with disease, it was only a very slight impediment in his walk, hardly noticeable.

Though never really out of his mother's tutorial influence, young Federico's education was left in the hands of Antonio Rodriguez Espinosa, friend of the family and local teacher. But all his education was not of the formal sort. Federico was an active and curious child whose interests were boundless. This lack of passivity made him:

> ... adopt a contemplative attitude which would enhance his imaginative capacity; he paid much attention to the external world, thus stimulating his tender perception of the small and delicate in nature and art, characteristic of Granada.[5]

One of the main-streams of this informal education was a peasant serving woman, Dolores, Francisco Lorca's nurse, who held the young children spell-bound with her folk tales, taught them the popular and salty speech of the peasant and gypsy, and sang them the ballads that had been handed down by word of mouth for hundreds of years in the tradition of the people. She awoke in Federico the deep love and hunger he was to manifest in later years for all that was Spanish.

With Dolores, Federico played games that were at once nonsensical and indicative of his future vocation. Out of his own savings, his brother reports, Federico bought a puppet theatre in a Granada shop. This led to his inventing plays with which to bring life to his little theatre. Dolores was the natural talent who helped him in carrying out his schemes. She and the other servants dressed as he pleased, acted out the parts he gave them, even formed an attentive and awed

---

5. R. M. Nadal, "Introduction," in *Poems, Federico Garcia Lorca* (Oxford, Oxford University Press, 1939), pp. vii-viii.

audience at the sermons he often delivered while acting out the Mass. Dolores often wept real tears during Federico's fiery utterances. Such was his power over these peasants. Perhaps these simpler folk felt the greatness and mystery that were to characterize Lorca's writings. But this must be a matter of conjecture. Along with these theatrical ventures of his early age, Federico also filled the role of impresario-director-actor in his "public" presentations of puppet plays. His audience—the servants and the village children.

This was his life in Fuentevaqueros. It was a good life for the young Federico. His father and mother endowed him with the love of music and good books, particularly *Don Quixote*. Dolores taught him the songs of Andalucia and Spanish tradition. And Federico devoured all with an insatiable appetite. Yet, there was little, if anything, to proclaim that a genius had been born in the person of Federico Garcia Lorca. The boy was normal—enthusiastic and talented, yes, but never showing the traces of abnormality that often accompany genius. His games were not those of other local boys, but neither were those local boys brought up in the love and respect for good music and books. Those evening hours which the family devoted to reading, to attending plays, to group singing accompanied by Don Federico's guitar, could not but be reflected in the way young Federico played, and in the way Garcia Lorca wrote.

With the passage of time came a change in scenery for the young Lorca. The family moved to Granada. His education was continued at the "Colegio del Sagrado Corazon de Jesus" in that city, where the pace of his studies was, no doubt, enlivened by the introduction of the greater part of the works of Cervantes and Victor Hugo. His first acquaintance with the latter had been in his own home since his paternal grandfather, Don Enrique Garcia, had been an avid reader of Hugo whose interest in that author was proclaimed in a sonnet advising future readers to beware of bad translations of the master's works. Cervantes, of course, was no stranger to Federico who had read *Don Quixote* as one of his first books.

The climate of Granada was perfect for Federico. Here he was close to the ancient subtleties of Arabic culture; he was intimate with the remnants of Roman and Greek civilizations; he was conversant with that most enigmatic life of all—that of the gypsy.

To Lorca the gypsy was the embodiment of the free spirit of man, the closest person to that mystic existence he longed for and sought after all of his life. While he lived in Granada he was closer to them than he would ever again be. He stayed with them, often writing his poetry among them, learning their speech and their soulful chants, painting them in his own mind forever. A gypsy dancer, Lola Medina, has given a rare portrait of the young Lorca in search of the muse:

"... In this very corner we are sitting in, Federico used to come to write his poems. That was when he was very young, perhaps eighteen or so, and nobody knew of him. I was thirteen then, when I first met him. He knew us all on the Sacromonte but I like to think he had a special fancy for me. He'd bring me sweets or money or food whenever he came, but he'd never just give it to me—always he'd make me dance for my *regalito*. He loved asking questions—about my mother and father, how they'd treated me and what they said, stories about the family, what we gypsies thought about this and that, and he'd make me teach him words of our language, *Calo*. He'd go away often for months at a time but I always knew he would turn up again. . . . And all this time he'd often come up to spend an hour or two in my cave when I wasn't there, and I'd ask him 'Federico, why do you come to my cave when you have your beautiful home in the valley?' and he'd say that he was writing poems for us gypsies and he liked to write in my cave, and, as I say, it was on a wooden chair in this corner that he wrote."[6]

---

6. Michael Swan, "Lorca's Gypsy," *The Atlantic Monthly*, vol. CXCIV, No. 3, (September, 1954), p. 37.

But Federico did not concentrate only on this search. After his studies in the Jesuit school, he enrolled, at his father's insistence, at the University of Granada and pursued studies for a career in the law. Pursued is too strong a word. Garcia Lorca showed no interest in this line and soon abandoned it for studies more in keeping with his talents— music, painting, literature. His earlier studies in piano now proved worthwhile. As a pianist he excelled, and because of this brilliance he was noticed by Manuel de Falla, the prominent composer, who took Lorca under his patronage. Under this guiding spirit Lorca profited in many ways. Falla was greatly interested in the backgrounds and antecedents of modern Spanish music, and in Lorca he found a person of similar bent. Together they penetrated into many of the crevices of the popular song and brought new light to a long-neglected art form. The closeness of this association between Lorca and de Falla was to develop into a deep friendship rooted in companionship and common artistic endeavor. It was with Falla that Lorca was later to present many puppet plays and musical interludes at functions jointly sponsored throughout Spain.

Lorca's knowledge of Spain was further enhanced through a long journey in the interior under the guidance of Martin Dominguez Berrueta, the distinguished Professor of the History of Art at the University of Granada. Together with other students of similar interest, Lorca experienced a new and definitely impressive feeling. He, for the first time, felt like a real Spaniard. No longer was Spain's beauty, life and history a mystery of the printed page. Now it was a reality that would prove unforgettable. This extensive journey resulted in an important first publication, a small but valuable book, *Impresiones y paisajes*,[7] which was more than a good travel guide. The poetry of its phrasing and the selec-

---

7. Federico Garcia Lorca, *Impresiones y paisajes* (Granada, Impr. de Paulino Ventura, 1918).

tivity it showed were good indications of a talent worthy of observation.

This talent had already manifested itself in other concrete ways—music, poetry and especially reading. It would seem that he devoured the works of nineteenth century Spanish Romantics, the Latin-American Modernists, Spanish contemporaries, Shakespeare, the French Symbolists and the classics of both Spain and Greece. He did not read haphazardly. The counsel of parents, friends and teachers was heeded, but always supplemented by his avid curiosity. The earliest poems he produced were patterned on favorite authors. Thus, he served his apprenticeship.

The young Federico, anxious to absorb the richness of his native Granada, joined "El Centro Artistico" in that city and there published his first article in 1917[8] on the occasion of the centennial of the birth of Zorilla y Moral, nineteenth century poet-dramatist. During this association with "El Centro," he gave many readings of his poetry and recitals of the folk tales he had collected through his young years, now comprising a formidable collection rich in tradition and extremely varied in theme. Lorca's presence in the intellectual life of the city is not something that has been manufactured by zealous Lorquians in order to give stature to his early years; it is a fact that his talents were recognized even by the older cultural leaders of Granada, and that his age was no impediment to the influence he had on the literary circles therein.

Perhaps the most influential of Lorca's patrons of this period was Fernando de los Rios, then President of "El Centro Artistico," who was later to become a famous jurist in Republican Spain. His first interest in Federico was kindled the night that he heard the young poet play a Beethoven sonata on the piano. Recognizing the rare talent before him, he undertook to help in its development. Lorca

---

8. F. Garcia Lorca, "Fantasia simbolica," *Boletin del Centro Artistico y Literario de Granada,* Granada (1917).

always acknowledged this guidance, often recognizing it to be one of the important elements in decisions on his art. One of these turning points in his career, a move which was to prove of great magnitude in Lorca's growth as the artistic leader of his generation, was recommended by Fernando de los Rios. The suggestion was that Garcia Lorca journey to Madrid and enroll at the university there. This Lorca did, joining the intellectual groups which had made the "Residencia de Estudiantes" their own.

The Spring of 1919 finds Garcia Lorca at his new home in Madrid. On and off his stay there would extend itself through 1928. The influence of this center of culture on the young writer was beyond evaluation simply because it was the intangible creative atmosphere there rather than actual courses of study which did most to influence Lorca. It was there that he met and formed deep friendship with Juan Ramon Jimenez and Gregorio Martinez Sierra, two of the lights of Spanish letters; with Luis Buñuel and Salvador Dali, the earliest leaders of ultraism and surrealism; with painters, poets, philosophers, musicians. This contact with the leaders of the past generation as well as with those of the new movements was mutually fruitful to all concerned for the genius and affability of the young Lorca were indeed beacons of attraction to all who came into association with him. It was never a case of the inexperienced seeking after or borrowing from the masters, but rather an active exchange of views, theories, works. Such was the system devised by the "Residencia."

Where the "Institucion Libre de Enseñanza" had been founded in 1898 by Giner de los Rios and other liberal-minded professors to promote wider education in a highly restrictive Spain, 1910 had been the year for the establishment of the "Residencia" by Alberto Jimenez. It was the direct descendant of the "Institucion," manned and guided by many already famous names in the world of letters and philosophy—Ortega y Gasset, Azorin, Pio Baroja, Perez de

Ayala, Antonio Machado, Juan Ramon Jimenez, Unamuno. These were largely the names of the "Generacion del '98." Because of the impetus that led to its founding—the intellectual and political turmoil of the times required new outlooks, better Europeanization of Spain, more opportunites to all—and because of a quickly-acquired reputation, the college was drawing to itself the best intellects in Spain and France. The influence of this select academy radiated not only through the literary and artistic worlds, but likewise spread through sectors of lower education. Its influence was complete.

Lorca matured rapidly in this ambient. But his maturity came about through a process largely divorced from the "academic" lines as they are usually considered; he became immersed in the literary life of Madrid to such an extent that he ignored many of the lectures offered at the "Residencia," eventually abandoning the idea of obtaining a degree there. Later this decision was somewhat reversed when, for no apparent reason, he completed his studies for the law at the University of Granada and received his degree in 1923.

As has been seen, the "Residencia" provided a meeting-ground for poets, painters, playwrights, musicians and philosophers; Lorca was perhaps more attracted by the stimulus of a conversation with his colleagues than he was by the formal proposals of the classroom. In view of his later achievements, and those of his contemporaries, it is hardly fair to condemn this position. Among those who knew Lorca well, and who would continue to be his friends until the end, was Salvador Dali. The Dali of these early years, confused, egoistic and volatile, knew the attraction that Lorca possessed and in his way—rebellious and antagonistic—he was led along, like the rest, to the poetic world of the Andalucian.

The personality of Federico Garcia Lorca produced an immense impression on me. The poetic phenomenon in its entirety and "in the raw" presented itself before me suddenly in flesh and bone, confused, blood-red, viscous and sublime, quivering with a thousand fires of darkness and of subterranean biology, like all matter endowed with the originality of its own form. I reacted, and immediately I adopted a rigorous attitude against the "poetic cosmos." . . . And when I felt the incendiary and communicative fire of the poetry of the great Federico rise in wild, dishevelled flames, I tried to beat them down . . .[9]

Poets were the primary participants in the Lorquian cult. These numbered many now famous names—Jorge Guillen, Rafael Alberti, Pedro Salinas, Gerardo Diego and Damaso Alonso. These close friendships, however, did not have the effect upon Lorca's writing which may well be imagined. He could not be more than a little influenced by his contemporaries, having always his own ideas and his personal way of arriving at them. Where many of the younger poets, some of them those mentioned, were practicing with the new forms borrowed from the French poets by Ruben Dario, and others were consciously rebelling against these very forms, Lorca wrote with an eye to revitalizing the ancient forms of Spanish poetry. He sought out the ballad pattern and the traditional stanzas of the Moors, he looked to the gypsy for inspiration, and to all of Spain for his subject matter. Where innovation was the keynote and others tried to achieve it diversely, Garcia Lorca became the leading innovator by *modernizing* the traditional values in Spanish literature. He was the most creative while being the most traditional and Spanish of all his contemporaries.

During the early part of his stay at the "Residencia" Lorca published only scantily. A few poems appeared in magazines. The most notable was *Balada de la placeta*.[10] However, his reputation as a poet grew, not in the usual

---

9. Salvador Dali, *The Secret Life of Salvador Dali,* trans. by Haakon M. Chevalier (New York, Dial Press, 1942), p. 176.
10. *Antologia de la Poesia Española* (Madrid, Novela Corta, 1919).

manner through the printed word, but in the mysterious circumstances of word-of-mouth. His poetry became well-known and admired in literary circles throughout Spain even before any of his poems appeared in print. His poems, first recited by Lorca at poetry readings in the "Residencia" and elsewhere in Madrid, were passed on through his listeners.

When Lorca found an encouraging audience who would listen to his poems and improvisations for hours at a time, he had no concern for publication. The way of the old troubadors—communication through enactment, through word-of-mouth—was more satisfactory. From the time of his beginnings as a lyric poet, he had the urge for dramatic representation that found full expression later in his writings for the theatre. The full flowering of his personality was essential to the growth of his art.... Thus the phenomenon arose, rare in contemporary literature, of a new poetic art appearing without the intermediary of publication.[11]

Along with his poetic development, Lorca was coming of age as a dramatist. His childhood games had not been in vain, nor had they been deserted as a child deserts old toys for new ones. His miniature theatre, his rough puppets, his fiery "sermons" had been but put aside temporarily. This early interest in theatre suddenly took definite form in 1920. On March 22nd of that year Lorca's first known play was premiered in Madrid at the "Teatro Eslava" under the direction of Martinez Sierra. Its title: *El maleficio de la mariposa*. Originally it had been titled *La menor de las comedias*, but upon the suggestion of Martinez Sierra the title was changed to assure better publicity. The production was unsuccessful, being greeted largely by laughter, whistling and rhythmic handclapping, but it did preview the power of the young writer in another medium and gave promise of that achievement which was to be his in later years as a result of the

---

11. Edwin Honig, *Garcia Lorca* (Norfolk, New Directions, 1944) pp. 8-9.

perfect blending of poetry and theatre. The play ran only one night. The same theatre, on whose stage Martinez Sierra presented the plays of Moliere, Shakespeare, Goldoni, Shaw, Ibsen and Barrie, closed its doors that evening upon the only performance of Lorca's first play.

The following year, 1921, Lorca published his first book of poems, *Libro de poemas*, verses which were written at the same time as *El maleficio de la mariposa*. Madrid took little notice of another collection of poems among so many, but the publication of this book showed that the poet was no longer hesitant to have his work circulated more widely. Later that year two of his poems, *El jardin de las morenas*, and *Suite de los espejos*, appeared in *Indice*, an important journal of poetry founded and edited by Juan Ramon Jimenez.

It must be remembered that most of this period in Lorca's life was spent at the "Residencia" in Madrid, and that the various literary movements of the day—dadaism, ultraism and surrealism—where very noticeable in that sphere. It has been suggested in many studies of Lorca that, because of his associations with participants in these movements, he was one of them. Such is not the case nor is the reverse true. Lorca was always on a different plane. This is not to say that he rejected any or all of these literary phases so as to dedicate himself to a purist traditionalism. Garcia Lorca was too aware of that around him, too curious and absorbing a person to let anything evade him. His work of later years bears this out. He absorbed these modern ideas, digested them fully, and let his subconscious store the best of this selection for future reference. If there is one point that is obvious in the poetry and drama of Lorca, it is that they are fluid—variable, non-conforming in influence, never of one seed. Through the use of new forms and new interpretations garnered in these years of exposure to the avant-garde, Lorca was able to arrive at a completely valid, yet new, interpola-tion of traditional elements of Spanish culture. This applies equally to the plays as to the poetry. Lorca's interests were

simultaneous rather than mere phases in a career. He prac-
ticed music and painting along with poetry and drama.

> His poetical transformation of gypsy chants and ballads,
> which is the fruit of those years, shows that he had
> learned from modern symbolist poetry, with its stress
> on the image instead of the narrative content.[12]

In June of 1922, he and Manuel de Falla organized a
folk-music festival in their native Granada. The idea was
to give tribute to the great tradition of the gypsy—*the cante
jondo*.[13] By presenting a well-organized celebration featuring
the best available proponents of this art, Falla and Lorca
made the festival a success. The following January Lorca and
Falla again collaborated. The new venture, though not as
ambitious as the first, had an equal reception. The program
of "The Children's Festival" in Granada included two plays
with music: the first, a short piece by Cervantes; the other,
a puppet play—*La niña que riega la albahaca y el principe
pregunton*—and old tale with dialogue and musical adaptations by Lorca.

The poet was again moving along the road to the drama.
In the period of 1923-1925 Lorca accomplished much in the
realm of playwriting. Although he continued with his poetry
(his interest and concentration on other endeavors was also
constant), he explored the theatre as a further outlet for his
creative intuition. These years represent work on two important dramas in his catalogue of theatrical productivity.
By 1924 he had conceived the idea for *Doña Rosita la soltera*
and written parts of this drama, and in January of 1925 he
completed *Mariana Pineda*, one of his most popular plays.
Later that same year he read the final version of the latter
play to Salvador Dali and his sister, Ana Maria, who in the

---

12. Arturo Barea, *Lorca: The Poet and His People,* trans. by Ilsa
    Barea (N.Y., Grove Press, 1949), p. xiii.
13. A highly complicated and ancient Andalusian gypsy musical
    form, primarily vocal, using rhythmic hand-clapping to accentu-
    ate its soulful chant.

earlier days of Lorca's career were influential and critical friends.

Canciones, a new book of poems, was finished in 1924. It contained poems written between 1921 and 1924, prior to the *Romancero gitano* also commenced at this time. Published at the instigation of friends, as was the case with most of Lorca's poetry, *Canciones*[14] was well received and a second edition followed in 1929. As can be seen in these poems, the poet was never far from the dramatist or the artist or the musician. Work on one project would often overlap into another resulting in mixed influences within the whole of his work.

His productivity never in question, Lorca wrote constantly, perfecting poems, developing old ideas or preparing new plots for his drama. Two major poems were published in 1926: *Oda a Salvador Dali* and *Reyerta de gitanos.* There is evidence that his brief scene, *El paseo de Buster Keaton,* was completed at this time for, in a letter to a friend, Lorca writes:

> "Everything I write now is long; but I'm preparing various dialogues in prose which will fit well into *La Gaceta. Dialogue of Buster Keaton,* a photographic dialogue, etc. I prefer to publish prose. I'm sending several prose essays to *Revista de Occidente,* and in *La Gaceta* I would like to make my debut this way."[15]

By the end of 1926, the playwright had conceived the idea for *La Zapatera Prodigiosa.*

The following year, Lorca began the most active period of his life. Hardly a month passed that he was not represented in a magazine by a poem or article, in the book market by a collection of poems, or in the theatre by a new play. The dates June 25 through July 2 were of double im-

---

14. Federico Garcia Lorca, *Canciones* (1921-1924), (Malaga, Litoral, 1927); (Madrid, Revista de occidente).
15. *Obras Completas, op. cit.,* p. 1568; letter to Guillermo de Torre, Granada, ("before March, 1927").

portance to Lorca because they marked his return to the
professional theatre, and because they also heralded the first
public exhibition of his drawings. The joint opening of the
exhibit at the "Galeries Dalmau" and the production of
Mariana Pineda in Barcelona were well received. The impetus for the showing of Lorca's drawings came from a group
of artists headed by Salvador Dali. Margarita Xirgu enacted
the role of Mariana at the "Teatro Goya." After a summer
hiatus, the play was taken to Madrid in October where it
opened at the "Teatro Fontalba" to public acclaim.

Having accomplished a successful return to the theatre,
Lorca journeyed to Granada. Several projects demanded his
attention, among them a celebration to honor Luis de Gongora, the Golden Age imagist, on the 300th anniversary of
his death. Lorca wrote and delivered a paper on the occasion:
La imagen poetica de don Luis de Gongora. The final months
of 1927 also ushered in an attempt on the part of Lorca to
publish a magazine that would serve as an incentive and a
showcase for his unpublished friends in Granada. But finan-
cial difficulties and delay in the preparations of the material
led to postponement of the venture, so that it was not until
1928 that Lorca could write with satisfaction:

"We have finally published, here in Granada, the young
writers' magazine, *Gallo*."[16]

As a gesture of recognition to the young poets, Lorca had
obtained material from his friends for inclusion with theirs.
Originally, the idea had been that only their work appear
therein, but the troubles encountered prior to publication had
changed this viewpoint. The names of established poets, playwrights and painters within the covers of the magazine would
aid the young unknowns in their search for recognition. And
so the second issue of *Gallo* appeared in April with two of
Lorca's short scenes: *El paseo de Buster Keaton* and *La*

16. *Ibid.*, p. 1588; letter to Sebastian Gasch, Granada (January 20,
    1928).

doncella, el marinero y el estudiante. A third playlet: *Quimera,* was to be included in the third issue, but *Gallo* had to be discontinued.

The following June 15th, in an interview with Ernesto Gimenez Caballero in *La Gaceta Literaria,* Lorca disclosed that he planned on presenting his puppet theatre, *Los Titeres de Cachiporra,* as soon as time allowed. The interview also revealed the completion of another play, *El amor de don Perlimplin con Belisa en su jardin.* The September publication of *Mariana Pineda* in *La Farsa,* a Madrid periodical, assured the survival of the play. But *Don Perlimplin* was not as fortunate. Although it was announced by Magda Donato, producer at "La Sala Rex," the Madrid production under Cipriano Rivas Cherif's direction never went beyond the rehearsal stage.[17]

But in spite of this theatrical activity, Lorca did not desert his other means of expression. His music and art were always at hand, if not in formal expression then at the service of his friends, who enjoyed his piano renderings and the occasional drawings he would include with his letters. The poet, too, continued writing verse, and published one of his major books of poems, *El Primer Romancero Gitano,* in 1928. It contained works created between 1924 and 1927. Other poems appeared in *Revista de Occidente* and *L'Amic de les Arts,* a magazine published in Sitges by Catalonian friends, among them Sebastian Gash and Salvador Dali.

Romancero Gitano, as it came to be known, was a hugely successful book. Accepted by intellectuals and the general public alike, it made its author more the poet of his era than he had ever before been. But the plaudits begot an unexpected reaction in the poet. Lorca, though pleased at first, began to resent the sudden fame the book had brought him. He began to experience the disillusionment of the artist who fears he will never again reach the prowess of his acclaimed

---

17. See the chapter on *El amor de don Perlimplin.*

creation. Martinez Nadal, a companion of the poet in those triumphant days, noted the spirit of depression that held Lorca in its grip:

> As the months passed and the popularity of the book (*Romancero*) increased, the poet felt the weight of his own work. This, added to other personal reasons, forced him into the only period of depression in his life. He became sad, sought seclusion, no longer spoke of his plans and, what is more strange, he ceased to recite his poetry.[18]

He delivered some lectures during this time, the most important of which took place in February of 1929 at the "Lyceum Club" of Madrid: *Imaginacion, inspiracion y evasion en la poesia.* But Lorca reached a state of desperation that forced him to leave Spain. The combined forces of artistic negation and personal crisis made the poet a foreigner in his own country. The decision to leave Spain, though unusual considering Lorca's former attachment to it, was not unplanned. His former teacher and friend, Fernando de los Rios, was on his way to New York. Lorca joined him in a move which took him to Paris, London and Scotland. After brief visits there, the tour arrived in New York in the summer of 1929.

Apparently under the counselling of Dr. de los Rios, Lorca took up his residence at Columbia University's John Jay Hall.[19] The academic surroundings of the university were pleasant enough, though noticeably altered from the atmosphere Lorca had known in Madrid's "Residencia." The language barrier and his own disorientation in the presence of New York at first made Lorca more of a social recluse. His contacts with the intellectual life of the city were brief

---

18. R. Martinez Nadal, *op. cit.,* p. xviii. These "personal reasons" were never disclosed by Lorca & the usual inference is that a love affair went awry.
19. Letter from Thomas A. McGoey to Federico de Onis (Feb. 13, 1939) giving the details of Lorca's residence in John Jay Hall, in room 1231.

forays and the sole consolation of the autumnal days was the companionship of a few friends: Angel del Rio, Federico de Onis, Damaso Alonso, Hershell Brickell, Mildred Adams, Ignacio Sanchez Mejias and Andres Segovia. With them he toured Harlem, the Bowery, Coney Island, Brooklyn and the far reaches of the city. Though he did not always understand the strangeness of his surroundings, Lorca did display an interest in them that awakened new sensitivities within his companions. Through his eyes they saw a different New York from that which they had come to take for granted, a city he would attempt to describe in English to the amusement of his friends. Lorca's surrender to the notion that he could never learn the language resulted in his withdrawal from an English course for foreign students—the only course in which he ever enrolled while at Columbia.

It has been erroneously suggested by Angel del Rio, in the introduction to Belitt's book,[20] that New York was the first foreign city visited by Garcia Lorca, and that in itself the experience was an overpowering force which jolted the poet's sensitivities. But the fact that Lorca had traveled extensively through the vastly opposite provinces of Spain and had ventured briefly into Paris, London and the countryside of Scotland contradicts the assumption which del Rio makes.

> During his stay in Paris he quickly grasped the enchantment of France. He spent long hours in the Louvre and lamented not having more time to lose himself in the literary haunts and "meet people." In London, he visited the British Museum and admired the lights of Piccadilly Circus with the pleasure of a provincial.[21]

The traces of these visits to the leading European capitals are not to be found in his writings; however, it is well to note that they did occur because they oblige the inference that Lorca was not abruptly transferred from the pleasant in-

---

20. Ben Belitt, *The Poet in New York* (New York, Grove Press, 1955).
21. Fernando Vazquez Ocaña, *op. cit.,* p. 240.

tellectual and social climate of Madrid to the brusqueness and indifference of New York. To what extent the transplantation was responsible for the prolongation of his acute melancholy is unfathomable, but Lorca had to leave New York temporarily in search of greater peace of spirit. The August of 1929 he spent with acquaintances in Newburg, New York and Eden Mills, Vermont, where he tried to forget what J. B. Trend calls the "mess of his love affairs."[22] That may or may not be correct and Trend recognizes the statement as only a logical theory. Lorca's correspondence with Angel del Rio from Eden Mills (August, 1929) contains this passage.

"I will probably leave Thursday. This is sheltering for me, but I'm drowning in this fog and tranquility which renew my memories in a burning way."[23]

It was during this time that Lorca began to write the poems of New York, impressions later collected under the title: *Poeta en Nueva York*. Several of these pieces were only indirectly concerned with the city as they resulted from Lorca's experiences at Eden Mills and Newburg, but their kinship derives from the similarity of outlook and experience they divulge.

Prompted by the renewal of his sadness, Lorca deserted what he had sought as a haven and returned to Columbia and his friends. Once in New York he became occupied with teaching his fellow students the songs and customs of Spain, entertaining them as best he could with his badly-pronounced English, greatly aided by a clever pantomime born out of necessity. These occasions, as well as the continuation of exploratory treks through New York, served to divest the poet of his burdensome thoughts. His renewed vigor was carried into responsible and important occasions such as the celebration to honor Antonia Merce, "La Argentina," the

---

22. J. B. Trend, *Lorca and the Spanish Poetic Tradition* (Oxford, Basil Blackwell, 1956), p. 7.
23. *Obras Completas, op. cit.*, p. 1603.

famed interpreter of the Spanish dance. Lorca, as one of the central participants, read many of the poems from *Poema del cante jondo* and played his arrangements of traditional songs.[24]

Lorca's "cure" had begun effectively, and the success of the celebration which he had helped to shape contributed to his acceptance of invitations to lecture at Vassar and Columbia. At Vassar his subject was: *Las nanas infantiles;* at Columbia's "Instituto de las Españas" his lecture topic was: *Imaginacion, inspiracion y evasion en la poesia.* But the real proof of Lorca's return to normalcy became evident when he resumed work on *La Zapatera Prodigiosa,* the play he had commenced in 1926.

Although Garcia Lorca was unable to read English or American literature in the originals, he did read several works in translation. Among these were *Manhattan Transfer* by John Dos Passos and Angel Flores' version of T. S. Eliot's *The Wasteland—Tierra Baldia.* The war classic—*All Quiet on the Western Front*—by Erich Maria Remarque was likewise on his list of preferred translations.[25] What interested Lorca most, however, were the poems of Walt Whitman, *Leaves of Grass,* which he read in a Spanish counterpart—*Hojas de hierba.* As a voice not too distant from his own, Whitman's poetry appealed to Lorca. It provided an escape from the imprisoning crisis that kept him in New York. They shared an appreciation of nature that seemed lost to the concrete and steel of New York. The influence of Whitman's poetry on Lorca has been debated, but as most things personal to Lorca it remains a matter of conjecture. Whatever that causation may be, it was strong enough to generate a sincere expression of sentiments in the striking poem, *Oda a Walt Whitman.*[26] And apparently it was Whitman who re-opened

24. Recordings are at Brander Matthews Dramatic Museum of Columbia University.
25. Ben Belitt, *op. cit.,* p. xxx.
26. Federico Garcia Lorca, *Oda a Walt Whitman,* in *Alcancia,* Mexico (1933).

the doors of surrealism to Lorca after Dali and Luis Buñuel had initiated him many years before. That previous contact was expressed in three brief theatre pieces: *Quimera, El paseo de Buster Keaton,* and *La doncella, el marinero y el estudiante* These are no more than self-contained scenes, whimsical and outlandish, but they disclose the very germ which would later develop into a work of such power as *Asi que pasen cinco años,* and lead to the writing of the two extant scenes of *El Publico.* These latter are indicative of this surrealistic tendency in its Whitmanesque expression. Angel del Rio recalls them as incomplete works:

> He also read to us, in addition to his new poems, the play *Don Perlimplin,* which he had revised in New York, and fragments of *The Shoemaker's Prodigious Wife, When Five Years Pass* and *The Public*—the last two of a surrealist character with themes and language close to those in *Poet in New York.*[27]

If Lorca ever completed *El Publico,* there is no evidence of it. All that is available of the play's content, intended as a five-act drama, is an unrelated sequence of two scenes— "Reina Romana" and "Cuadro Quinto"—which makes an objective study impossible. What does exist, however, serves as an indication of the tendencies his drama was encountering:

> *El Publico,* unpresentable drama, with Whitmanesque ideas, is a valiant affirmation full of tormented ingenuity, of some gay truths, of the poet who rebels against certain pressures and prisons of contemporary morality.[28]

The expression of these ideas had received its fundamentals of existence in *Asi que pasen cinco años.* Apparently in *El Publico* Lorca planned a more extensive analysis of society than he had undertaken before. But as far as is discernible, he intended to concentrate on the psychological aspects of

---

27. Ben Belitt, *op. cit.,* pp. xv-xvi.
28. Rafael Solana, "Mapa de afluentes en la obra de F.G.L.," in *Letras de Mexico,* Num. 29 (1938), p. 8.

behaviour rather than on particularized causation as had been his habit of procedure.

It seems to be inspired by the problem of poetic reality and superreality in the theatre and in life. It also reveals in different episodes a vein of perverse and abnormal sensuality which responds to preoccupations which must have tormented him in these years. The characters are creations from fantasy as well as from real life without distinction between them. They all work and speak with the same incoherent automatism. The bloody and violent image abounds, dissolved in humor. The poetic idea of the supplanting of forms, the basis of all surrealist esthetic, is already formulated in the first scene of those published.[29]

This mixture of fantasy and reality through the interchange of form, more advanced than in *Asi que pasen cinco años*, is the basis for the scene titled: "Reina Romana." In it two neutral figures—Figura de Pampano (Vine Figure) and Figura de Cascabel (Bell Figure)—hold a complex dialogue in words and dance which depicts the abstract negation of love. Cruelty and devotion seesaw on the frail fulcrum which divides fantasy and reality, each figure, in turn, adopting both expressions. Finally, another character, the Roman Emperor, enters in search of the one who represents unity in its beautiful nakedness. The Vine Figure sheds his covering and is immediately embraced by the Emperor who thinks he recognizes the figure as that which he sought. The Bell Figure remains alone, denouncing the treason that has been perpetrated by the Vine Figure, as the scene ends.

In the other fragment, "Cuadro Quinto," the reference of the play's title to the public is somewhat explained through the bizarre plot-line. The scene takes place in a theatre wherein various characters from plays are interlaced by the dialogue. Constant reference is made to the theatre public

29. Angel del Rio, "Federico Garcia Lorca," *Revista Hispanica Moderna,* New York, Vol. VI, Nums. 3 & 4 (Julio y Octubre, 1940), p. 240.

which is attacking an enactment of *Romeo and Juliet* wherein the director has substituted a young boy for Juliet. Aware of the deception, the patrons have risen from their seats and stormed the stage. As the noise of the struggle reaches the ears of an old man who is crowned with thorns and nearly naked, his words are those which Christ uttered during his final hours. The two situations, therefore, are brought together through a clever use of dialogue. And when the public kills the real Juliet, the old man utters the last of the seven phrases of Christ—that which He said as He died. A group of students and other assorted characters enter then, and comment on the behaviour of the public.

It would be absurd to attempt an interpretation of the play in the feeble light of these separate scenes. It becomes obvious, nonetheless, that like Lorca, his drama was seeking to escape the bonds of formality and decadence. Through the influence of Whitman and the surrealists, the playwright was able to comment in this manner on the society of his era—cruel and insensitive in most instances in the playwright's eyes.

But escape could not be complete until Lorca had also withdrawn from the stifling atmosphere of New York. In spite of the fact that he had left Spain to forget his triumphs and despairs, the playwright had to return to his mainstream, even if only in a compromise. The opportunity came in the spring of 1930 when Lorca was invited by the "Institucion Hispano-Cubana de Cultura" to lecture in Havana. The expectation of his visit to Cuba had a two-fold effect on Lorca. These opposite emotional aspects are represented in two poems written as Lorca was preparing to leave New York, and which were joined under the heading: *Huida de Nueva York*. The first, *Pequeño vals vienes*, shows Lorca's light-heartedness at the prospect of disembarking on a shore where he could again breathe the air of contentment; the second, *Vals en las ramas*, recalls the futility of life in the city.

Unlike New York, Cuba could and did provide Lorca with

a compatible setting. Introduced to Havana's active life by his old friend, Adolfo Salazar, Lorca became easily acclimated. The attention paid to him by new friends such as the Cuban Negro poet, Nicolas Guillen, and Emilio Ballagas was very helpful in restoring Lorca to his rightful state of mind. Under this new influence he completed two poems begun in New York—*Pequeño poema infinito* and (*La luna pudo detenerse al fin*)[30]—and composed a third, *Son de Negros en Cuba*.[31] Another of his works, a short narrative—*La Degollacion del Bautista*—was also published during his stay in Havana.[32]

Lorca's lectures were very successful. The series consisted of four discussions: *Soto de Rojas*,[33] *Lo que canta una ciudad de noviembre a noviembre, Las nanas infantiles*, and *La teoria y juego del duende*. This last of the lectures is of particular interest in that it is concerned with *duende*, or the strange and undefinable spirit that inspires Andalusian art and tradition. Lorca attempts to put into words, and attempts is the best description by his own admission, the circumstances and manner in which *duende* becomes obvious to the spectator of a dance, song or other serious creative form of Andalusian tradition. Lorca, himself, had experienced the visitation of *duende*, first as spectator and then as a participant:

> "...he (Lorca) told me to dance, told me to wear an Oriental costume I had... I lit some incense and then began to dance. Not flamenco, something much softer than that—Eastern—I love the East. I just stood where I was and danced with my body, my arms and my face— moved my body like a snake. Then something began to come over me in the way it often does when I dance. I felt I was leaving my body, that I wasn't Lola Medina any longer, that I was watching her dance from a corner. And Federico seemed to know what had happened. He

30. The first is dated (January 10, 1930, New York); the second: (October 19, 1929, New York).
31. Published in *Musicalia*, Havana (1930).
32. *Revista de Avance*, Havana (1930).
33. A lecture on the 17th century Spanish poet.

began to speak, not ordinary words, and he didn't seem
to be speaking to me at all. It was like a huge poem that
I couldn't understand, except that he was making it up
as he went along. We went on for what seemed like hours
and got wilder and wilder. Ay, yes, it was real ecstasy.
Then, suddenly, I collapsed and Federico had to pick me
up. We didn't speak for some minutes and then he said,
'Lola, we shall never know whether we've been in heaven
or in hell. We shall never know anything like this
again."[34]

The *duende* which Lorca experienced in the early years of
this account, however, was to visit him often in later life as
attested to by his poetry, be it in its pure form or as an
integral part of his drama. The rich and unusual imagery
which characterizes his work is the expression of Lorca's
duende. Perhaps the greater part was in the poet when he
read his own poems or plays. The sheer magnetism of his
voice, the dedication of his spirit to the words, the inspired
gestures of his hands as he read, have all been remarked
upon by countless friends who would sit for hours in rapt
attention as Lorca recited. They would be transported to
Lorca's world depicted in the story, poem or play. Such
occasions were not rare, for Lorca read often and always with
equal results.[35]

Duende is so typically Andalusian that it defies natural
comprehension and must be relegated to the realm of the
phenomenal. Lorca's lecture on the subject, one of his longest
and most interesting, cites many examples of *duende* and
definitions of the same, among them:

"... Manuel Torres, the man with the greatest culture
in the blood whom I've known, spoke this splendid phrase
while listening to Falla play his own *Nocturno del Generalife*: 'Everything which has black sounds has *duende*.' And there's no greater truth.
    These black sounds are the mystery, the roots which

---

34. Michael Swan, *op. cit.*, p. 38. Interview with Lola Medina.
35. See accounts of many of these readings in Carlos Morla Lynch,
    En España con Federico Garcia Lorca (Madrid, Aguilar, 1957).

imbed themselves in the slime we all know, which we ignore, but from whence comes the substance of art. The Spanish man of the people said "black sounds" and he concurred with Goethe who defines *duende* in speaking of Paganini by saying: 'Mysterious power which everyone feels and no philosopher can explain.' Therefore, *duende* is a power and not something constructed; a struggle and not a mere thought. I've heard an old guitar teacher say: '*Duende* is not in the throat; *duende* ascends from within, from the soles of the feet'. That is, it isn't a question of physiological power, but rather of real living style; of the blood; of ancient culture; of instantaneous creation."[36]

By the summer of 1930 all traces of depression had deserted Lorca, and the playwright prepared to return to Spain. A changed man from the one who had hurriedly left his country, Lorca embarked with a greater maturity of spirit and a more experienced outlook on life. He was to need both these qualities to cope with the turbulence that was to mark Spanish life in the years that would follow. After a short stay in Granada with his parents, Lorca resumed his life in Madrid.

But what he found in Madrid's intellectual climate was hardly conducive to creativity. Where, formerly, politics had only entered the conversation with his friends distractedly, Lorca now found that it had become the center of daily life. It was so throughout the rest of the country. Everywhere the topic seemed to be the historical decadence of Spain and her role in the future. Revolution and a new democracy were the outstanding demands of the people in the streets of Madrid. The city was a tense and expectant hot-bed, breeding plots and counter-plots, deceit and heroism. Every Spaniard, including Lorca, though unversed in the intricacies of politics and government, found himself swept along by the tempo of the tense situation. Lorca was tutored by his friend Rafael Alberti whose interest in the "new democracy"

---

36. *Obras Completas, op. cit.,* p. 37; "Teoria y juego del duende."

was active and belligerent. Alberti, a poet of great talent, turned from a theoretician in political ideology to a die-hard revolutionary who sought to recruit his many friends. But Lorca could not be approached. All that he could foresee was the tremendous wave of fear that would engulf Spain if the rebellion gained ground. Fear ruled the people, and, as one of them, Lorca was afraid.

The government which ruled Spain was a contractual monarchy under Alfonso XIII. The king had appointed Primo de Rivera Prime Minister many years before but the former general had become a self-styled Mussolini whose strong governmental measures, though clothed in phrases of traditionalism, made him a dictator. The abuses of the regime were the cause of the tension throughout Spain. King Alfonso XIII, seeking to avert a crisis, dismissed Primo de Rivera and replaced him with another general, Berenguer. The attempted compromise, however, failed to satisfy many of the groups causing the friction and Berenguer had to be removed within a few months of his appointment. His replacement was likewise unsuitable for Admiral Aznar could not meet with the problematical situation to everyone's satisfaction. Strikes and military uprisings were quickly suppressed and their occurrence caused many of the former laws of Primo de Rivera's dictatorship to be restored. As the spirit of revolt gained ground, the monarchy began to feel the throes of death. Many of the officers of the army turned against the dictatorship, laws were openly scorned, and the streets bore great multitudes to protest rallies. Finally, on April 12, 1931 the general elections declared in favor of the Republic and the suppression of the monarchy. Two days later, a car slipped unobtrusively out of Madrid; its passenger—Alfonso XIII—was going into exile.

Though the Second Republic was faced with problems that it would never fully resolve, the optimism of the times was at a maximum. The monarchist faction, however, refused to extinguish its flame and made its most serious threats through the presence of an officer-burdened army. To relieve the pressure of the situation, the new government pensioned nineteen thousand officers, leaving a cadre of seven thousand men. The government settled down to the preparations for its land reform program, the biggest of its proposed measures, which would resettle the large peasant population in new lands forged from the confiscated estates of the nobility.

During the perilous days of 1930-1931, Lorca became a passive member of the reactionaries. It was the participation of an observer carried along by the tide of his friendship with many of the active members in the movement to overthrow the monarchy. But his own work, always the primary force in his life, did not suffer because of the association. On December 24, 1930 *La Zapatera Prodigiosa* was given its premiere presentation by Margarita Xirgu in Madrid's "Teatro Español." Thereafter, an interview with Gil Benumeya in 1931 related Lorca's continued attention to the manuscripts he had commenced in New York.[37]

In January of 1931 some of the New York poems appeared in *Revista de Occidente* and caused much comment, even in a press that was dedicated largely to the communication of political activities. Having received many requests to read his new poems, Lorca acceded to them and in March gave a reading at the "Residencia de Estudiantes" in Madrid. The May publication of *Poema del cante jondo*,[38] containing poems written between 1921 and 1922, caused another stir in the literary centers because it seemed to be a contradiction to the surrealist poems of New York. But as Lorca's works were often withheld from publication long after their completion, the two events are reconciled easily in this light.

At the invitation of the "Comite de Cooperacion Intelectual," Lorca journeyed to Galicia, northwestern province of Spain and home of the renowned University of Com-

---

37. Gil Benumeya, "Estampa de Garcia Lorca," *La Gaceta Literaria,* Madrid (January 15, 1931).
38. F. Garcia Lorca, *Poema del cante jondo* (Madrid, C'I'A'P', 1931).

postela. There, during the summer of 1931, and in the city of La Coruña, Lorca initiated a lecture on *La arquitectura del cante jondo*, the theme of which had been mastered during his early venture in Granada.[39] While in Galicia, the desire to learn its language came to the poet and with the aid of various books, as well as friends, he began the pleasant task.

Upon the completion of his brief stay in Galicia, Lorca returned to Granada and the many projects which merited his attention—the surrealist plays: *Asi que pasen cinco años* and *El Publico;* the puppet piece, *El retablillo de don Cristobal;* and the poems titled *El divan del Tamarit:*

> ... (the) book with which he proposed to mark a new period of creation, of pure poetry, based on the naked images of intellectual asperity.[40]

By 1932, the new government of Spain had many of its social reforms under way. One of the principal programs undertaken under the leadership of Azaña, Fernando de los Rios, and others, was the expansion of the school system throughout the nation. The hope was that the thirty thousand new schools planned would eventually reduce the rate of illiteracy which had grown alarmingly during the monarchial period. Complementing this ambitious attempt was a program dedicated to the idea of uniting the Spanish people by more than mere geography. The education of the populace in its historical and traditional heritage was entrusted to the newly created "Ministry of Culture and Public Information," headed by De los Rios.

The "Ministry" established various means to accomplish its task. Chief among them were the "Misiones Culturales"

---

39. F. Garcia Lorca, *El cante jondo*—lecture read in "Centro Artistico y Literario," Granada—(Feb. 19, 1922); published in *Noticiero Granadino,* (February 1922).
40. F. Vazquez Ocaña, *op. cit.,* p. 283. The book was not published until 1940 when it was included in *Revista Hispanica moderna,* vol. VI, *op. cit.,* pp. 307-311.

consisting of traveling museums and libraries, and two theatre companies—"Teatro del Pueblo," directed by Alejandro Casona, and "Teatro Universitario," led jointly by Garcia Lorca and Eduardo Ugarte. Through the thespian endeavors, the most remote villages of Spain would be regaled with the music and plays of its great past.

The actual birth of "La Barraca," as the "Teatro Universitario" was affectionately called, came about in November of 1931 at the "Segundo Congreso de la Union Federal de Estudiantes Hispanos" in Madrid. Then, in the early part of 1932, Fernando de los Rios became its official sponsor. Others rapidly volunteered their services, talented men such as Benjamin Palencia, Manuel Angeles Ortiz, Miguel Prieto, Alberto Sanchez, Ponce de Leon and Santiago Ontañon.

Among the members whom Lorca and Ugarte selected for the troupe were young actors from the University—Ernesto Da Cal, Joaquin Sanchez Vocisa, Rafael Rodriguez Rapun and the three Iguera brothers—as well as Laura de los Rios Giner and Isabel Garcia Lorca, the playwright's sister. Properly uniformed in dark coveralls which bore the insignia of the new theatre, they set out in a converted truck to tour the provinces.

The first presentation was unambitious but successful. Following its aim of bringing the classical drama to the small villages of Spain, the group introduced two "entremeses" by Cervantes—*La guarda cuidadosa* and *La cueva de Salamanca*— to the eleven hundred inhabitants of Osma, a very ancient town in the province of Castilla la Vieja. The setting was reminiscent of *commedia dell'arte* improvisational staging; with the cathedral as a background for the simple platform raised a few feet above the large plaza, the devoted actors faced an awed public. From these small beginnings developed full-length dramas which were added to the repertory as the group mastered techniques; the comedies and historical romances of Cervantes, Tirso de Molina, Lope de Vega and Calderon de la Barca were performed throughout the country.

However, Lorca realized the danger of staging these plays with the false respect that characterized recent productions. Instead of observing the crusty traditions that had dictated an almost religious adherence to ancient style in manner and language, Lorca and Ugarte approached the plays with the modern audience in mind. Thus, Lorca proceeded to adapt the language, movements, music and style of each play—comedy or historical romance—in a version that would prove more appealing to the diversified audiences that would view it. In that way the plays, which had been created in an era when Spain was less unified, were given a greater feeling of being Spanish. That the revision was worthwhile is attested to by the great appeal the plays had for the peasant audience who understood and enjoyed even the most subtle references:

> "The characters had wigs of metal, of silver, of various materials, green beards; gentlemen dressed in suits with outlandish shoulders. Everything exaggerated to common sense. And yet—oh, what a consolation—everything was understood, even in its minutest details, by that public which thus encountered Calderon for the first time. No one found anything which clashed with his sense of reality. And the reason is that we, with our green beards, our copper hair, our tremendous shoulders, speak the truth. And these country people have ears and souls made to receive, house and ripen that truth which we give them."[41]

The reputation of these adaptations circulated within theatrical circles with the result that two leading actresses—Margarita Xirgu and Lola Membrives—later used Lorca's interpretations in their own repertories. From France and Italy came invitations to present "La Barraca" in those countries. Jean Prevost, French poet and translator of Lorca, and Ezio Levi, a professor at the University of Naples, issued the con-

---

41. F. Garcia Lorca, *Poema del Cante Jondo,* "Garcia Lorca en Montevideo," by A. M. Ferreiro, (Santiago de Chile, Edit. Veloz, 1937).

gratulatory messages that bore the invitations. But the plans which were immediately formulated by Lorca could not be put into effect because of the demands of his many commitments.

In March, Lorca lectured at Sevilla's "Sala Imperial" where he once more described *La arquitectura del cante jondo.* Meanwhile, the text of another study, *La imagen poetica de don Luis de Gongora,* was published in Madrid,[42] and several of his New York poems appeared in an anthology, along with a short preface: *Poetica.*[43]

The following year, 1933, Lorca continued to direct the classical re-creations of "La Barraca." By the end of March, the group had toured Spain with such significant plays as Calderon's *La vida es sueño,* Lope de Vega's *Fuenteovejuna* and *El caballero de Olmedo,* Tirso de Molina's *El burlador de Sevilla,* and Cervantes' "entremeses": *La guarda cuidadosa* and *La cueva de Salamanca.*

On March 8, 1933 *Bodas de sangre,* the first tragedy in a trilogy planned by Lorca, was enacted by the company of Josefina Diaz de Artigas at the "Teatro Beatriz" in Madrid. The playwright directed the production. The critics and public alike greeted the powerful play with enthusiasm, recognizing it as Lorca's most mature and theatrical work. The success of *Bodas de sangre* reached across the Spanish border to France and across the Atlantic to the United States. Jean Prevost and his wife translated the play into French for Gaston Baty,[44] and, in New York, Irene Lewisohn sought the rights to a translation into English.[45] Neither of these versions, however, was immediately produced, the

42. (Madrid, Residencia de Estudiantes, 1932.)
43. Gerardo Diego, *Poesia Española: Antologia* (1915-1931), (Madrid, Signo, 1932).
44. *La noce meurtriere,* trans. by Marcelle Auclair and Jean Prevost, *La Nouvelle Revue Francaise,* Paris, No. 295-297, (1938). The play was presented under the title: *Noces de sang.*
45. *Bitter Oleander,* trans. by Jose Weissberger, unpublished typescript in New York Public Library—Theatre Collection.

French premiere being postponed until 1938 and the American presentation until 1935.[46]

Having learned many of the intricacies of the theatre through his tour with "La Barraca," Lorca felt confident that he could direct plays with greater insight and feeling. *Bodas de sangre* gave him the opportunity and its acceptance as a valuable contribution to the Spanish stage urged Lorca to continue along these lines. Shortly after *Bodas de sangre* was launched, Lorca began the final preparations for a new venture—the physical realization of the "clubs teatrales"—an idea similar to the off-Broadway-theatre. The first "Club Teatral de Cultura" was inaugurated in Madrid on April 5th with two of Lorca's shorter plays: *El amor de don Perlimplin con Belisa en su jardin* and *La Zapatera Prodigiosa*. The brief version of the latter work was added to the program to provide a more complete evening. Both plays were directed by Lorca who had conceived the idea for these theatre clubs during his tour of Spain. He and Pura de Ucelay, a prominent lady in Madrid society, collaborated in the cultural enterprise with the thought of expanding it to cover all the provinces of the Republic.

In an interview[47] which preceeded the first presentation, Lorca divulged that Max Reinhardt—the prominent director —had requested his permission to produce *La Zapatera Prodigiosa* in Berlin and Vienna as a full-scale pantomime. To this end Lorca began to prepare a musical score that would accompany the stage action.[48] Always aware of the necessity to be creative in more than one field, Lorca continued his musical and poetical life even in the face of the great demands made upon him by the theatre. Two of his New York poems—*Oda al rey de Harlem* and *Oda a Walt Whitman*— were published at this time. The first appeared in a Madrid

---

46. Paris, Theatre de l'Atelier and New York, The Lyceum Theatre, respectively.
47. *Obras Completas, op. cit.,* pp. 1619-1622, "Una interesante iniciativa," *El Sol,* Madrid (April 5, 1933).
48. There is no available information as to the outcome of this plan.

magazine[49] and the second was printed in a Mexican periodical.[50] Prominent among his many participations in musical events of the Spanish capital was the collaboration with Falla in the presentation of *El amor brujo*, Falla's captivating ballet, at the "Residencia de estudiantes." The ballet was staged by Lorca and its principal dancers were the prominent interpreters of Spanish terpsichore: "La Argentinita" and Ortega.

In mid-September of 1933 Lorca received an invitation to attend a special presentation of *Bodas de sangre* in Buenos Aires, and to lecture in the Argentinian capital. After hasty preparations Lorca left Spain once more, towards the end of the month. This time his journey took him to Brazil, Uruguay and Argentina. His brief stay in Rio de Janeiro was made memorable by the renewal of his acquaintance with Alfonso Reyes who in earlier days had, together with Juan Ramon Jimenez, edited two of Lorca's poems for *Indice*. Remembering Lorca's fondness for butterflies, as manifested in his first play, Reyes made the playwright a gift of a colorful collection of Brazilian specimens prior to his departure.

An even shorter period in Montevideo prepared the way for Lorca's arrival in Buenos Aires on October 13th. *Bodas de sangre* was already a successful play in Buenos Aires when Lorca arrived, and Lola Membrives, who headed the cast, had invited him to witness and collaborate in an outdoor production of the tragedy. Two more of his dramas—*Mariana Pineda* and *La Zapatera Prodigiosa*—were similarly received as the enthusiasm for the Spanish playwright mounted. Everywhere that his name was displayed on a theatre marquee, attendance records were set and the demand for seats unprecedented. The climax of this popularity was reached during performances of Lope de Vega's *La dama boba*, adapted and directed by Lorca, held in a stadium. At one of

49. *Los Cuatro Vientos,* Madrid (1933), no. 1, pp. 5-10.
50. *Alcancia, op. cit.*

these showings a crowd of sixty thousand spectators was on hand.[51]

The lecture series which he delivered in Buenos Aires was comprised of previously treated topics: *Teoria y juego del duende, La imagen poetica de don Luis de Gongora, Las nanas infantiles, Lo que canta una ciudad de noviembre a noviembre* and *El canto primitivo andaluz*. Besides these lectures and theatrical productions, however, Lorca was involved in many interviews in newspapers, magazines and on radio, as well as in poetry readings and various cultural activities. One such affair, in which Lorca and the Chilean poet Pablo Neruda participated, was a dialogue in honor of Ruben Dario. The joint dissertation on the Nicaraguan poet whose influence had reached even to Spain was held at the PEN Club of Buenos Aires and was attended by many notable figures in the cultural life of the city.

Lorca in Argentina was, in a sense, the symbol of the spiritual union that had always existed between Spain and that nation. Realizing this, and as a true Spaniard, Lorca received all plaudits in the humility and grateful quietness that had endeared him to many new friends—Victoria Ocampo, Lola Membrives, Gonzalez Carbalho, Amorin and Blanco Amor. Before his return to Spain, planned for the end of March, 1934, Lorca was made the recipient of a singular honor. Representatives from many of the Latin-American republics met to pay homage to the effervescent artist, proclaiming him "ambassador of Spanish culture to Latin-America." It was the perfect, if unexpected, end to Lorca's most triumphant journey.

The resounding success which *Bodas de sangre* achieved both in Spain and abroad made Lorca financially independent for the first time in his career as a writer, and allowed his family to breath easier in the assurance that he was finally settled. The generosity and understanding which his mother

---

51. Edwin Honig, *op. cit.,* p. 17.

and father showed during the years of hardship and apprenticeship were beginning to bear more than artistic fruit. With new prospects before him, Lorca returned to Madrid, and immediately planned the new repertory for "La Barraca" which was to be initiated at the University of Santander. Then, too, he began to write *Yerma*, the second tragedy, choosing to complete his trilogy before returning to the farces and lighter fare of his earlier theatre:

> "I am hard at work. I'm now finishing *Yerma*, a second tragedy. The first was *Bodas de sangre*. *Yerma* will be the tragedy of the sterile woman. The theme, as you know, is classical. But I want to give it a new development and intent. A tragedy with four principal characters and a chorus, as all tragedies should have. We must return to tragedy. We are obligated by the tradition of our dramatic theatre. There will be time to write comedies, farces. In the meantime I want to give the theatre tragedies. *Yerma*, which is nearly completed, will be the second."[52]

But Lorca had not been as decidedly opposed to the popular theatre in May when he had distinterred his puppets and given a special rendition of Cervantes "entremeses" for a public which had gathered at Madrid's "Hotel Florida" to honor him upon his return from Argentina. Now he was momentarily concerned with the need to further satisfy the tragic outlook on Spanish life which had pressed him to write *Bodas de sangre*. And late in the summer of 1934, in August, Lorca was given even greater reason for approaching the theatre from the tragic side. Ignacio Sanchez Mejias, the famed bullfighter whose friendship with Federico was deep, was gored in the abdomen and died a few hours after the accident. The man, already over forty, had returned to the bull-ring after several years of absence to regain the glory that his younger competitors now possessed. His death af-

---

52. Juan Chabas, "Federico Garcia Lorca y la Tragedia," *Luz,* Madrid (July 3, 1934).

fected Lorca and other friends—Rafael Alberti, Marcelle Auclair, "La Argentinita," Carlos Morla Lynch most particularly—and resulted in one of Lorca's most beautiful poems, the plaintive elegy, *Llanto por Ignacio Sanchez Mejias.*

Lorca reached the height of his achievement in his *Llanto por Ignacio Sanchez Mejias;* here he remained true to his native Andalucia, to the earth and the landscape from which his verse derived its strength, flavor and perfume; yet he was not under the restriction he imposed upon himself in the *Romancero,* that of the coldly impartial and ironic spectator. On the contrary, he was expressing his grief for a beloved friend, one of the greatest bullfighters of all time, who was also a cultured literary man, a good farmer, a great horseman, and a popular figure . . .[53]

Lorca completed the poem on November 4th and read it to Carlos Morla Lynch that evening. The sincerity of his voice and the feeling in the words prompted Morla's annotation:

The concept is of titanic grandeur and it leaves the impression that Federico has given to it all the measure of his genius. Greater height or greater magnitude cannot be reached. The monument he has raised to his fallen friend sprouts from the bloodied earth and breaks from it to ascend and lose itself in the clouds.[54]

The poem, however, was not published until 1935 when it caused much discussion.[55]

Yerma was completed by December 3rd, at which time, as was his custom, Lorca read the play in its entirety to the Morla household. On December 29, 1934 the second tragedy was presented in the "Teatro Español" with Margarita Xirgu enacting the principal role. And again the theatre-going public of Madrid was treated to a poetically striking, dramatically moving slice of life translated, through Lorca's un-

---

53. Roy Campbell, *Federico Garcia Lorca* (New Haven, Yale University Press, 1952), p. 95.
54. Carlos Morla Lynch, *op. cit.,* p. 422.
55. Federico Garcia Lorca, *Llanto por Ignacio Sanchez Mejias* (Madrid, Ed. Arbol, Cruz y Raya, 1935).

equivocal genius, into an unforgettable tragedy of frustration and sacrifice.

The last months of 1934 were full of governmental discord and renewed revolutionary activity. The Republic, which had inherited a tradition of corruption developed through decades of mismanagement, was expected to resolve the precarious situations of education, commerce and labor immediately. When it found it impossible to cure all the evils promptly, strikes erupted everywhere and the goodwill which had greeted the Republic began to sour. The miners of Asturias province succeeded in forcing a change in the government and with the assistance of the Socialist party installed Alejandro Lerroux in the principal cabinet post. But shortly thereafter, the miners were suppressed by the Moorish legions under General Franco. The former ministry resumed its rightful place and, under the guidance of Gil Robles, remained in power until the elections of 1936 when this Christian Socialist party was replaced by Azaña and his Republican government. The election fortunes of the Republic, therefore, were sketchy; having been popularly acclaimed in the election of 1931, the Republic was forced to give way to the Robles government in 1934's unquiet balloting and to forsake its program of agrarian reform. The new leadership, composed of anti-Liberals and Monarchists, as well as fascist elements, tended to imitate the strong centralized control that had characterized monarchial rule, and leaned discreetly towards the example of Italy and Germany.

For a week, while the Lerroux government was in power, Madrid became an armed camp. Lorca found it unsafe, as others had, to walk the streets, or even to be in his home for stray machine gun bullets had penetrated the privacy of his kitchen while his sister Isabel had been in the room. Such was the atmosphere in which Lorca lived during the latter months of the year. It was providential that his work occupied his mind and distracted him from the tense life of the city.

"I'm writing a comedy on which I place all my illusion: *Doña Rosita la soltera o el lenguaje de las flores.* 'Family reveille divided into four gardens.' ... I expect my tragedy, *Yerma,* to be ready for production within the month. The rehearsals are well under way. ... I would like to finish the trilogy of *Bodas de sangre, Yerma* and *El drama de las hijas de Loth.* The last is yet to be written. Afterwards, I want to do other things, including topical comedy of our times, and to bring to the theatre themes and problems which people are afraid to consider."[56]

Lorca's reference to the last play in the trilogy as *El drama de las hijas de Loth* is troublesome in that the title casts a certain doubt as to the lineage of *La casa de Bernarda Alba.* However, as the drama had not been written at the time of the interview, it is probable that the title cited by Lorca was more contemplated than actual, and that it was eventually resolved into the title of his final completed play. As a tragedy on the theme of frustration, *La casa de Bernarda Alba* fits perfectly into the pattern of its sister plays—*Bodas de sangre* and *Yerma.*

There are other plays which can be added to the list of unknown dramas. Vazquez Ocaña[57] cites several: *La destruccion de Sodoma,* which Lorca announced to be complete on January 1, 1935; and *El sacrificio de Ifigenia,* to which he alluded frequently in conversation. C. Rivas Cherif, in three consecutive articles for a Mexican newspaper,[58] uncovers other proposed plays: *La bestia hermosa,* a rural drama which Lorca had promised to Carmen Diaz, an Andalucian actress; *La sangre no tiene voz,* a treatment of the theme of incest based on a true episode in the life of a Barcelona workman whom Lorca had known; and *La bola negra,* a tragedy of an individual in conflict with society. Lorca himself, in an in-

---

56. Alardo Prats, "Los artistas en el ambiente de nuestro tiempo," *El Sol,* Madrid (Dec. 15, 1934).
57. *op. cit.,* p. 356.
58. C. Rivas Cherif, "Diorama de la cultura: FGL," *Excelsior,* Mexico, D.F. (January 6, 1957).

terview not published until after his death, revealed other plays in preparation:

> "I will write the tragedy of the 'Soldiers who do not want to go to war.' I also wish to give the Spanish theatre a mystical and human Saint Theresa. This figure attracts me irresistibly. But before this one the other play, the one of peace . . . In it, a chorus of mothers of men from all nations will direct their apostrophes and their lamentations to the representatives of the great powers."[59]

And his brother, Francisco, in the "Prologue" to *Three Tragedies*,[60] mentions yet another play:

> . . . in the same way that he (Lorca) appears in person in his poetry . . . he appears in his plays. In some of them the author himself takes a part, and it is not by chance that in his last play, *The Dreams of My Cousin Aurelia*, of which he was able to write only the first act, the leading character is Federico himself as a child.

The text of his first act remains in the possession of the playwright's brother as an unpublished manuscript.

Several further citations, of plays which Lorca had in mind or actually had begun to write, exist. Jose Mora Guarnido, a companion of Lorca in Granada and Madrid between 1915 and 1923, recalls a conversation in which Lorca delineated the plot to a play which dealt with the second coming of Christ, placed within the context of Spanish life:

> . . . it was nothing other than the reiteration of the theme of frustrated love, but elevated to summits of thought superior to the human.[61]

The play never went beyond the playwright's thoughts, though its presence therein must have lasted many years, awaiting

59. *La Vanguardia,* Barcelona (Sept. 22, 1936). Lorca had uttered these words a year before, during the premiere of *Doña Resita.*
60. James Graham-Lujan, Richard L. O'Connell, *Three Tragedies of Federico Garcia Lorca* (New York, New Directions, 1955), p.4.
61. Jose Mora Guarnido, *Federico Garcia Lorca y su mundo* (Buenos Aires, Ed. Losada, 1958), p. 173.

the precise moment when its creation would be complete. The final instance where the title of one of Lorca's plays conflicts with the actual facts is seen in another interview:

He has finished *Yerma* and will soon complete *La hermosa*, another great tragedy of love.[62]

Apparently the reference is to *Doña Rosita la soltera*, the play Lorca did write immediately following *Yerma*. Therefore *La hermosa* cannot be considered a "lost" play as its title appears to be a "working" one, used merely to facilitate reference to the drama.

The month of January, 1935 proved a full one for Lorca. With Pura de Ucelay he presented one of Lope de Vega's plays under the auspices of the newly founded "Teatro de la Anfistora," descendant of the former "Club teatral de cultura" in Madrid. Some days later, on the 30th, Lorca took part in a tribute to the Galician poet, Feliciano Rolan. The festivities were held in Madrid's "Lyceum Club," and among the other principal participants were Juan Ramon Jimenez, Benjamin Jarnes, Recasens Siches, Azcoaga, Nieto Pena and Burgos Lecea, with Enrique Diez Canedo presiding. These proceedings were later collected and published as a pamphlet.[63] On the 31st, the cast of *Yerma* gave a special showing after hours to satisfy the petition from the theatrical unions whose members could not otherwise view the play. Lorca faced a full house as he stood on the stage to welcome the members of his profession whom the early morning hours could not distract from open anticipation.

The success of *Yerma*, even brighter than that which had been bestowed on *Bodas de sangre*, gave occasion to many attempts to extol publicly the virtues of the gifted playwright, but Lorca, though never ungrateful, resisted all such plans:

---

62. *Obras Completas, op. cit., p.* 1624; "Vacaciones de 'La Barraca'," *Luz,* Madrid (Sept. 3, 1934).

63. *Homenaje a Feliciano Rolan,* (Madrid, Lyceum Club, 1935), contains a short article: "De mar a mar" by Lorca.

"Some time in the past I made a firm promise to refuse
every type of tribute, banquet or feast which might be
dedicated to my simple person; first, because I know
that each one adds more mortar to our literary tomb,
and second, because I've seen nothing more desolate
than a prepared speech in our honor, nor a sadder
moment than that of organized applause, even if in good
faith . . . For poets and playwrights, I would organize
attacks and challenges instead of tributes . . ."[64]
His friends and admirers, however, were not dissuaded from
their purpose, finally presenting Lorca with a written testimonial of their appreciation. The impressive list of signa-
tories included Juan Ramon Jimenez, Adolfo Salazar, Alejandro Casona and Ramon del Valle-Inclan. The tribute
ranked with that which was given the playwright on his departure from Argentina.

Events of importance in Lorca's creative life followed
quickly upon each other. Though Lorca had little contact
with the American group which was to present *Bodas de
sangre* in New York, it must have pleased him to learn that
the play made its debut there on February 11, 1935.[65] And
on March 1st, Lola Membrives, the Argentinian actress, performed *Bodas de sangre* in a limited engagement at the
"Teatro Coliseum" of Madrid. As usual, Lorca delivered a
short talk during the course of the evening. This revival
served only as a prelude to the principal reason for Lola
Membrives' presence in Madrid: the opening of *La Zapatera
Prodigiosa* in a full-length and final version under Lorca's
direction. The play premiered on March 18th at the "Coliseum," a few days after *Yerma* reached its 100th performance mark. On that occasion Lorca was called upon to read
some of his poems; he chose *Llanto por Ignacio Sanchez
Mejias*, thereby giving the elegiac poem its first public
reading.

64. *Obras Completas, op. cit.,* p. 33; "Charla sobre tetro."
65. Jose Weissberger, the translator, had been in Madrid previously
    to confer with Lorca. This is the only known participation of
    Lorca in the American production, *Bitter Oleander*.

Another of his poems, *Tierra y Luna*, was published during this period[66] while the playwright worked diligently to meet deadlines on two plays: *El retablillo de don Cristobal* and *Doña Rosita la soltera*. After the final performance of *Yerma*, on April 2nd, Lorca was able to concentrate fully on these two works so that the first was enacted on May 11, 1935. The puppet play figured prominently in "La Feria del Libro" held in Madrid under the sponsorship of the "Residencia." Lorca's dedication to his many theatrical ventures left him little time for poetry and music, though in past years he had been able to cope with all aspects of his creativity. But he did not cease to write poetry. However, he was unable to select from his new poems those best suited for publication:

"I have embraced the theatre because I feel the necessity for expression in the dramatic form. But I have not abandoned the cultivation of pure poetry, although it can equally be contained in the dramatic work as in the poem itself. What is happening, however, is that I am now wary of publishing books of verse. I am overcome by a great laziness and discouragement in selecting from the poems I write those to be published."[67]

It is for this reason that only one or two single poems were actually published at this time besides *Llanto por Ignacio Sanchez Mejias*[68] and *Seis poemas galegos*.[69] Likewise, Lorca prepared the typescript for *Poeta en Nueva York* but the collection of poems was never published during his lifetime. Various problems in collecting the poems necessitated a long and often fruitless search by Lorca, as evidenced by a letter from Madrid in August, 1935:

"I'm typing my New York book to give to the printer next October; I beg you earnestly to return by mail the

---

66. In *El tiempo presente,* Madrid (March, 1935).
67. Alardo Prats, "Los artistas en el ambiente de nuestro tiempo," *op. cit.*
68. *op. cit.*
69. Federico Garcia Lorca, *Seis poemas galegos,* (Santiago de Compostella, Ed. Nos, 1935).

poem *Crucifixion* as you're the only one who has it and I've been left without a copy."[70]

The frustration of not being able to collect the poems was due partially to Lorca's carelessness in handling them. He hardly ever knew the whereabouts of many pieces, often sending the only copy to a friend, or leaving a manuscript at someone's house or where it had been written:

> Federico made me a present of the original pencil-script, on the occasion of his stay in Barcelona. I kept it, according to my custom, in a copy of one of his books. When he asked mc for the manuscript—as the letters reproduced here testify—I could find it nowhere. When the civil war was at an end, I resumed my search for it eagerly. I had moved to Madrid during the first days of August (1936), leaving all my books in Barcelona. Not until the May of 1939 did I have access to them again, and one day, between the pages of the *Romancero Gitano*, I discovered the manuscript, which is now a relic.[71]

Although Lorca himself did not accept the tribute of his friends in official acts, he was always present when his services were needed to honor a fellow artist, whether at a testimonial dinner or other such act of recognition. There were outstanding occasions in which Lorca's participation was the principal force: the act of homage at the grave of Isaac Albeniz, for example. Another such tribute, this time to Pablo Neruda, was held on June 14, 1935. Lorca's laudatory remarks on the poet whom he had met in Buenos Aires were motivated by Neruda's book, *Residencia en la tierra*, which had recently been published, and appeared many years later in a volume of Neruda's poetry.[72]

Lorca had completed *Doña Rosita la soltera* in June

---

70. *Obras Completas, op. cit.*, pp. 1605-1606; letter to M. Benitez Inglott.
71. Federico Garcia Lorca, *Crucifixion*, notas de Miguel Benitez Inglott, (Las Palmas, Imprenta Ortega, 1950); trans. by Belitt, *op. cit.*, pp. 188-189.
72. Pablo Neruda, *Seleccion* (Santiago de Chile, Nascimento, 1940).

when he read the piece to some friends gathered at the house of Carlos Morla Lynch. Then in September, after first polishing the play tediously, he gave a private reading in Barcelona's "Teatro Estadium" for the actors of Margarita Xirgu's troupe. After extensive rehearsals, the play opened in Barcelona on December 13th at the "Teatro Principal Palace"; Lorca's theatrical return to Barcelona (*Mariana Pineda* had been the last of his plays to be inaugurated there) was marked by festivities after the final curtain, at which time the playwright read various poems from his New York collection.

Three of his poems, widely separated in subject matter and treatment, were published during the last months of the year. The first, *Nocturno del hueco*, appeared in Pablo Neruda's magazine.[73] Another poem, *Epitafio a Isaac Albeniz*, was composed for the posthumous dedication of a statue at the composer's grave, read on December 14th, and printed in a Barcelona newspaper that evening. The third publication was of a group of four poems from Lorca's unedited collection: *Divan del Tamarit*. The poems were included in a magazine edited by Guillermo de Torre.[74] These last poems, written under the influence of Arabic poetic forms and content, caused much comment for they showed yet a third influence on the poet's mind (the surrealist and flamenco tendencies in his writing have already been discussed).

As always with the coming of something new, the spirit regains its composure in the buoyancy of hope and new plans take the place of others long ago worn thin by despair. Such was the atmosphere in Spain at the start of 1936, the new year. Lorca kept himself on the treadmill of varied projects. *Bodas de sangre* was edited and published on January 21st,[75] while several poems from *Divan del Tamarit* were readied for magazines. *Gacela de la huida*, one of these,

73. *Caballo verde para la poesia*, Madrid (October, 1935).
74. *Almanaque literario*, Madrid (1935).
75. F. Garcia Lorca, *Bodas de sangre* (Madrid, Cruz y Raya, 1936).

appeared in February.[76] That same month, all Spain held its breath in anticipation of the election. Therein would be decided whether the Republic would be returned to power or whether the regime of Gil Robles would continue. But it was clear that Manual Azaña and his liberal program would carry on the work interrupted by the defeat in 1934. The Republic emerged victorious.

In the meantime of tranquility embroidered with threats of war, Lorca continued to be active in the literary life of Madrid, publishing a collection of early poems, *Primeras canciones* (1922),[77] at the instigation of Manuel Altolaguirre and Concha Mendez. Later, on April 18th, he again took part at an honorary banquet, acting as the master of ceremonies for the affair which celebrated Luis Cernuda's success with his recent collection of poems: *La realidad y el deseo.*[78] Lorca's comments appeared later in a Madrid newspaper.[79] Along with these activities, however, Lorca found time to concentrate deeply on his drama. But an interview reveals that he was all too aware of the greater drama that was being fashioned in Spain, a drama of poverty and hunger:

"I'm now working on a new comedy. It will not be like its predecessors. It's a play which I cannot write, not a line, because truth and falsehood, hunger and poetry, have fled and roam the air. They have escaped from my pages. The truth of the comedy is a problem both religious and socio-economic. The World is detained by the hunger which devastates the common people. As long as economic unbalance exists, the World doesn't think. I've thought it out. Two men are walking by the edge of a river. One is rich, the other is poor. One has a full stomach, and the other dirties the air with his yawns. And the rich one says: 'Oh, what a beautiful boat on

---

76. *Floresta de Prosa y Verso,* Madrid (February, 1936).
77. F. Garcia Lorca, *Primeras Canciones* (1922), (Madrid, Ed. Heroe, 1936).
78. Luis Cernuda, *La realidad y el deseo,* (Madrid, Ed. Cruz y Raya, 1936).
79. *El Sol,* Madrid (April 21, 1936).

the water! Look, look at the lily blooming on the shore.'
And the poor man prays. 'I'm hungry, I can't see anything. I'm hungry, very hungry.' Naturally. The day
hunger disappears the World will experience the greatest
spiritual explosion which Humanity has ever known.
Man cannot conceive the happiness that will burst on
the day of the Great Revolution."[80]

With this statement, Lorca clarified the feelings which dominated many of Spain's intellectuals. But the difficulty of
treating such a thesis in play form, in the face of the reality
of Spanish necessity, detained Lorca's usual dexterity and
prevented the drama's full conception. Thus the plot detailed
in the interview never developed and the play did not even
reach the stage where a tentative title was assigned to it.

Lorca reached his largest audience in a broadcast over
"Union Radio" in Madrid when he read his lecture: *Semana
Santa en Granada*. In it he looked back fondly on the memories of childhood impressions made by the traditional
festival, traditions which he later saw diminish in importance
as commercialism overpowered the real significance of the
celebration. The text of the lecture became, then, a plea for
the reinstatement of the real values in the symbolic ceremony. As such it was reproduced the following day in *El Sol*,
the Madrid newspaper.

In the early days of May, Margarita Xirgu, who was
planning a tour of Mexico and other Latin-American nations, almost convinced Lorca to accompany her. The allure
of Mexico was opportune in the presence of Spain's precarious political state and was made even more so by an offer
to lecture in Mexico City where former friends such as Alfonso Reyes, Salvador Novo and Gabriel Garcia Maroto
would welcome Lorca with enthusiasm. Then, too, there was
the incentive of seeing various of his plays performed in the
Mexican capital. But Lorca's destiny was in Spain.

---

80. Felipe Morales, "Declaraciones de Garcia Lorca sobre teatro,"
    Heraldo de Madrid (April 8, 1936).

Among the projects which prevented what could have been a providential exodus was his last play: *La casa de Bernarda Alba*. Completed by June, Lorca read the play to his fellow poets—Damaso Alonso, Jorge Guillen and Guillermo de Torre—who had gathered at the home of Eusebio Oliver in Madrid.[81] Also in June, on the 10th, a conversation between Lorca and the caricaturist, Luis Bagaria, was printed[82]—the last interview to appear before his death. In the waning days of June and in the first weeks of July, Pura de Ucelay announced the rehearsal of Lorca's *Asi que pasen cinco años* by the "Teatro Anfistora" which she and the playwright had founded. But the worsening situation throughout Spain—the assassinations of important Republican leaders, the attempts on the lives of others[83]—forced Lorca's return to Granada on July 16th for a reunion with his family.

On July 18, 1936 the garrison of troops stationed in Spanish Morocco under General Franco openly revolted against the Republic and began preparations to invade the homeland through an air and sea lift provided by German and Italian planes and ships. The long-feared Civil War had begun explosively, two days after Lorca decided on the trip to Granada. Once in the city, Lorca and his family moved to their farm nearby. In Granada itself, workers' representatives tried in vain to convince the governor, Cesar Torres Martinez, that the workers should be armed in the event the city might be endangered by the revolt of the

---

81. Another reading took place on June 24th (five days after the play's completion) at the home of the Count of Yebes where Carlos Morla Lynch, who reports on the occasion (*op. cit.*, p. 483), and others were invited for dinner. Lorca mentioned that the play was to be produced in October.
82. *El Sol*, Madrid (June 10, 1936). "Dialogo con un caricaturista salvaje."
83. The most significant assassination was that of Jose Calvo Sotelo, chief of the Spanish renewal program, on July 13, 1936. An attempt on the life of Lorca's brother, Francisco, then secretary of the Spanish Consulate in Cairo, brought the decision to return to his family in Granada.

troops stationed there. General Campins, commander of the Granada garrison, however, remained uncommitted. But the pressure from his officers finally wore down his resistance to military protocol and the city came under siege on July 20th.[84]

After the fall of Granada, various groups, known as "black squads," were formed to maintain order and carry out directives from the military or civilian leaders. Many of these orders led directly to executions. Among the first executed was Lorca's brother-in-law, the mayor of Granada, Manuel Fernandez Montesinos. His death occurred on August 3rd. Hundreds more were to follow in the months of terror that ruled Granada thereafter. Lists were prepared and submitted to the "black squads" and many innocent persons, whose sole crime had been to gain the disfavor of those now in power, found themselves facing the firing squads because their names were on one of the lists as a Communist, Socialist, Intellectual, Liberal, Republican or under other similar designations.

Lorca's family lived in constant fear that Federico's name would be included in one of those fatal lists. Their anxiety was enhanced when one day an armed group came to the farm seeking the poet. When Lorca presented himself, they abused him with words and warned him not to leave Granada. After their departure Lorca was taken to the apparent safety in the home of Luis Rosales, a fellow poet who had influence in the Falange through his brothers.

> The fact that Rosales brother, who also lived there, was a leading Falangist appeared to offer complete protection, yet a couple of days later, during the temporary absence of his hosts, a car manned by gunmen drew up at the door and carried him away. None of his friends ever saw him again.[85]

---

84. General Campins was later executed for his hesitation.
85. Gerald Brenan, *The Face of Spain* (New York, Grove Press, 1951), p. 147.

The story of the last hours of Lorca's life is difficult to piece together, but several narrations of the events that led to his death are helpful, if only informatively rather than conclusively. Luis Rosales' account is one.

"They (the individuals referred to) went to my house. Only the servant was there and she did not know enough to deny that Federico was inside. (From this came the confusion that someone among us had betrayed him.) They took him away. When we returned, I became most indignant. Lorca's father and mine went to look for him in all the possible places where they could have taken him. He couldn't be found during the entire night. But the following day my brother brought the news that he was in the 'Gobierno Civil.' I went there. You can imagine my state of mind. I arrived at the 'Gobierno' and asked: 'Who has violated my house and taken Garcia Lorca?' The one responsible came forward and said 'I' . . . I became so angered that the governor himself suggested I return to my house. I obeyed relatively calm. The following day, when we expected that all would be remedied, my brother returned with the horrible news: Action was no longer needed!"[86]

Jean-Pierre Chabrol hints that the Rosales story is incomplete,[87] while Claude Couffon acts as witness to Luis Rosales' efforts and those of his brother to save the unfortunate Federico.[88] But the disbelief centers mainly about the point of the power which the Rosales family held in the Falange. Though Luis was not a member of the new regime, his brothers participated actively in Granada. Pepe Rosales was the party leader in the city; another brother, Antonio, was the treasurer; Miguel, the fourth brother, was an attorney for the movement. It seems to dissenters from his story, that if Rosales' account is true, Lorca should have been easily freed through the sheer weight of influence. But the hold

86. C. Rivas Cherif, *op. cit.*; Luis Rosales' account given to C. R. C.
87. Jean-Pierre Chabrol, "J'ai retrouve les assassins de Lorca," Paris (October 18, 1956).
88. Claude Couffon, "Como murio Garcia Lorca," *Nueva Democracia,* New York (July, 1953), XXXIII, No. 3, pp. 64-81.

which his adversaries had on Lorca could not be broken, based as it was primarily on hatred rather than authority:

> The first open blow to this controversy had already been struck by the Falangist ex-minister, Serrano Suñer. In December 1947 he gave an interview to a Mexican journalist, Alfonso Junco, in which he asserted that the man who had given the order to kill Lorca was the Catholic Conservative deputy to the Cortes, Ramon Ruiz Alonso.[89]

As the government of the Falange had not been centrally organized because of the war, each section acted with great freedom. Thus the Granada government, hastily improvised, could hardly cope effectively with the many quick actions taken by individual groups who now found in the new power a license for sadism and revenge. What Ruiz Alonso's motives could have been, if he was indeed responsible for Lorca's death and not merely the government's scapegoat, is not easily ascertained. A former linotypist for Granada's newspaper, *El Ideal,* and a member of the C.E.D.A.,[90] his motivation could have been political, since Lorca's relatives and friends were principally Republicans, or personal, based on some jealousy or disagreement. But no matter what the reason may have been, all accounts mark the deputy as the instrument, the culpable party in the detestable act.

Chabrol asserts that on the night of August 18th several men, among them Ruiz Alonso, came to the Rosales house and presented an order for Lorca's arrest to Miguel Rosales. Being alone in the house with Lorca, Rosales allowed him to be taken away. This version varies from that of Luis Rosales, and both are at odds with that proposed by Schonberg,[91] wherein he affirms that Ruiz Alonso and his henchmen went to the Rosales house with the order signed by

---

89. Gerald Brenan, *op. cit.,* p. 148.
90. "Confederacion Española de Derechas Autonomas."
91. Jean Louis Schonberg, *Federico Garcia Lorca: L'homme, L'ouvre* (Paris, Plon, 1956).

Valdes, the civil governor of the city. However, according to Schonberg, the time was five o'clock and both Miguel and Antonio Rosales were with Lorca who was reading in the patio. Miguel helped him dress and then accompanied him in a car to the "Gobierno Civil" where Valdes promised that no harm would befall Lorca. Miguel left to seek out Pepe, the Falangist leader. But the action against Lorca was swift and by morning he was dead, an unidentified corpse lying in some pit excavated by himself in the nearby mountains.

Lorca's brief life ended a few months after his 38th birthday, but his years had not been a deterrent to a valid and full life as a creative artist. His bibliography attests to the scope and diversity of his production, be it musical, poetical or theatrical. The universality of his appeal as a writer is evidenced by the ever-increasing volume of studies, the continuous presentation of his theatre throughout the world, and the never-ceasing magic which his poetry brings to those who became acquainted with it either in the original or in translation. But perhaps the truest testament to Lorca as a man is seen in the devotion of his friends, who still recall the vivid personality that illuminated many of their days, and who deeply regret the tragic action which ended his life so unnecessarily.

THEATRE

"The theatre is that poetry which rises from the book and becomes human." F.G.L.

II. EL MALEFICIO DE LA MARIPOSA

Lorca's first play, *El maleficio de la mariposa*, was given its only presentation in Madrid's "Teatro Eslava" on the night of March 22, 1920. The company, headed by Catalina Barcena and "La Argentinita," was directed by Gregorio Martinez Sierra. The decor was by Mignoni; the costuming by Rafael Barradas.

Few of the spectators of this two-act fantasy, written entirely in poetry, remained sympathetic to the play or its author after a few minutes had elapsed. The first-night audience behaved in the tradition of European publics in its reaction against the play—hissing, yelling, laughing, stomping —not because the presentation lacked artistry or the acting genuine talent, but because a public suckled in the tradition of Benavente, Calderon and Lope de Vega, and accustomed to the drama of Martinez Sierra, the Quintero brothers and other such romantics, could not be expected to take pleasure or even passive interest in a new poetic theatre whose first offering was a play about cockroaches.

Whatever else the unpleasant reception may have stirred up within the playwright, it served to convert Lorca to a principle that his later drama was to preserve: the public must be served, not by forcing new ideas upon it, but by the slow process of subtle education in the experiments of theatre. The very traditions which destine a people to act, rejecting something seemingly foreign to their lives, must be adopted and used to make the same public aware of progress. Thus, it can be conquered. It was well that Lorca tasted defeat and felt the quicksand footing of disapproval on his first theatrical venture, for the lesson remained within him during his creative life.

In all of Spanish theatre history there did not exist a basis for a full-length play like *El maleficio de la mariposa*. Where, then, did such a play originate and what were the

55

reasons for its creation? Several authors have attempted to trace a connection between this work and those of other writers, persisting in their search in spite of the historical and geographical barriers, not to mention that many of the works cited were not available in Spanish translations. Alfredo de la Guardia, one of these researchers, fabricates such far-flung mentors (in time and locale) as Maeterlinck, Rostand, La Fontaine, Aesop, Linares Rivas, Cervantes, Lope de Vega and Kipling.[1]

While it is true that these authors' works have included writings, of one sort or another, on animal life, there is no basis beyond conjecture for making them antecedents of Lorca's insect fantasy. Although Lorca was known to be an extensive reader, it is highly unlikely that he read every dissertation presented by De la Guardia, works such as: Maeterlinck's *The Blue Bird*, Kipling's *Jungle Book*, Cetina's *La Pulga*, Aesop's *Fables*, Cervantes' *Coloquio de los perros*, Rostand's *Chante-cleer*, Quevedo's *Cabildo de los gatos*, and Aristophanes' *The Birds*. The influence of Capek's *The Insect Comedy* cannot be claimed because Lorca's play preceded it by several years.

But the only point that can be established with certainty is that the principal source is to be found in the playwright's imagination. Jose Mora Guarnido, who accompanied Lorca during the period of the play's conception, attests to this in his account of real ancestry, traceable to an earlier poem:

> . . . "The Discoveries of an Adventurous Snail," saved from burning by my intervention and that of Garcia Maroto. One of those fables (to give them a name) told the slight adventure of a butterfly who, with broken wings, falls into a nest of roaches; there they shelter her, aid her and nurse her; and there the roach's son falls in love with her. But when the butterfly recovers the power to fly, she ascends to the sky deserting the poor lover . . . recited by Federico, they (the fables)

---

1. Alfredo de la Guardia, *Garcia Lorca, Persona y Creacion* (Buenos Aires, Ed. Sur, 1941).

abounded in grace and appeal. Don Gregorio Martinez
Sierra, writer and playwright ... heard that recital and felt
so overcome by its tenderness and grace that he saw in
it an interesting theme for "poetic theatre" (it hardly
was that), and proposed immediately that Lorca adapt
it, assuring him it would be presented in his theatre.[2]

Since Lorca had destroyed the poem which gave birth to *El
maleficio de la mariposa* upon the play's failure, the only
direct line to the fable's ancestry is found in the poem which
Mora Guarnido saved: "Los encuentros de un caracol aven-
turero." The poem centers on the meeting of a snail and a
colony of ants. The snail first encounters two old frogs who
tell him that he must believe in eternity; the snail, never
having prayed or strayed from home before, becomes afraid
of their insistence and departs as quickly as he knows how.
The two frogs then question each other as to why they told
the snail to believe in eternity when they themselves did not.
As the snail journeys to his home, he meets a group of ants
which is dragging one of their members, antennae shorn, to
his death. The puzzled snail questions their behavior. The
unfortunate ant says sadly: "I have seen the stars."[3] Never
having seen the stars, the other ants have condemned him
to die for his lie which has brought dissatisfaction to their
colony. The snail, who by now is very confused, asks that
they let their fellow die in peace. Then, as a bee crosses
above him, the dying ant says: ". . . She's the one who's
come to take me to a star."[4] The visionary dies and the
others flee, afraid more of their consciences than of anything
else. The snail can do no more than sigh and go on his way,
full of confusion about eternity.

The parallel between *El maleficio de la mariposa* and
these two poems leaves no doubt that the play grew out of
the further contemplation of the poems' theme. The play, as

---

2. Jose Mora Guarnido, *op. cit.*, pp. 123-124.
3. *Obras Completas, op. cit.*, p. 106.
4. *Ibid.*, p. 108.

a dramatized fable, presents lessons that are not hidden, but openly arranged in a simple and direct manner. These themes or lessons are first outlined in the "Prologo" of the play:

". . . broken comedy of one who wants to scratch the moon and scratches his own heart . . . Love, just as it passes through man's life with its mockery and failures, in this case passes through a hidden meadow populated by insects. . . . There was an insect who . . . seized a vision too distant from his life . . . the lovelorn insect died. . . . That poetry which asks why the stars move is very dangerous for uninitiated souls."[5]

The final theme sets the scene for the opening dialogue of the play proper:

"And why is it that you men, full of sins and incurable vices, are repelled by the good insects who pass tranquilly through the meadow?"

The scene upon which these insects live and die is a green field, shaded by a giant cypress; nearby there is a small pond, flowers and blue rocks. The early morning dew gives a freshness to the setting.

Doña Curiana, ancient and with one leg missing, is talking with Curiana Nigromantica, the local conjurer, who wears a Merlinian hat with authority. The latter relates a dream wherein a swallow imparted to her that: "All the stars will be turned off." Her pessimism continued when she beheld a star depetalled in the sky. She could not help but think: "A fairy has died." The good fairy of the sea and fields had been slain by love! Doña Curiana tries to make her friend see the brighter light that comes with the dawn, but Nigromantica can only recall the strangeness of her dream as she departs.

The second french scene poses Doña Curiana and Curianita Silvia, the ingenue—young and suffering out of love for Doña Curiana's son. Curianito, the beloved, is indifferent to

---

5. All textual quotations, unless otherwise specified, are from *Obras Completas, op. cit.,* pp. 579-631.

the lovely Silvia. He waits for something other than Silvia's love, an unknown thing that will make his existence worthwhile. But she cannot be distracted from her longing.

"He detests me . . .
The princess
he awaits will not come."

Silvia reveals her love for Curianito to his mother. Overjoyed at the prospect of a wealthy marriage for her son, Doña Curiana promises to speak to him. Silvia cannot contain her joy now that hope is reborn:

". . . I will be Queen
of this green meadow
for I have love and riches."

Curianito, the object of Silvia's passionate dialogue, comes on the scene carrying a piece of bark upon which he has written a poem. He is young, a poet and visionary, and pupil of Nigromantica. He seems removed from his surroundings; his eyes have a look of distance as if they were searching for a dream with desperation bred in quietness. Silvia, meanwhile, has coquettishly placed herself among the flowers trying to capture Curianito's interest as his mother tries to convince him that he should marry. But Curianito is obstinate: "I won't marry without love." And when his mother leaves him to be convinced by Silvia, Curianito tells her blankly, as her young face looks at him tenderly:

"My illusion
is suspended from the star
which is like a flower."

This star, for which he waits so patiently and devotedly, lies within his imagination pre-empting other thoughts or capabilities. Silvia realizes that Curianito cannot love her while the illusion dominates his thoughts, and begins to cry. And in a moment of irony, the neighboring roaches pass by interpreting the nearness of Curianito and Silvia as the facade of lovers. Curianita Silvia exclaims through her tears:

"If what that voice says
were only true."

Curianito can do no more than try to calm her in his awkward way.

The mood, however, turns from despair to apprenhension as Alacranito, a drunken, loud-mouthed, irreverent, and totally evil scorpion, approaches. Caring little for anyone's feelings, Alacranito takes pleasure in his notoriety. He enjoys watching the faces of those to whom he reveals his many evil deeds; their fear is now shown by Silvia and Curianito as Alacranito tells of his latest feats:

"I have just finished eating a delicious worm
it was soft and sweet, exquisite!
Next to him was a cocoon, a small child...
But I didn't eat him because he was a suckling
And I like them large, tasty!"

Curianito and Silvia are appalled by the account and bravely accuse Alacranito, warning him that his murders will not be forgiven by Gran Cucaracho, their deity. But the cynical scorpion replies threateningly:

"... You'd better be quiet
as you're both most edible."

The two poets, for both are that in different ways, run to the apparent safety of the rocks near Doña Curiana's house as Alacranito laughs drunkenly. Doña Curiana appears in their defense and the intimidator finally falls to the ground in a fit of laughter, but not until he has eaten Silvia's pet fly and threatened to devour all of them.

As if to coincide with Alacranito's stumbling gesture, a group of cockroaches enters in the midst of great confusion. They carry a beautiful butterfly which has fallen, wounded, from the sky.

"Sweet star fallen from a sleeping cypress,
What bitter dawn did your eyes behold?"

The white aviatrix lies unconscious, unable to respond to

Nigromantica's question or to see the curious faces of the roaches as they excitedly minister to her in the hope of curing her broken wing. And Curianito looks upon the fallen star of his dreams with sadness. La Mariposa sighs audibly and his attention becomes more concentrated. Without moving, and as if asleep, Curianito's fairy utters a plaintive cry —"I want to fly!"—and then:

> "The thread leads to the star
> where my treasure lies;
> my wings are silver,
> my heart is gold;
> the thread is dreaming
> with its sonorous hum."

Now Curianito is certain that this is the mysterious "something" he had been awaiting. Realizing that his fate is in the stars and that this beautiful messenger has come to take him there, Curianito begins to fall in love with La Mariposa. But Nigromantica warns him of the dangers of such a love:

> "Curianito, your fate
> depends on the wings of that great butterfly.
> Do not look at her with desire, for you can be lost . . .
> If you fall in love with her, beware you will die."

The poet expresses his sad love gallantly and then sits upon a rock to cry. The curtain falls slowly on the first act as the boisterous song of Alacranito, who has awakened from his drunken slumber, contrasts with the plight of Curianito. The stage is filled with light as the scorpion exits with his song.

The second act discloses a different setting. The dominant green of the first act is now replaced by a flower garden in which giant periwinkes reign. A great cascade of ivy adorns the farthest reaches of the setting, acting as a backdrop to a spring whose waters glitter welcomingly in the pastel hues that light the scene.

Two old roaches enter discussing Curianito's plight. One of them, Curiana Santa, is reputed to be a very learned and saintly matron. Her sympathy extends to the sad poet, but her companion, a more practical roach, does not share her views. She sees Curianito as a worthless vagrant whose fate it will be to starve to death because he refuses to work for his food. Santa responds to these accusations with philosophic gusto reminiscent of a Christian beatitude:

> "They who sing and laugh are more worthy in my kingdom than they who spend a lifetime working."

The quotation from Gran Cucaracho hardly impresses her companion who becomes argumentative. But Santa, true to her name, continues:

> " 'Suffer upon you the stranger's wounds,
> another's pain,' spoke San Cucaracho."

Not being able to oppose such obvious holiness, the companion returns to her cave; Curiana Santa goes on to offer her prayers for Curianito whose poetry reminds her of her own youth.

Doña Curiana and Nigromantica, preceding another group which bears the wounded butterfly, prepare the ground where La Mariposa will be placed for her moonlight bath. Nigromantica, who has taken charge of the patient, assures herself that she will be protected by leaving one of the stronger roaches on guard. Alacranito, she warns, must not be allowed near the butterfly. The sentinel remains nearby while the rest of the roaches depart.

Slowly, La Mariposa awakens, her wings moving very slightly. Her soliloquy, which accompanies the movements, expresses a longing to fly to distant fields, to the fog, to the wind, to the stars:

> "I will fly on the silver thread.
> My children await me,
> there in the distant fields,
> spinning on their wheels.
> I am the spirit
> of silk.
> I come from a mysterious ark

and travel towards the fog.
....
I spun my heart over flesh
to pray in the darkness,
and death gave me white wings,
but blinded the fountain of my silk.
Now I understand the waters' lament,
and the lament of the stars,
and the wind's lament in the mountain,
and the piercing buzzing
of the bee.
Because I am death
and beauty."

And her lament likewise expresses her recognition that she
is beauty and death joined, an omen of sadness for anything
that caresses her. But her wings will not let her fly, and La
Mariposa surrenders to exhaustion.

Alacranito, meanwhile, has been watching the butterfly
with a gleam of never-appeased hunger in his eyes. He approaches her cautiously. As he is about to touch his intended
victim, however, the guard intervenes with his shouts. Failing to convince La Mariposa's protector, Alacranito returns
to his own cave to satisfy his hunger with ten captive flies he
has saved for such an occasion.

La Mariposa remains immobile, as if dead, unaware that
Alacranito had attempted to dispose of her. The guard, now
reinforced by others whom his shouts brought to the scene,
stands apart, but ever watchful, as three old glow-worms
enter slowly. They speak of the mysteries of nature and one
is prompted to say resignedly:

"We shall never understand
the unknown."

They are, in fact, searching for love. The analogy between
love and the dew, in the short speech of one of the insects,
is a sweetly precise one:

"... We old ones
know that love

is like the dew.
The drop which you drink
does not fall anew on the field;
like love, it is lost
in the peace of forgetfulness.
And tomorrow other drops
will glisten on the grass
and shortly cease
to be dew."

As the three approach La Mariposa, she stirs and speaks
weakly; her words are a mixture of disillusionment and despair.

"I do not know what love is,
nor will I ever know."

And the butterfly, whom they think is a fairy, tells them of
the life of the dew drops, of the grains of sand, of the tree
leaves. Their ignorance accentuated by this revelation (for
like men they see themselves as the only animate things),
the puzzled glow-worms return to their quest: "We search
for a lover."

After a short french scene in which Curianito laments his
sad state, and a neighbor roach listens to his moans with
little enthusiasm, the young poet kneels by La Mariposa. His
gesture of love and his impassioned speech, however, do not
touch the butterfly's sensitivities. She begins to dance slowly,
attempting to poise herself for flight. Curianito's questions
are ignored by her as her dance becomes more desperate.

"I will cure your wounds with kisses
if you marry me;
and my friend, a huge nightingale,
will take us flying through the morning."

Still no response. Curianito becomes more dedicated as La
Mariposa falls from exhaustion. He pleads his love with increasing fervor. But though she has not answered him, neither
has she refused his closeness. Curianito embraces La Mariposa suddenly and she remains unconcerned. But it is not

the surrender of a lover and La Mariposa brusquely frees
herself from his clinging darkness which had seemed a tres-
pass upon the virginal whiteness of her body. Curianito,
stunned by her coldness, cries out:

> "Have you no heart? Haven't you been seared
> by the light of my words?"

But the butterfly, his dream, dances on with renewed vigor.
Curianito's love becomes madness as he realizes he has lost
the only thing that could have satisfied his hopes. As she
dances, his words become more and more agonized:

> "Who gave me these eyes I do not want
> and these hands that try
> to grasp a love I do not understand?
> It drains my life!
> Who loses me in shadow?
> Who ordains my suffering without wings?"

These are Curianito's last words. The other roaches rush to
him, but it is too late as the unfortunate poet has died from
a broken heart. "And it is that Death disguises itself as
Love!" The words spoken in the "Prologo" have their vindica-
tion as the play ends.

The themes which Lorca treated in his first play were
not unusual topics for the theatre. Only the manner in which
they were presented was at odds with the traditions of Spanish drama. The themes had been treated in most of the romantic literature of that and preceding periods. Hadn't Don
Quixote been driven to madness in his search for honor,
beauty, justice and virtue? Hadn't Sister Joanna, in *Cancion
de cuna*, been greatly saddened upon her parting from Teresa,
the child who had fulfilled her unrealistic dream of motherhood? Hadn't St. John of the Cross and St. Teresa of Avila
devoted their attentions to the mysticism of the Catholic
faith and longed for death so as to possess its very mysteries?
But Lorca chose to handle these themes in a different manner. The insect world, in his hands, became a world of fantasy wherein the inhabitants spoke and felt as humans, pos-

sessing even the most sensitive feelings and desires of which mankind is capable. His insects had souls.

The very simplicity with which these themes are presented as well as the obviously didactic tone first observed in the "Prologo" lend their support to the classification of the insect play as a fable. But *El maleficio de la mariposa* also extends into the area of social satire, containing elements which implicate society in a plot against the idealist, the poet, the seeker after truth. Principally viewed through character types, the insect world becomes a stultified society with its petty evils and petty goodness. It is a group of individuals which fails to see values beyond its immediate cognition. There is no place in such a society for the visionary and so he must, of necessity, find another means through which his hopes can be expressed, and perhaps fulfilled. And as he seeks his particular elixir, the sure process of withdrawal begins. This, in time, leads to the only path through the maze of frustration—Death. Thus, Death itself becomes the goal, though it is seldom clear to the character that he or she or it is eliminating all other possibilities. And so it is that Curianito dies of a broken heart when La Mariposa's attractiveness eludes him; it is as if she were leading him with her dance towards Death. The quest for Beauty or Love or any ideal, through the agency of time, reaches the state of frustration and this, in turn, leads unequivocally to Death. The process is inescapable.

Within this early framework of thematics are contained the seeds for Lorca's later plays, all of which, with the exception of *La Zapatera Prodigiosa*, deal directly with the many aspects of the Love-Death relationship. However awkward, the intuitive leanings of *El maleficio de la mariposa* are the core around which a strong poetic drama is to evolve. Clearly a work of mixed values, particularly because of its inexperienced technique, the play, nonetheless, serves as a valid starting point from which Lorca's development as a dramatist can be traced.

III. LOS TITERES DE CACHIPORRA

SECTION 1: *La niña que riega el albahaca y el principe pregunton*, the first of Lorca's puppet plays, was presented in the playwright's Granada home on January 6, 1923 as part of the "Children's Festival," organized by Lorca and Falla. A second performance of the play took place in Madrid's "Sociedad de Cursos y Conferencias."

UNFORTUNATELY, the text of *La niña que riega el albahaca . . .* is unavailable. Whether it is lost or being withheld from publication is a matter for the future to uncover. The puppet comedy is significant because it was the first theatre piece written by Lorca after his failure with *El maleficio de la mariposa*, and therefore shows the rebirth of his interest in the theatre.

> Curious about all the theatrical forms, accomplished in the handling of real characters as well as wooden puppets, he adopts the *guignol*, "expression of folk fantasy, indicative of its grace and innocence," not basing it on foreign types, but reviving a popular Andalusian character. His *Titeres de Cachiporra*, first presented in his Granada home in 1923, in his youth, with the musical collaboration of Falla, belong to that spirit.[1]

Manuel de Falla arranged the music—excerpts from the compositions of Debussy, Albeniz, Ravel and Pedrell—and accompanied the stage action on the piano. The watercolorist Hermenegildo Lanz created the puppets used in the production, while the settings as well as the miniature stage were designed by Lorca. The only record of the proceedings is found in a magazine article which contains a duplication of the program notes:

> "Gentlemen, listen to the program for this children's festival which I proclaim from the window of the puppet

---

1. Guillermo de Torre, "Prologo," *Obras Completas de F. G. L.* (Buenos Aires, Ed. Losada, 1940), vol. I, pp. 15-16.

stage, before the brow of the world. First, we will present
our Cervantes' *entremes*, titled: *Los dos habladores*
(with the appearance at the end of the picaresque Cristobita). Second, you will see the ancient Andalusian
tale in three prints and a chromolithograph: *La niña
que riega el albahaca y el principe pregunton*, with
dialogue and adaptation to the Andalusian Puppet
Theatre by Federico Garcia Lorca."[2]

Though the play was conceived by Lorca, its roots lay in
Andalusian folk tradition. Lorca based the puppet comedy
on the ancient tale, reviving the well-known plot through
dialogue, plasticity and music. The result was an apparently short piece in "three prints and a chromolithograph."
The term "Chromolithograph" would, of course, have a
meaning totally divorced from its obvious definition, such
as the term "Photograph" in Lorca's last play, *La casa de
Bernarda Alba*, serving only to indicate a colorful re-creation
of the plot. Lorca often used such sub-titles to convey his
intent. The program notes, this section cited in another article, continue:

> "The little heads of the characters in both works have
> been sculptured by the watercolorist Hermenegildo Lanz.
> The decorations have been painted by the poet Feder-
> ico Garcia Lorca."[3]

The final part of the program consisted of a thirteenth century play, *Misterio de los Reyes Magos*, a Spanish mystery
play which had remained intact. The notes conclude with
other credits and an admonition:

> "The music in the entire program will be executed by
> Manuel de Falla, piano and cymbal; Jose Gomez, violin;
> Alfredo Baldres, clarinet; Jose Molina, lute. The first
> invitatory and the 'Carol of the Three Magi Kings of
> the Orient' will be sung by Isabelita Garcia Lorca and

2. Juvenal Ortiz Saralegui, "Federico Garcia Lorca y Rafael Barradas," *Romance*, Mexico, (1940), vol. I, no. 19.
3. Guillermo de Torre, "Federico Garcia Lorca y sus origenes dram-
   aticos," *Cinco Farsas Breves* (Buenos Aires, Ed. Losada, 1953),
   p. 9.

Laurita de los Rios Giner. Goodbye, gentlemen. Good afternoon and be quiet as it will begin promptly. Once the play begins the doors will be closed and entrance will not be permitted. The show begins at three o'clock in the afternoon, on the day of the Three Kings. The Owner of the Theater."[4]

SECTION 2: Second in Lorca's repertory of puppet comedies is *La tragicomedia de don Cristobal y la seña Rosita*. The date of its completion is uncertain, but in an interview in 1928,[5] the playwright revealed that he was preparing the piece. Its premiere, however, was delayed until after Lorca's death although plans existed for a 1935 production.[6] Felipe Lluch Garin directed the live production in 1937 at Madrid's "Teatro de la Zarzuela."

La tragicomedia de don Cristobal was to be produced in 1932 by the company of Margarita Xirgu, not as a puppet play but as a farce. The dances were to be executed by "La Argentinita." To this end Lorca prepared the music for the play, often rehearsing the score at a friend's house:

> He's studying—he says—"a crystalline music" for his *Titeres de Cachiporra*, which the company of Margarita Xirgu will present with the valuable cooperation of 'La Argentinita.'[7]

But as was to be true of many projects envisioned by Lorca, the play had to be postponed indefinitely. The affairs which concerned him most intimately at the time, those of his theatre troupe—"La Barraca"—no doubt prevented his efforts from reaching fruition.

Written in six scenes and a short "Prologo," the play is

---

4. J. O. Saralegui, *op. cit.*
5. Ernesto Gimenez Caballero, "Itinerarios Jovenes de España: Federico Garcia Lorca," *La Gaceta Literaria,* Madrid (June 15, 1928).
6. *Obras Completas, op. cit.,* pp. 1604-1605; letter to Angel Ferrant.
7. Carlos Morla Lynch, *op. cit.,* p. 175.

the longer of the two extant "guiñolesque" works. Its characters, members of a long line of Spanish comedy creations, bear some resemblances to *commedia dell'arte* types, but generally fall into a diversified genealogy as delineated by Lorca in a letter to the sculptor who created the puppets:

"Cristobal's head is energetic, brutal, like his club. Currito el del Puerto is young and of melancholic turn. Cocoliche is the 'pretty boy,' the leading man. Mosquito is Shakespeare's Puck, part *duende*, part child, part insect. Figaro is a Figaro."[8]

The "Prologo," announced by two trumpets and a drum in a comical overture, is delivered by Mosquito—part duende, part ghost, part insect—who "represents the joy of free living and the poetry of the Andalusian spirit." He speaks these preliminary words with rare gusto allowing them to flow as from an endless spring—effortlessly and with direction—as he introduces the history of his troupe to his audience:

"My company and I come from the bourgeois theatre, from the theatre of counts and marquis, a theatre of gold and crystal. . . . My company and I were imprisoned. . . . Then I got word to my friends and we fled through the fields in search of plain folk, to show them life, the small and smallest things of the world. . . ."[9]

Once his task is completed, Mosquito begins his exit. As he does so, a frail musical triad accompanies him and the stage slowly changes into a large room in the house of the heroine, Rosita.

The first scene opens with Rosita sitting near a window and sewing on a large embroidery frame. Behind her, through the grill on the window, can be seen a small orange grove. Rosita pricks herself constantly because her mind is not on her sewing but on Cocoliche, her lover, and the thought of marriage overcomes all others. A whistling from outside the

---

8. letter to Angel Ferrant (1935), *op. cit.*
9. All textual quotations, unless otherwise specified, are from *Obras Completas, op. cit.,* pp. 633-690.

window brings her back to life. She drops her embroidery to answer its call. But no sooner is she thus engaged than the voice of her father forces a hasty retreat to the chair. Cocoliche is left with only a glimpse of her face. El Padre enters unceremoniously, a caricature of the impecunious old man who plans that his daughter's marriage will provide handsomely for his old age. He laments their impoverished state which forces Rosita to embroider for their support, all the while crying profusely and loudly into a large colored handkerchief. Thinking of Cocoliche, Rosita confesses that she is willing to marry, in fact that she longs for it. El Padre's tears turn to sobs of excitement. He exits in buoyant spirits which confound Rosita for she knows that Cocoliche is poorer than her father, having inherited only three coins and a box of quince from his grandmother. Nonetheless, Rosita loves him:

"Ay! But I love him, I love him, I love him and love him. Money is for the rest of the world; I'll take love."

Having become absorbed in the reflection on love for love's sake, Rosita has failed to see the implication of her father's remarks. Obviously, though not to Rosita, El Padre has found a profitable marital arrangement. While Rosita was consenting to marriage with Cocoliche, El Padre was planning the match with another person.

In this manner Lorca introduces one of the earliest, yet most effective, refinements of comedy into this puppet play —talking at cross purposes. Expertly used by past masters such as Lope de Vega and Moliere, Lorca revives the technique at the very beginning of the farce rather than in a later segment as had been the custom. With this procedure he is able to incite interest immediately. But it is because he is dealing with stock characters, well-known types in Spanish literature and theatre, that Lorca can proceed directly to the situation and not be detained with the development of such personages. Especially, too, since Lorca places these human caricatures within the confines of a smaller world —that of the marionette stage—he has the advantages of the plastic arts (which create characterizations at the height of their distinction) in giving an audience an instant and revealing look into the characters.

The situation is further complicated when Rosita coquettishly tells her lover that their marriage is arranged. In his joy, Cocoliche exclaims: "I'll write to Paris immediately requesting a baby." But Rosita thinks it is better to write to Madrid for the baby. Their naivete becomes even more comical as Cocoliche tries to embrace Rosita through the fancy grill that guards her window. She kisses him but manages to stay out of the reach of his outstretched arms. When the sound of bells announces someone's approach, Cocoliche departs reluctantly.

Don Cristobita, the villain of the piece, can be seen outside the window in his carriage which has stopped to let him admire Rosita's charms. The old man casts mischievous looks upon Rosita and compliments her highly:

"She is the most beautiful child in the village . . . I'll definitely take her . . . what a figure, what gentility!"

Rosita receives his compliments graciously but no sooner is he out of sight than she begins to mimic his words, delegating him as "one of those crazy foreigners." Suddenly, a pearl necklace is thrown through the window from the direction where Cristobita had been. Without as much as questioning her good fortune, Rosita places it around her neck and admires the way it suits her. Her father, however, interrupts her daydream with the announcement of the wedding. Still thinking her father has arranged her marriage to Cocoliche, Rosita is jubilant. But the talking at cross purposes finally resolves itself when El Padre reveals that her prospective bridegroom is Don Cristobita who had just passed the window. In a fit of temper, Rosita tears off the necklace recognizing it as a gift from the old man. El Padre

confronts her defiance with his authority and she becomes
outwardly calm. When he leaves, she returns to her sewing,
ignoring the window where she knows Cristobita lurks although every word he utters to his servant is audible in the
room: "She's a succulent wench. And all mine! All mine!"

Meanwhile, Rosita sews. The large clock which stands
against one of the walls strikes a solitary note. As Rosita
looks up, the front of the clock opens and a figure, Una
Hora, dressed in yellow, appears. Its words of hope attempt
to calm Rosita's dissatisfaction.

"There, Rosita, be patient, what can you do? How do
you know how things will turn out? While it's sunny
here, it rains elsewhere. How do you know what winds
will make your weathervane dance on the roof tomorrow?"

But as the figure, perhaps a personification of her hope,
returns to its receptacle, Rosita's face once more inherits its
former melancholic look. Outside, Cocoliche's voice is heard
sufferingly wondering:

"My lover's sighs
are borne by the air."

Rosita continues to cry, and the scene ends as she repeats
his words to herself.

The short second scene takes place in the small plaza
outside Rosita's window; a large palm tree, a bench and the
grill-work are the only decorations visible. Cocoliche, a dash-
ing figure in the popular costume of the nineteenth century—
a dark green cape trimmed in black brocade and the Andalusian hat worn at a rakish angle—strolls pensively near
the window hoping to discover why Rosita's sighs have been
so despairing. A guitar, held dejectedly in one hand, completes his appointments. His patience is rewarded when
Rosita appears at the window. But her news that their wedding is ill-fated stuns him and Rosita does not explain the
reason. Cocoliche begins to cry and kick in an infantile man-

ner, throwing himself on the ground. He thinks that Rosita never loved him and fails to realize that she, too, is crying. El Padre's voice, however, calls to his daughter and she dutifully responds, leaving Cocoliche with his doubts.

Contrasting with Cocoliche's comic cries, a merry group of his friends appears singing the praises of the ladies whom they have been serenading successfully. Refusing to have their evening spoiled by their friend's troubles, the group takes Cocoliche along to buoy his spirits. They all exit singing and drinking, heading for a tavern.

While their song and laughter are still in the air, El Padre and Don Cristobita exit from the house discussing the final arrangements for the latter's wedding. Recognizing the more obvious faults of the lecherous Cristobita, El Padre begins to doubt his judgment in delivering his daughter to the confessed villain. But the attractiveness of the price keeps him from objecting more than tokenly. Cristobita, meanwhile, thinks covetously of Rosita as: "Un bocatto di cardinali!" Surprised at the intrusion of Italian into the conversation, El Padre asks Don Cristobal if he speaks the language. The old man replies:

"No; as a child I was in Italy and France, serving a certain Don Pantaloon . . ."

Cristobal thus reveals his connection with "a certain Don Pantaloon," presenting himself more clearly as part of the same tradition which made his patron and his cronies renowned throughout Europe. And true to the type he represents, he threatens El Padre with his club when his hesitation becomes more evident. The club poised, Cristobita approaches him:

"Who said no to me? I don't know why I haven't pushed you into the ravine where the others lie. This club has killed many Frenchmen, Italians and Hungarians. . . . I have the list at home. Obey me! Don't end up with the others. The club hasn't been working for some time and it escapes from my hands. Be careful!"

Confronted with the sad choice of fulfilling the bargain or
facing Don Cristobal's boisterous wrath, El Padre receives
the hundred coins agreed upon. Inside the house, as if realizing that her life has been sold, Rosita sings a lament. Cristobita listens with disdain. He will make her sing a more
natural song, he says. The scene closes with the villain's
version of the proposed tune in which the ridiculous lyric
becomes even more so at his rendition:

> "The frog sings out cuac, cuac,
> cuac, cuac, cuarac."

The father, intimidated and despondent, thinks half aloud
on his daughter's fate now that he has consented to the
thoughtless and selfish marriage.

The third scene is set in the town's tavern, a typical
Spanish inn decorated with bullfight posters, hand fashioned
tables and chairs, large wine barrels and oil lamps. Espantanublos (literally, Scareclouds), the tavern keeper, stands
behind his counter surveying his customers. The Contrabandistas, smugglers, sit at the tables. They are reminiscent
of legendary smugglers whose romantic exploits were tinted
by an air of mystery and intrigue, partly due to the velvet
capes, the hidden faces and the imposing muskets. These
men are dressed likewise. One of them sings a gay ballad of
the carefree life of the smuggler as popularized in legend.
As he sings, the door opens and another mysterious figure,
fully covered by his large cape, stands on the threshold. The
song stops and everyone looks at the silent man who sits at
a corner table without revealing his face. Espantanublos tries
to converse with him but his questions are answered only
by sighs. Fearing that the stranger might be a danger to
them, the Contrabandistas waste no time in leaving the
premises. When they have left, El Joven utters his first
words: ". . . I'm shaking inside. . . . I shouldn't have come."
Hearing these spoken thoughts, Espantanublos reacts as
anyone might hearing a man speak to himself: "He's worse

off than Don Tancredo . . ."[10] This opening sequence, very similar in tone and gesture to several scenes in Duque de Rivas' *Don Alvaro*, serves to implant mystery in the seedbed of comedy.

The mood of mystery is broken, however, when Cocoliche and his friends enter the tavern in gay spirits. As Cocoliche is very drunk, his companions place him on a chair while he plays the forsaken lover in a loud voice that catches the attention of El Joven. He listens while the young men try to cheer up Cocoliche by telling him that Don Cristobal can be ignored because of his age, that he will fall asleep by midnight, that Cocoliche will then be able to go to Rosita. This is done in great gayety with the guitars playing furiously. Interested by the curious situation, El Joven offers a toast in honor of the absent Rosita, at the same time seeking information about her. But Cocoliche and his friends join forces in putting off the stranger's questions with various insults. El Joven manages to remain calm and finally learns the details of the wedding, but only to be disconcerted at the mention of Rosita's full name. Before he exits, he tells them that he, too, had once been affianced to a Rosita but that she now preferred a "dabbler in love." His eyes singe Cocoliche as he leaves with clenched fists: "I don't know how I've held back."

Cocoliche seems disturbed at El Joven's word, but before he can explain himself or his suspicions, Espantanublos announces the arrival of Don Cristobita. Cocoliche, who becomes belligerent upon hearing his rival's name, is dragged out of the tavern by two of his companions. The other two hide behind the large barrels to observe the villain. Espantanublos, afraid that their proposed jests may irritate the old man, tries to make them leave also. Before he can further his attempts, however, Cristobita enters in his usual bois-

---

10. The phrase refers to Tancredo, a character in Tasso's *Jerusalem Liberated* who fights with Clorinda, the Saracen heroine, and, without realizing who she is, slays her.

terous manner. The expected abuse of Don Cristobal takes
place from behind the barrels. The derogatory remarks of
the young men, unseen by their subject, seem to Cristobita
to be the responsibility of the innkeeper. Slowly, Espantanublos is turned from spectator to suspect, finally being chased
out of the tavern by Don Cristobal in typical *commedia
dell'arte* fashion, his slapstick working feverishly to catch
Espantanublos in its punishing arc. Their exit brings the
culprits to their feet, convulsed with laughter. The squeals
of the innkeeper, growing ever fainter outside, close the
scene.

Another short scene follows immediately. The same two
friends who carried Cocoliche out of the tavern now deposit
him where they first found him, outside Rosita's window,
and depart. Cocoliche is unaware of his state as he sleeps
contentedly. The sound of a flute, persistent as the noise of
a mosquito, traces its way ever closer to the plaza. Mosquito,
who delivered the "Prologo," is the composer of these irk-
some notes. Seeing Cocoliche, he mischievously crosses to
him. The light has become brighter since Mosquito's entrance and reaches its high point as he plays his flute in
Cocoliche's ear. But a swat discourages further efforts and
Mosquito begins a slow exit, philosophically commenting:

> "Of course he doesn't know what's happening, he's only
> a child . . . But what's certain is that Rosita's heart,
> the tiniest of hearts, escapes him. Her soul is like one
> of those mother-of-pearl boats sold at the fairs; little
> Valencian boats carrying a scissor and a thimble. Now,
> he'll write on that sail, 'Remembrance,' and it will keep
> drifting, drifting . . ."

As Mosquito leaves, the light diminishes, seeking its earlier
level of illumination. Soon Cocoliche is alone once more.

A few moments later, El Joven and another man, Mozo,
appear from the shadows discussing Rosita's forthcoming
wedding. As he talks with his friend, El Joven tells him that
he has returned to Rosita because he did not find in the

world, which had called to him five years before, that which he had sought:

> "I used to think that bells were always ringing throughout the world and that the roads were full of white inns with fair girls, their sleeves rolled to the elbow. But it isn't so! It's very dull."

His strange dream of a vibrant world found false, El Joven has retraced his steps. Rosita, now, becomes the symbol of that which he had sought elsewhere. Mozo tries to discourage his hopes, but even the proposed marriage does not stop his plan of seeing Rosita.

A figure crosses in the shadows opposite the two men. Recognizing him as the shoemaker Cansa-Almas (literally, Soul-exhauster), Mozo calls to him. The old man toddles across the stage, half-afraid and half-curious. Only then does El Joven unburden himself of his cloak and the shoemaker realizes it is Currito el del Puerto who had sold oranges on the town's streets. Mozo proceeds, after the greetings, to convince Cansa-Almas to allow Currito to take his place. This would give Currito an opportunity to speak with Rosita when he would deliver her wedding shoes. After his hesitation has been weakened by an offer of money, Cansa-Almas agrees to follow the plan. The three men exit together arm in arm, partners in the conspiracy formulated near the drunken Cocoliche.

He tosses restlessly as he experiences a dream wherein he warns Rosita of Cristobita's bad habits and extols his own virtues. Then, the ghost of Rosita appears. She sings a bittersweet quatrain to the lively music of "vito"—a popular dance.

> "With the dancing, vito, vito,
> with the singing, vito, clearly ...
> Every hour, little darling,
> I am drifting more from you."

The Rosita of Cocoliche's dream is dressed in a dark blue gown, crowned with a garland of tuberoses. In her hand she carries a silver dagger. The vision, however, is brief, disappearing as Cocoliche awakens to the sad lyric which mourns the lovers' separation. But Rosita's real voice picks up the song. As the curtain closes, Cocoliche begins to cry: "This is the first time that I've really cried!"

In scene five, the setting represents an Andalusian street with its white houses, varied stores—a shoemaker's shop, a sidewalk barbershop—and a large gate which bears the impressive sign: "Refuge of all the undeceived of the world." A heart pierced by seven swords completes the adornments of the gate. Cansa-Almas and Figaro (the barber of opera fame) sit in front of their respective shops awaiting the early morning trade. While the shoemaker sews a boot, Figaro, a very comical figure in green costume and wearing a hair net to hold his curls, prepares his instruments for Don Cristobita's appointment.

The two men's conversation is necessarily brief as the sound of a flute punctuates each of Cansa-Almas' phrases with a scale similar to the proposed word endings. It is as if Mosquito were hiding off-stage, ready to annoint any of Cansa-Almas' words with the ointment of the mischievous flute. Adding to the annoyance, an urchin taunts the elderly shoemaker but Figaro chases him away nobly. Currito, who has entered meanwhile, pushes Figaro aside and goes to Cansa-Almas. The old man trembles at Currito's demand that he be given Rosita's slippers, but his better judgment forces him to succumb. Figaro observes the candid scene as Currito caresses the slippers:

> "Oh, little shoes
> of Doña Rosita!
> Oh, to have her
> dear legs inside!"

When, at the insistence of Cansa-Almas, Currito departs on his mission, Figaro watches with an amusement that matches the shoemaker's chagrin. He knows that as a barber he will soon receive all the details of what will transpire:

"The news reaches the world after passing through the sorting house of my barber-shop."

Cristobita enters hurriedly in his usual gruff manner. But Figaro is the perfect host, maneuvering him to the chair with the skill of a wise man. Cansa-Almas, on the other hand, afraid that Cristobita will discover the deception that substituted Currito in his own place, runs into his shop to hide. Cristobita waves his club menacingly, first at Figaro and then at Cansa-Almas. Completely nervous with fright, the old cobbler hides himself entirely. But Figaro's calm approach soothes the vociferous Don Cristobal, who falls asleep. Figaro works diligently and accompanies himself with an operatic aria. The song is then taken up by a young girl who follows the lead of an old accordionist as the stage is filled by a chorus. Everyone marches around the sleeping Don Cristobal admiring his painted wooden head which the barber has discovered. Even Cansa-Almas leaves the security of his shop to observe the great marvel. Cristobita remains unaware of the concentrated analysis, the muffled laughter and the general gayety at his expense. The "pianisimo" revelry continues as the scene ends.

The final scene is the longest in the play. It is set in Rosita's house, in a pink room whose appointments number two large latticed cabinets, an oil lamp hanging from the ceiling and a painting of St. Rose of Lima over the doorway. Rosita paces nervously through the room in her rose-colored wedding gown. The beauty of the dress is contrasted with the jet beads she wears, an effective touch of mourning over her fate:

"Everything's lost! Everything! I'm going to my execution like Marianita Pineda."

Rosita compares her suffering with that of the Granadine heroine, thinking of Cristobal's embrace as the "iron necklace" which had joined Mariana and Death. With sobs of bitter resignation, she sings a small ballad which ends: "When will I see my love?"

A response to her question, a voice entoning a song of its own offstage, recalls Currito's words in the previous scene. Rosita listens, surprised that her solitude has been intruded upon:

> "Rosita, if only
> I were able to see
> the tip of your foot
> then we'd see indeed."

Currito, carefully disguised by his cape, enters slowly. Rosita retreats for fear. His enigmatic answers to her questions serve to prepare her for his very theatrical uncovering. Recognizing her former lover, Rosita's alarm mounts:

> "Ay, I am unfortunate! ... Do you want to ruin me? ... Get out, thief!"

But Currito is not so easily dissuaded from his purpose. He advances on Rosita with outstretched arms and a short chase ensues. However, before the comic sequence can be completed with an embrace, El Padre enters. Currito hastily frames an excuse for his awkward presence and proceeds to fit the shoes. El Padre sits nearby reading a newspaper. Reluctantly, Rosita sits and allows Currito to begin what he considers such a pleasant task. As he whispers his admiration of her legs and lifts her skirts ever higher, Rosita protests with insults. Currito takes advantage of his position and demands that she lift her skirt and El Padre, who is unaware of his real intent, instructs Rosita to be obedient. When he leaves the room Rosita jumps up and the chase is renewed until Cristobita's approach is heard through her screams. Aware of his danger, Currito tries to open the door which El Padre had shut behind him. But to no avail. Rosita is also frightened by the thought of being discovered in another man's company by Don Cristobal. Finally, she has recourse to a quick prayer to the saint over her doorway. The result is a sudden inspiration which makes Rosita grab Currito and place him in front of one of the large cabinets. Once he is safely inside, she sighs with relief and then renews her sad ballad.

But she has little time to give way to her emotions. Don Cristobal, promising to be much less than a tolerant husband, enters suspiciously and searches the room:

> "I smell human flesh
> in this room;
> unless you give it to me
> I will eat you up."

Don Cristobal's words sound somewhat like Alacranito's in *El maleficio de la mariposa*, and no doubt there is a similarity in the two characters, a kinship which shows them both to be boisterous, and given more to alarm than to action. Like Alacranito, Cristobal can also admire Rosita's charms with hungry eyes: ("Oh, how appetizing! What a pair of nice hams she has!")

His aside is not heard by Rosita who tries to overcome her reluctance to Cristobita so as to arrest his attention and prevent his discovery of Currito. The old man grows more ridiculous as he talks. Brandishing his club, he brags about the men he has killed and promises Rosita that soon she will witness his talent. Rosita's relief is evident when an acolyte appears to announce that the church is ready for the wedding and Cristobal exits temporarily: "I'm going to put on a magnificent hat and hang ribbons on my club."

When he has left, Rosita begins to open Currito's cabinet. But she is not to be so easily freed from her predicament. Cocoliche suddenly enters through the window. Exhausted from her ordeal, Rosita falls in his arms confessing that she loves only him. The jealous Currito, still imprisoned in the cabinet, screams his disapproval. Soon the scene becomes a series of insults of which Rosita is made the central recipient. Her nervousness is heightened once more by the sound of Cristobita's footsteps and only after a dedicated struggle is she able to hide Cocoliche in the second cabinet. The scene resembles the famous "screen scene" in Sheridan's *School for Scandal*, promising hilarious results.

Again Rosita has to calm Don Cristobita's suspicions, aroused by the sounds of the recent quarrel. Not entirely convinced but willing to wait until after the ceremony to investigate, Don Cristobal escorts Rosita to the church through a group of wedding guests who enter with garlands of paper roses.

The two suitors have been left to face each other through the cabinet's shutters which conveniently open outwards. Their animosity, however, quickly turns to self-pity in the realization that Rosita has forsaken them for the lecherous Cristobita. They become very dramatic in interpreting their joint sorrow as their renunciations of life lead to a chorus of tears.

Mosquito, who appears at opportune moments when he can sermonize properly, now enters and advises the young and rejected suitors:

"There's no need to cry, little friend, no need to cry. The earth has many little white paths, smooth paths, silly little paths. . . . After all . . . the moon is not waning, nor the air coming and going."

His words serve to end the flow of tears, but their practicality goes no further. Without a visible solution to their problem, Currito and Cocoliche are left with their sighs as Mosquito exits playing his flute. His optimistic words are lost in the notes of his song.

Meanwhile, the wedding of Rosita to Don Cristobita has taken its course and the newlyweds return to the house. As they enter the room, Cocoliche and Currito retract their heads grudgingly. Though curiosity over the old man's amorous intent makes them apprehensive, the promise of safety from his wrath is momentarily more alluring. The villain approaches his bride with lustful eyes, and she exclaims aside: "He'll kill me with his club!"

Cristobita's advance stalls at Rosita's reluctance to be

embraced but his ill-fitting generosity—a result of the wed-
ing—does not permit his suspicions to find new outlets; he
sees Rosita's hesitation as a prerogative of the bashful bride
who really loves her husband:

> "You're sighing! But it must be because you like me.
> I am old and understand such things .... Aren't I very
> handsome? I shall kiss you! There, there."

Currito and Cocoliche react violently when they hear his
narcissistic words and see Rosita being kissed. Their angry
shouts cause Cristobita to grab his club. But Rosita succeeds
in vanquishing his suspicion by distracting him with lies and
amorous words. For a few moments he remains convinced,
distracted from reality. When again he kisses Rosita, however, the rebellious screams of the forsaken lovers bring Cristobal back to reality. His rage mounts as Rosita tries a final
lie:

> "Now, don't get like that. It was only a bird passing by
> the window with wings ... this big!"

Seeing that he doesn't believe her, Rosita resorts to crying.
Torn between reason and love, Cristobita succumbs finally
to his wife's tale and drops his club. As he has been drinking
heavily all day, he is not himself nor does his attitude indicate any real reform in the villainous character. Dazed by
the wine, Cristobita sits comfortably as Rosita recalls her
childhood. Her voice, sweetly monotonous, serves, along with
the wine, to dull the old man's senses. Within a few moments
Cristobal falls asleep.

Rosita stealthily starts to open Currito's cabinet. As she
does so, Mosquito re-enters with his flute and begins to play
annoyingly in Don Cristobita's ear. The latter intermittently
slaps at him, but to no avail. Mosquito continues as Currito
is helped out by Rosita. She disavows any love for him;
Cocoliche, hearing these unexpected words, becomes ecstatic
until he remembers that Rosita is married. Mosquito, meanwhile, plagues Cristobal so ardently that the old man awakens.
When he sees Currito standing unguarded, he grabs his club

and charges drunkenly. Half in fright, half in valor, Currito draws his knife and faces his adversary. Cristobal walks menacingly around Currito. Rosita opens the door. Then, Currito plunges his knife into Cristobal's chest and flees into the street. Stunned only for a minute by the knife which dangles strangely from his chest, Cristobita finally pursues his opponent. The hysterics of the scene have been aided by various noises provided by a small orchestra off-stage and by Rosita's shrill screams.

Cocoliche, too, adds to the noise as he demands to be let out so that he can kill Don Cristobal. Rosita fluctuates between doubts, eventually releasing him from the second cabinet. The lovers embrace as if nothing else mattered. But suddenly Cristobita returns. The old man fumes as they kiss in front of him:

> "So, you have lovers by pairs! Get ready for the ravine. Pin! Pon! Brrrr! Impossible! I who have killed three hundred Englishmen, three hundred Constantinoplans! You'll remember me."

As he lunges towards the helpless Cocoliche, Don Cristobita falters. He drops his club as a great creaking of springs resounds in the room. Holding his stomach, Cristobal falls to the floor:

> "Oh, my belly! My poor belly! It's your fault I'm broken, that I'm dying! Oh, I'm dying! Oh, call the priest! Oh!"

Rosita runs wildly through the room yelling for her father. Don Cristobita moans a few more times and dies face up. Cocoliche timidly circles the body and confusedly observes:

> "...Hey! He has no blood!... Look! See what's coming out of his bellybutton!...Do you know something?... Cristobita was not a person!"

The discovery shocks Rosita. Cocoliche gladly comforts her as the main door opens and many puppets, carrying torches, enter. Carrying a white flag and playing a trumpet, Mosquito leads the ceremonious group. The puppets wear red capes and black hats as they escort a huge coffin into the room. Several priests are among those present. An attempt by the undertakers to lift the body results in a general scramble when it emits a bassoon-like noise. A second try is likewise rewarded, but the sound is less powerful. The sounds diminish steadily until there remains only a noise similar to piccolo notes. When they are sure that the frame is harmless, the puppets place Don Cristobal in the coffin and exit. Cocoliche and Rosita embrace happily while Mosquito leaves with a musical flourish. The play ends as a symphony accompanies the slow descent of the curtain.

La tragicomedia de don Cristobal is the more serious of the two extant puppet plays in that it is composed more skillfully within a philosophical attitude. Not that this is what prevails. The comedy itself is what is most interesting and arresting. But the attempt to imply a solution to the social problems that Lorca sees is of importance also. In a light manner, the play ridicules the conventions of society and the characters who help make these conditions so predominant. However, being an early and youthful dissection, the play is not as damning or as revelatory as Lorca's more mature work would prove to be in this very area.

If viewed in the light of Lorca's theatre experience, the play can be seen as a "spoof" of that romantic and extremely ornate drama which dominated the Spanish stage during his apprenticeship. Though Lorca's appreciation of the classical theatre was never in question, he did object to the heavy-handedness which characterized modern productions of these traditional works. In line with this thinking, Lorca rejected the public acceptance of trivial plots encased in a thoroughly syrupy rendition. Attempting to follow in the path of Cervantes, Lope de Vega, Calderon de la Barca and other masters of the form, many of the playwrights in Lorca's era sought a magic formula that would please the public. That form was extreme romanticism. Therefore, Lorca's puppet farce, besides being an entertaining piece, becomes also a satirical study of the then modern Spanish stage with its thin plots disguised by ornamentation and its contrived "happy endings."

But, as if to prove the adage that talent will tell, Lorca's theatricality of expression, be it scenic or auditory, is obvious in every well-fashioned act:

> Here appear the stock characters of the popular puppet theatre of Spain, especifically of Andalucia. Don Cristobita is, for example, as native to that tradition as is Punch, his fellow-clubman, to the English puppet theatre. And here also are the conventional devices and plot of the traditional marionette play, but with this difference —almost every detail has been refashioned and given the charm and freshness and vigor that are characteristic of Lorca's most unusual genius.[11]

SECTION 3: The puppet trilogy is completed by *El retablillo de don Cristobal,* written in 1931. Its premiere was held on May 11, 1935 on the occasion of "La Feria del Libro" in Madrid. Lorca manipulated the puppets which now went under the name: "Guiñol 'La Tarumba'."

El retablillo de don Cristobal is very similar to the puppet play just considered, even containing sections where the dialogue is exactly that of its predecessor. This is particularly true in those places where Cristobita converses with Rosita (both are the same characters seen before, now appearing in an altered situation). Here, Cristobita emerges as a doctor of suspicious capacity and obviously evil intent. Though his role is different, his attitude is much the same—selfish, domineering, cruel and lecherous. Rosita, who does not enter until the second part of the short play, has an altered character. She is now represented as an over-sexed woman who conducts her affairs while Cristobita sleeps. Again, the plot is made more comical by its many ridiculous elements and situations.

The play begins with the "Prologo" which, unlike that pronounced by Mosquito in the previous piece, is in the

---

11. William I. Oliver, "The Tragicomedy of Don Cristobita and Doña Rosita," *New World Writing No.* 8 (New York, Mentor, 1955), p. 188.

manner of an "apologia." Lorca defends and explains the puppet comedy, giving its origin as popular tradition, its un-expurgated language as that of the people, its outlook as innocent and comical:

> "The poet who has interpreted and gathered this *gui-ñolesque* farce from popular sources has the evidence that the cultured public here this afternoon will know how to receive the delicious and hard language of the puppets with intelligence and a pure heart.
>
> All popular *guiñol* has this rhythm, this fantasy and this enchanting freedom which the poet has preserved in the dialogue.
>
> *Guiñol* is the expression of folk fantasy and presents the environment of its innocence and grace.
>
> Thus, the poet knows that the public will listen joy-fully and simply to the words and expressions which are born from the earth and which will serve as purification in an age in which iniquities, errors and twisted senti-ments reach even into the recesses of the home."[12]

Once the first part of the "Prologo" has been expressed, preparing the audience for the occasional bad language of the play, one of the characters, El Poeta, the supposed author of the entertainment, appears and commences his section of the introduction. Here, for the first time in the comedy, are heard echoes of *La tragicomedia* as El Poeta's words resemble those of Mosquito. As a drum roll announces the start of the play, the author takes the liberty of adding a few extra words that reveal his suppressed sensitivity:

> "I want to tell you that I know how roses are born and how the stars of the sea are nurtured, but..."

But the divergence from the strict wording prepared for the prologue brings El Director on stage:

> "Be kind enough to shut up.... You, as a poet, have no right to disclose the secret of our lives.... Don't I pay your wages?"

Trying to explain his forwardness, El Poeta answers meekly and ashamedly:

---

12. All textual quotations, unless otherwise specified, are from *Obras Completas op. cit.,* pp. 929-953.

"Yes, sir, but I know that deep down Don Cristobal is
good and that perhaps he could really be."

His attempts at recognizing some goodness in Don Cristobita, however, irritate the director to the point where he
threatens the author with physical violence. Humbly resigned to his fate, El Poeta follows the only route to apology
the director has left him: reiterating Cristobal's evil nature
so as to reassure the audience whose doubts the poet has
aroused. A final insult is heaped on El Poeta before he exits
as El Director pays him for his services. Feeling like a Judas
who has sold himself and his ideals, El Poeta rejects the five
gold coins and accepts instead five pieces of silver. "Silver
coins appear to be reflections of the moon." Laughing because
he has profited by the transaction, El Director helps to es-
tablish the symbol by paying him in silver.

Through this purposely pathetic episode, Lorca uncovered
one of the problems that concerned him greatly in relation
to the contemporary theatre in Spain. He defines his reason
for the apparent decline of the modern stage as the excessive
control over the creative elements by economic pressures.
On the physical level, this control over authors is exercised
from producer, to director, to actor. Joined under inter-
dependent necessities, these three important cogs in the
theatrical machinery exert pressure on the artist, the poet,
and control his very words. The author, as Lorca explains
here, must give in, abandoning his creative goals and sacrificing his integrity, if he wishes to survive. The director, El
Director, represents all the powers which are arrayed against
the poet and who savagely curtail his honest efforts to reveal
humanity in its true tonality. Not allowed to create his
subject in the most faithful colors, the author is instructed
by management as to how to depict or design his characters.
The result is a monochromatic delineation whose tones lack
truth and depth. It is this debasement of theatre that Lorca
objects to and gives more extensive coverage in various interviews.

"Today, the majority of authors and actors in Spain

occupy a place which is hardly a middle-ground. Theatre writing is directed to the main floor while the balcony and the 'floors of paradise' are left unsatisfied. Writing for the main floor is the saddest thing in the world... The actors are partly to blame. Not that they are intentionally bad, but... 'Look, so-and-so, I want you to write me a comedy in which... I play myself. Yes, yes, I want to do this and that. I want to wear a Spring suit. I want to be twenty-three years old. Don't forget.' And theatre cannot be created that way. All that is achieved is the perpetuation of a young woman in spite of her epochs and of a young gallant in defiance of arteriosclerosis."[13]

And he adds, particularly commenting on the hold of the wealthy producer on theatrical matters:

"No matter what they say ... the theatre will not decay. What is absurd and decadent is its organization. That a man who has a few millions can set himself as censor of plays and governor of the theatre is shameful and intolerable. It is a tyranny which, like all, can only lead to disaster."[14]

But the problem, as viewed by Lorca, is not one whose causation can be placed at the feet of one group alone. The situation cannot be resolved unless the three principal offenders—producer, public and author—are held equally accountable. The circle of influence is the basis for the low state of the theatre—the producer accepts what he knows the public will like, the public accepts, through custom, what it is given, and the author accepts the responsibility for creating what the norm indicates is acceptable.

"Here, the gravity lies in that the theatregoers do not want to be made to think upon any moral theme. Besides, they go to the theatre as if displeased. They arrive late, leave before the play ends and depart without any respect. The theatre must win because it hasn't lost authority. The authors have allowed the audience to have

13. Felipe Morales, "Declaraciones de Garcia Lorca sobre teatro," *Heraldo de Madrid,* Madrid (April 9, 1936).
14. Alardo Prats, "Los artistas en el ambiente de nuestro tiempo," *op. cit.*

its way through its incitements. . . . I always await the arrival in the theatre of the light from above, from 'paradise.' "[15]

With these consistent comments in mind, it becomes obvious that the inclusion in the play of such a scene as that between El Director and El Poeta is no mere theatrical device, but a well-executed thrust on behalf of strong beliefs. And so, when the author leaves the stage, it is under the yoke of El Director. He, beaten and with the lack of spirit common to the hopeless, exits calling weakly to Rosita to prepare herself for her entrance.

The introduction ended, Cristobal is summoned by El Director who advises the villain that if he wishes to marry he must play the part of a doctor. In that way he will be able to find a rich patient from whom he can steal a sum sufficient for Rosita's dowry. Don Cristobita favors the project and immediately fetches his infamous club. Thus prepared, Cristobal receives his first patient—Enfermo. The unfortunate man is hardly on stage when he meets with an argument from Don Cristobita as to the time of day. Aware of the old man's club poised over his head, Enfermo agrees to let Cristobal treat his sore neck. Cristobita also succeeds in making the patient reveal that his money is hidden on his person:

> "Twenty *duritos* and twenty *duritos*,
> and under my little vest
> six *duritos* and three *duritos*
> and in the crack
> of my little ass
> there's a little roll
> with twenty *duritos*."

With a few well-placed strokes, Cristobita kills the sick man and then takes his money, happily proclaiming another conquest. Thus, another body is to be delivered to Cristobita's preferred ditch which he seems to fill with gusto. The instigator of the affair, El Director, reappears and again instructs

---

15. *Ibid.*

the villain: "Rosita's mother is coming. It is imperative that you speak with her." El Director, always the figure of good manners, steps aside as La Madre enters. Her monologue explains the desire that her daughter soon be married because:

> "... she has two breasts
> like little round oranges
> and cute little buttocks
> like little round cheeses."

The conversation between Cristobita and La Madre is ingeniously handled. It is made to seem innocent, even natural, although it contains phrases of questionable taste and words never used in the discussion of wedding arrangements. Most of these expressions are issued by Don Cristobal, not reserved merely for this moment as he employs them frequently from the time of his first entrance until the final curtain. But La Madre, though not as openly vulgar, does not lag too far behind the lecherous Cristobita, enflaming his already excessive appetite with her description of Rosita. Nonetheless, La Madre manages to act offended by Don Cristobal's language. It is this very naturalness which Lorca described in the "Prologo" as the "delicious and hard language of the puppets." Even without the playwright's explanatory note, however, the words could not be offensive because of the singular situation wherein they are pronounced. Expressed by puppets in an openly farcical satire, the language has a quality that endears rather than alienates. Under such circumstance of execution, laughter alone can result.

Cristobal and La Madre leave the stage discussing the dowry. As they exit, Cristobita dripping with expectation, Rosita appears in a sensual monologue which introduces her as well as the names of her many lovers:

> "... I want to lie
> on the divan
> with Juan,
> on the bed
> with Ramon,

on the settee
with Jose,
on the chair
with Medinilla,
on the floor with my lover,
against the wall
with handsome Arturo
and on the 'chaise-lounge'
with Juan, Jose and Medinilla,
with Arturo and with Ramon."

Rosita is revealed, not as the faithful lover of Cocoliche in
La tragicomedia, but as a capricious girl concerned with the
physical aspects of varied love. Her attitude on love com-
plements the lax spirit of the play and draws vividly her
erratic character. A few moments later, as she meets Don
Cristobita, Rosita says:

"I want to marry
a Caesarean calf,
an alligator,
a little donkey,
a general,
because after all
it's all the same."

Having resolved the dowry negotiations, La Madre runs
ahead to arrange the ceremony as Don Cristobita and Rosita
follow. Everything occurs in a smooth sequence that passes
over the common intricacies of life and goes directly to the
point—the union of Rosita and the old man. Such is the
general scheme of the play. The plot is never allowed to
invade the lightness and appeal of the action. The fantasy-
like structure provides a continuous pattern for enjoyment.

It is the proper time for a comment since all the characters have made their exits. El Poeta returns stealthily. He
has regained some of his former bravado and, addressing the
public with an "I told you so" sureness in his voice, makes
his plea for greater freedom:

"Do you see what I mean? However, it's best that we
all laugh . . . . neither Don Cristobal nor Doña Rosita see

the moon. If the stage director would allow it, Don Cristobal could see the water nymphs and Doña Rosita could bathe her hair in white frost during the third act, where the snow falls on the innocents. But the theatre owner has the characters locked in an iron box. . . . Because Don Cristobal is not like that, nor Doña Rosita."
But he is again forced to retreat by the entrance of El Director. Followed by his employer, El Poeta exits as Rosita and Don Cristobita return from the church.

The drunken Don Cristobal, in a tableau similar to that in the previous play, follows Rosita's suggestion and immediately falls asleep. No sooner is he snoring than Currito, the adventurous lover of *La tragicomedia,* enters and embraces Rosita. Thus begins the parade of lovers which includes El Poeta and Enfermo. Each time a new one appears, Cristobal is awakened by the passionate noises. But Rosita calms his fears with her imaginative excuses. Cristobal again sleeps. La Madre then enters hurriedly, announcing that the doctor has arrived. Rosita cries suddenly and exits, holding her womb. Puzzled, Cristobal tries to sleep, but El Director reveals that Rosita has given birth to quadruplets. Don Cristobita grabs his club and attacks La Madre with a demand as to the parentage of the quartet. She replies: "Yours, yours, yours."

Cristobal chases her through the room, often landing his blows. The announcement of yet a fifth child infuriates the old man and with greater vigor he strikes La Madre until she, dishevelled, is forced over the stage banister. Cristobal, then, exits and returns momentarily with Rosita. But before he can castigate her infidelity, El Director gathers all the puppets and calls an end to the farce. Holding the once lively figures, he adds the epilogue:

". . . The bad words acquire ingenuity and freshness when spoken by puppets which indulge the enchantment of this ancient rural farce. Let us fill the theatre with fresh stems, underneath which will be coarse expressions that will struggle on the stage with the tediousness and the vulgarity to which it has been condemned; and let us

today, in 'La Tarumba,' greet Don Cristobal, the Andalusian—cousin of the Galician Bulubu and brother-in
law of Aunt Norica of Cadiz; brother of Monsieur Guig-
nol of Paris; and uncle of Don Harlequin of Bergamo—as
one of the characters in which the old essence of theatre
remains pure."

With this small but worthy appreciation of Don Cristobal,
which also details his connection with the leading comedy
types in Europe, El Director officially ends the puppet play.

These two extant puppet comedies are typically Spanish
and represent Lorca's imaginative re-creation of folk traditions in song, word and action. Having perceived the misuse
into which these rich popular forms had fallen, Lorca sought
to bring his public to a new acceptance of its past through
modern interpretations of the classical drama. During his
years with "La Barraca" the very classics themselves were
revitalized and then taken on a tour of Spain; in these earlier
years, Lorca sought the creation of a drama akin to that of
its predecessors of the Golden Age. It is in these puppet
farces that the sincerity of his plan can be measured.

His modern interpretations of the spirit of classical drama,
however, do not lean solely on the stock characters of the
Andalusian puppet theatre. Lorca created his own personages,
types conceived in that spirit but expressed well beyond the
limitations of ancient comedy. The simple plots remain but
the embellishments fall primarily on the characters, adorn-
ing them with poetry and song. Through them he preserves
the gusto and vivacity of the Spanish *comedia*.

The very forces of comedy which Lorca first explored in
these puppet plays were to find later amplification in two
of his best-loved dramas—*La Zapatera Prodigiosa* and *El
amor de don Perlimplin*. Both of these contain, in fuller
measure, the picaresque tradition of Spanish theatre, a tradition first employed by Lorca in these highly amusing plays
as a tool of the modern drama. The use of such antique elements in combination with a rare theatrical insight made
of these puppet farces gems to be enjoyed in any era.

IV. MARIANA PINEDA

LORCA'S FIRST SUCCESSFUL play, *Mariana Pineda*, was not produced until 1927 although it had been completed before then (see below). In June of that year Margarita Xirgu's troupe enacted the historical romance in Barcelona's "Teatro Goya;" the play was directed by Lorca and the decor was created by Salvador Dali. The Madrid premiere was held on the following October, at the "Teatro Fontalba."

GARCIA LORCA'S *Mariana Pineda* is unlike his other plays because its basis lies in the mixture of historical fact and popular legend which has kept the memory of Granada's heroine alive. Lorca knew her story well, having been reared in the traditions of his native Granada. One of the city's plazas bore her name, a marble statue at its center serving as a more obvious reminder; the children's nurses still sang them the ballads that told of her heroism. Mariana's name was never too far from Lorca's reach:

> Not far from Federico's house in Granada, there was the small plaza of Mariana Pineda, an emphatic municipal homage to the local XIX century heroine. ... Yet, in spite of such a stunted monument and a historic painting preserved in the foyer of the City Hall's Assembly Room in which Mariana is depicted as surrounded by nuns upon leaving the jail on her way to the scaffold, the romantic figure of the unfortunate woman has instilled in the soul of the people a fresh aroma of unchanging esteem which is translated into the tone and lyric of her *romance* .... Lorca had within reach the impersonal documentation of the trial which is preserved in the archives of the Chancery, the warm surviving memories in the hearts of some people, and the effusive and tender story of the little ballad ...[1]

Lorca laboured arduously in the selection and editing of the

---

1. Jose Mora Guarnido, *op. cit.*, pp. 133-134.

great body of material, factual and otherwise, that was available. The story, however, as Lorca tells it, is dependent on fact only in the general plot-line, centered on a core of the important events in Mariana's life.

The widow of the liberal Manuel Peralta, Mariana aided rebellious elements in Granada who sought the overthrow of Ferdinand VII. These republican conspirators induced her to sew a flag of liberty which would be the symbol for their cause. Mariana did so. Her carefully embroidered words— "Ley, Libertad, Igualdad"—were to be the beacon for the early nineteenth century revolt against the crown. But Mariana's participation was revealed to the king's emissary, Ramon Pedrosa, a brutal and exacting man whose only concern was the suppression of the planned coup. The flag was confiscated and Mariana taken into custody. An illness overtook her during the imprisonment. She tried to escape, but the efforts of the ailing woman were not sufficient. During her illness she was confined to the convent of Santa Maria Egipciaca, located well beyond the city. Thereafter, the prosecution demanded her death and the best efforts of her lawyer, Jose Escalera, could not forestall the judgment pronounced on May 26, 1831.[2] Upon her decease, Mariana became a martyr in the eyes of the people and her unselfish acts and life were preserved in folk ballads and stories. By Lorca's time, the selection of pieces—musical, literary, artistic—had grown impressively so that the playwright had to decide on a new and totally untouched aspect of Mariana's life as the center for the proposed play. To achieve this end, Lorca approached his subject from the human rather than the historical view. Through his imaginative powers he was able to embellish and augment the hard facts of her later life. In Lorca's rendition, Mariana becomes more than a martyr for a cause; in *Mariana Pineda* she is disclosed as a very warm, very human figure whose dedication to the rebellious cause is decided by love. She, then, achieves a further

2. Francisco Pi y Margall, *Historia de España en el siglo XIX,* vol. II.

dimension, endearing herself much more to the populace in her guise of love-martyr. Thus, she is more understandable and believable than if Lorca had chosen to let her remain the cold figure which history adopted.

> Thus, his Mariana Pineda is a phantom who sews her flag, not as a symbol of liberty, but as the poetry of love; and only when she understands that in her lover's soul the love for liberty triumphs over the love for her, is she transfigured and converted into the symbol of that same liberty. ...It is here that a poet makes of the woman in which we incorporated it (liberty) more genuinely a heroine of love.[3]

Though the play was not publicly presented until 1927, that Lorca had completed the play by 1923 is clearly attested by Mora Guarnido:

> ... I left Spain late in 1923 and I already knew this play through a first reading by its author. I have also at my disposal an autograph of Manuel de Falla, dated June 17, 1924, in which he states: "... in Madrid he (Federico) told me that Martinez Sierra had postponed the opening of Mariana Pineda, and that he was improving the play ...".[4]

Martinez Sierra's interest in the play, however, must have been reserved since it never reached the production stage under his guidance. No doubt the changes which Lorca saw as necessary at that time were first pointed out by the playwright-impresario, but even after their correction the play failed to reach its goal. The previous misadventure with El maleficio de la mariposa may have warned the more experienced man not to irritate his public with another offering by Lorca. And then again, the drama's political overtones, though not applicable to the current events, may have caused his hesitation. But whatever causation is true, neither had reason for existence. The play, though written in poetry,

---

3. Enrique Diez Canedo, "Mariana Pineda, de F. G. L., en el Fontalba," El Sol, Madrid (Oct. 13, 1927).
4. Jose Mora Guarnido, op. cit., p. 134.

was at an opposite pole from the author's first theatrical
attempt; its political content was necessarily minimal since
Lorca's concern, as stated above, was with Mariana as a
person, a human being caught in the web of love. It is her
sacrifice that becomes important and the political intrigue
serves only to achieve the dramatic result.

From the very first moments, after a musical prologue
which sets the tone of the play, the playwright interprets
Mariana's actions as those of a woman dedicated to a very
real love rather than to an idealistic quest; Clavela and
Angustias, the latter being the adoptive mother of Mariana,
speak of her while she sews the secret flag in another room:

Clavela: "Why does she sew that flag?"
Angustias: "She says
          that her liberal friends force her . . ."
Clavela: "If I thought like an ancient woman, I would
          call her bewitched."
Angustias: "Enamored."[5]

Mariana, out of love for Don Pedro, sews the blood-red emblem. To Angustias, who has observed her at her work, the
red thread prognosticates that her involvement will lead to
a bitter fate:

          "Between her fingers the red thread seemed
          like a knife wound in the air."

This first french scene which is the beginning of the act,
"estampa" as Lorca designates it, together with the "Prologo" set the mood of concern and tension that will characterize the play. Contrasted with the predominant tone and
included to disperse slightly any over-heaviness, the second
scene introduces two sisters—young and vivacious—who enter
laughing. They are Amparo and Lucia. Their shouts bring
Mariana, who, in spite of her pleasantness and joviality, has
an aura of sadness about her. She greets her young friends:

---

5. All textual quotations, unless otherwise specified, are from *Obras
   Completas, op. cit.,* pp. 691-801.

> "How good you are for me
> with your girlish happiness!"

But these are words that hardly are sufficient to hide her sadness. Her visitors notice Mariana's anxiety, her distraction as she gazes constantly at the door, until Clavela, the servant, enters. Mariana jumps up suddenly. Seeing her concern over the possible arrival of someone, the girls try to leave. However, Marianita, again the correct hostess, insists that they remain and that Amparo tell her of their trip to Ronda:

> "Tell me! If you knew,
> how much I need your fresh laughter,
> how much I need your youthful humor.
> My soul is the color of my dress."

Obligingly, Amparo tells of the bullfight at Ronda. The narrative ends, after an impassioned retelling, with a true sentiment that touches Mariana:

> "I always thought of you;
> I thought: if my sad friend
> could only be with me,
> my Marianita Pineda."

The story of the bullfight contains a passage which uses two of Lorca's predominant symbols—the sword and the butterfly—in an ingenious metaphor:

> "With the point of his rapier
> he cut open five flowers
> and every moment it scraped
> the snouts of the beasts
> like a grand butterfly
> of gold with burnished wings."

The sword is poised between the horns of the bull like an immense butterfly. Again the butterfly, as in *El maleficio de la mariposa*, is equated with Death. The symbol is transferred to Mariana through the last lines of the narration in which Amparo relates how she remembered her when the sword was poised like a butterfly.

As Amparo and Lucia depart, Mariana remains alone in the room, waiting for the night to come. The night could bring news of Don Pedro, the leader of the revolution.

> "If the afternoon were
> like a great bird, how many
> hard arrows I would fling
> to close its wings!
> ....
> How very hard it is
> for the light to leave Granada!"

As if to emphasize the slow departure of daylight, Fernando, a boy of eighteen, enters the room and greets Mariana. Mariana turns hopefully upon hearing his voice, but quickly her face reflects disappointment on seeing that the visitor is not the person she expected. Instead, it is Fernando, the brother of the two girls who had just left.

Regaining her composure, Mariana attends to the young man who is obviously very dedicated to her. His halting and nervous voice is symptomatic of his true feelings for the older woman, though it is also evident that Mariana is not an abetter of his devotion. But as a fabrication of the playwright and with no basis in reality, Fernando is placed in the drama to serve two purposes: the first, to serve in the role of the ancient Greek messenger, changing the mood of a scene or precipitating some action by the message he bears; the second, to act as a foil to Don Pedro in the contrast of their different loves for Mariana. At the moment, however, it is his message that is important:

> "A captain whose name is,
> I can't remember . . ., a liberal,
> a prisoner of importance,
> has fled the jail
> of the High Court."

The news startles Mariana; she realizes the missing name is that of Don Pedro and now that he has escaped, she becomes even more worried. Unaware of her concern for the patriot,

Fernando tells her that the soldiers are already in pursuit:

> "...and it's certain they'll detain him
> on the road to Alpujarra."

Even the dreaded Pedrosa, the king's emissary, has joined the search for the valiant Don Pedro:

> "Pedrosa knows the place
> where the vein is widest,
> where the blood gushes out
> most warm and crimson."

But Mariana does not need to be told of Pedrosa for the vile man is known to her; presuming on his authority, he had visited the house often in spite of her disgust:

> "He's a man who frightens me...
> I can't look at him!"

The evening has given way to night. Clavela answers Mariana's call and brings the candles into the room. Mariana becomes more excited in the hope that night will aid the escape of Don Pedro, but Fernando is less optimistic:

> "Now the rivers of Spain
> instead of being rivers are
> long chains of water."

A sudden pounding on the door sends Clavela running out of the room. Mariana trembles with expectation. The waiting while the servant descends the stairs seems interminable; the confused Fernando does not understand Mariana's nervousness. The mystery deepens as Clavela finally enters with a letter:

> "A rider gave it to me. He was muffled
> to his eyes. I was very afraid."

Receiving the letter, Mariana hesitates in opening it, fearful of the news it might contain. It could herald Pedro's death and thus destroy Mariana's greatest love. Fernando, meanwhile, slowly takes his cape and hat. At the door he

promises to send his sisters to cheer Mariana. Clavela accompanies him down the stairs.

Alone, Mariana reads the letter. The note of relief as she
reads that he is well, however, is replaced by fear as she
recognizes the urgency of Don Pedro's request. In a quick
decision she runs to the window and calls to Fernando.
Gathering all her courage, Mariana prepares to ask Fernando
for his help. He could assure Don Pedro's safety by delivering the papers he requires. Fernando enters and, sensing the
urgency of his recall, tries to overcome Mariana's reluctance
to speak. Finally, she begins:

> "I need
> your help, Fernando,
> to keep breathing."

Fernando, his love flowing in his every word and look, pledges
his help. Mariana then gives him Don Pedro's letter. As he
reads, all of the evening's mysteries become clear. They are
explained by Mariana's love for Don Pedro. When he finishes,
Fernando exclaims:

> "How you've cut the path
> of all my dreams!
> It is not your fault, no;
> now I must help
> a man I begin to hate,
> when it is I who loves you."

But Fernando rises above his sentiments and accepts the
dangerous mission which will take him through Pedrosa's
men:

> "I go on this mission
> so I won't see you suffer."

Mariana gives him the identification papers for Don Pedro
and the crestfallen suitor departs hurriedly after a long look
at her sad face. She follows him out.

Mariana returns when Angustias' shouts bring her to
another reality. The children, whom she had neglected during

the day of waiting, have discovered the flag. Angustias tells
of their game in which they use the banner:

> "Mariana, the flag
> that you secretly sew ...
> .... they found it
> in the old cabinet
> and are lying on it
> playing dead!"

It is another omen. The two women rush out of the room
as the first act—"estampa"—ends, and the stage remains
illumined only by candlelight.

The expert handling of the expository elements in the
first act shows Lorca's growth as a dramatist since the un-
timely advent of *El maleficio de la mariposa*. The plot complications are smoothly inserted. The result is an even-paced
act with a climactic point which creates and sustains the
interest of the audience. The climax, reached upon the
reception and reading of Don Pedro's letter to Mariana, however, is not allowed to become an end in itself as far as the
act is concerned. It leads promisingly into an even graver
situation—the necessity to aid the leader of the revolution.
The suspense and danger which such a mission entail are
the outstanding considerations as the act ends.

The second act—"estampa segunda"—commences with a
facile scene set in the main room of the house. Clavela is
trying to get the small boy and girl—Mariana's children—
to bed. She is conspicuous by her lack of success, and finally
surrenders to their whim. Clavela begins the story, but all
three take turns in retelling the tale of the young lover who
sews a red flag, for her captain, the Duke of Lucena. The
parallel to Mariana's situation is obvious. It is accentuated
even more by her entrance as the story progresses. Neither
the children nor Clavela notice the solitary Mariana. Her
presence gives an uneasy sense, one of foreboding, to the
words, re-creating a feeling similar to that in the "Prologo"
and the first scenes of the play.

Once the story is ended, Mariana sends the children to
bed. The girl retires with the words:

> "We'll say
> the prayer to Saint John and the one
> for travelers and sailors"

And again, as in reciting the romance, the appropriateness
of the words does not go unnoticed by Mariana. Her sadness
again overtakes her:

> "Sleep soundly, my children,
> while I, lost and crazed, feel
> this rose of blood on my breast
> burning in its own vivid light."

But Mariana's pensiveness is distracted by the entrance
of Angustias announcing Don Pedro's arrival. Mariana runs
to the door as he enters. Don Pedro is a man of thirty-six,
virile and powerful. The lovers' restraint, a pose in consideration for Angustias, is broken when she exits. They embrace
passionately. Don Pedro's grateful words caress her ears:

> "All my blood is renewed because you've given it
> by exposing your fragile heart to danger.
> Oh, how greatly I feared for it, Mariana!"

Close to Don Pedro, Mariana rests her head against the
hollow of his shoulder and speaks to him as his breath touches
her brow:

> "... Leave your breath on my brow. Cleanse
> this anguish and this bitter taste I have;
> this anguish of walking without knowing where,
> and this taste of love that burns my mouth."

But her tension and fears cannot be disposed of so quickly.
She returns to the reality of Don Pedro's peril, afraid that
Pedrosa will somehow divine his whereabouts. Pedro tries
to calm her fears, but he too falls temporarily under the
threatening weight of the sentiments her voice have uttered.
His words are ponderous:

"But if it isn't like that; if Pedrosa . . .
. . . should surprise our group and we should die . . ."

Only liberty will cure their fears, the liberty which her flag
will herald, Don Pedro tells her. Then, in an impassioned
confession, Don Pedro reveals his true feelings:

"Mariana, what is man without liberty? Without that
fixed and swelling light that is felt inside?
How could I love you not being free, tell me?
How could I give you a firm heart if it isn't mine?"

It is at this moment that the first hint of possible conflict
between the lovers appears. To Don Pedro, love cannot be a
consideration until his battle for freedom has been won. He
is the man of destiny. Mariana, on the other hand, follows
a different path:

"My victory consists in really having you!
In looking at your eyes while you're unaware.
When you're by me I forget what I feel
and I love all the world . . .
. . . Pedro, when there is love
one is beyond time . . ."

Mariana is a woman in love. Her love is for Don Pedro, but
it also embraces his cause because it is his. Thus the conflict.
Although Don Pedro loves Mariana, his love for his ideal is
the greater of the two passions. For Mariana the process is
reversed. Each of these loves is pure—each seeks its object,
sacrificing all else. Don Pedro temporarily relinquishes his
love for Mariana to attain a greater goal; Mariana gives up
her life, its spiritual aspect is sacrificed here when she loosens
her hold on Don Pedro, also to attain a higher end. And the
tragedy lies in that their sacrifices are never concurrent.

But Mariana does not realize that Don Pedro's dedication to his ideal of liberty will prove to be far greater than
his love for her. Blinded by subjectivity, Mariana cannot
sense the truth. Don Pedro, however, in encarcerating his
passion for her, shows that he is aware of the dangers and

disappointments that may befall them during the course of his struggle. Liberty first and then their selfish happiness. Mariana longs also for that ideal, not because it is important to her as such, but because with it will come their union. Outside, the rain begins to fall in torrents swirled viciously by the wind. Having covinced Mariana that their sentiments must wait upon the larger cause, Don Pedro prepares to meet his fellow conspirators.

The sixth scene, a french scene as all the others, is ushered in by Clavela who announces that someone is at the main door. Mariana's brief instructions received, Clavela departs. Don Pedro is obviously gratified that his subordinates have been so prompt. But Mariana, apprehensive as before, can only utter a small invocation to Providence.

When they enter (Scene VII), Mariana and Don Pedro greet them warmly. The three men remove their coats and warm their hands, speaking of the cruel weather which made their journey almost impossible. Pedrosa, too, had a hand in their uncomfortable and dangerous trip, as one discloses:

> "Pedrosa has not ceased spying on me,
> and, though I put him off the scent,
> he continues in ambush, and knows something."

Mariana's fears of the man are more personal as he has visited her for unstated reasons, and her secret has imposed upon her a sense of danger whenever his eyes meet hers across amiable conversation:

> "He was here yesterday. . . . . .
> but as he spoke, so amiably,
> he looked at me . . . as if he knew!"

The mood becomes one of impatience. The men wait tensely for the arrival of the messenger who is to bring news of the rebellion. Don Pedro, meanwhile, speaks inspiringly of the city of Granada and of the other cities which wait only for his word to rise against the crown. But his phrases have a ring of uncertainty to the vigilant Mariana. Time passes. The lateness of the messenger troubles the conspirators, though they doubt that he will be apprehended since the rain and the darkness are his companions.

Mariana, who had been by the window, hears someone's approach below. In a few moments the emissary arrives. But his rapid voice pronounces only syllables of ill omen:

> "............ All in vain.
> We must be cautious. The Government
> is lying in ambush everywhere.
> We must postpone the uprising,
> or, on the other hand, fight or die."

His message that the government troops are aware of all their plans jolts Don Pedro. But the rest of the news is graver. It details the bloody death of General Torrijos, one of the leaders of the revolt. Torrijos and his company, betrayed by one of his men, had been slaughtered on the beach of Fuengirola where he had disembarked to attack the garrison of government troops in Malaga, one of the centers of the rebellion.[6] Torrijos' death only makes Don Pedro more resolved than before to carry out the plans. The messenger's warnings do not find sympathy in him; the eyes of Mariana, even, fail to dissuade him from his determination. The struggle which is taking place within the man is physically depicted by the torrential rains and the driving winds outside. Shutters slam strongly against walls. The sound continues while Mariana and the conspirators drink wine which she has given them subtly to delay the departure of Don Pedro. Even her conversation, centered on the storm, tries to deter their impulse to leave.

Suddenly, a loud pounding is audible. This time it is not the shutters and everyone instantly becomes alert. Clavela enters despairingly to announce what they feared:

---

6. Lorca employed poetic license in enrolling this event in the plot of the play. The incident of Torrijos took place on Dec. 10, 1831, months after the death of Mariana. This incident in the play recalls such events of betrayal, particularly that depicted in Jose Marmol's *Amalia,* the anti-Rosas Argentinian novel.

" .... Two masked men,
and Pedrosa is with them!"

In the confusion which follows her words, Clavela removes
the glasses and other traces of the men's presence. Mariana
tries to devise a way of escape. The pounding below grows
louder. Deciding quickly while the conspirators gather their
coats, Mariana points to a hallway window:

"You'll jump easily from that
hallway window. The roof
is close to the ground."

But she will remain in the house to entertain Pedrosa's attention and dissolve his suspicions. To the messenger's objection to escape without Mariana, Pedro answers energetically:

" .... It's necessary!
How can we justify our presence?"

His concern with the cause he embodies is again evident in
the selfish remark with its ungallant overtones. The conspirators exit rapidly. Clavela and Mariana remain in the room,
eliminating all traces which might betray them to the waiting Pedrosa. As Clavela leaves to open the door, Mariana sits
at her pianoforte and sings a ballad, "Contrabandista," with
disguised desperation; the heavy footsteps of Pedrosa and his
men accompany her song discordantly.

The last scene of the act begins with Pedrosa's entrance.
Preceded by Clavela, he appears in the room; Mariana stops
playing and rises to greet him. Pedrosa's controlled manner
adds to Mariana's terror; his sureness, contrasted to her tension, invites even greater reason for uncertainty on Mariana's
part. Frequent pauses punctuate the dialogue and Pedrosa's
eyes fill these moments with searching looks that seem to
pierce the curtain through which the conspirators found their
way to a redeeming window. The rain, too, makes these moments of silence almost unbearable. Pedrosa speaks, lightly
at first, of the weather, but as the conversation progresses
his words take on insinuative tones:

" . . . . I've just come
from patrolling the silent streets;
I'm soaked to the bones by the rain.

I'm carrying out the duties of my hard office.
But you, splendid Mariana,
make lace or embroider
in your house, protected from the wind. . . .
Who could have told me
that you embroidered very well?"

Mariana tries to maintain outward calm at the pertinent nuance, but her fidgeting reveals that inside her mind there is horror at the thought that Pedrosa may know of the secret flag.

Pedrosa is a variation on the police inspector in Victor Hugo's *Les Misérables*, relentlessly taunting, evil and conniving. He plays with Mariana's feelings as he wishes, enjoying her discomfiture. But unlike Javert, who in spite of his intolerance had a sincere dedication to duty, Pedrosa has a double motivation; neither is clear enough, however, to give him the stature of Javert. His concern with his mission—the suppression of the revolt—is sadistic rather than the result of driving dedication to an ideal; his motivation is also tempered by his desire for Mariana. So, where Javert's road is marked only by his consuming ideal of justice, wrong as it may be, Pedrosa has a lesser reason for his acts; where Javert could only redeem himself for failure to carry out his code by suicide, Pedrosa easily deserts his goal when he embraces Mariana and kisses her, promising her safety if she will be his. But Mariana's furious refusal deters his separation from the commands of the king whom he serves. At first, apparently willing to accept her love without condition, Pedrosa now reveals his scheme:

"Mariana! And the flag?
The one you sewed with those white hands
against the laws and the King?
 . . . . I also know

that many people are involved.
I think you'll tell me their names, no?
No one will know what happened. I want you
mine, do you hear me? Mine or dead. . . .
and you'll love me because I give you life."

The choice is a hard one: the names of the conspirators for
her life; the safety of her person but the possession of her
body by Pedrosa. Breaking away from his embrace, Mariana
refuses his cruel terms:

> "Never that! I'll shed my blood first!
> It will hurt me, but it is honorable.
> Get out!"

Faced by her heroic stance, Pedrosa returns to his cynical
and calculating manner, his passion replaced by authority
and power:

> "Very well! I'll continue my business
> and you'll be your own downfall.
> . . . . Torture
> will make you confess! The irons are cruel,
> and a woman is always a woman!"

He exits, leaving Mariana under house arrest until she decides to do his bidding. Escape is impossible. Angustias and
Clavela join Mariana, the three women clutching each other
in a vain attempt to lessen the terror left behind by Pedrosa.
Mariana cries without hope. The curtain descends on the
second act as the sobs of the women and the sound of the
heavy rain parallel its rapid descent.

The fast pace of the scenes which comprise this second act
and the exciting moments of suspense which characterize
them, make this "estampa" significant and very dramatic.
It remains the best of the three acts: forceful, interesting and
theatrical. The triple image of Mariana receives excellent
definition herein. Her motherliness is the least treated of the
three, but Lorca places the actions which define this aspect
at the beginning and end of the act to give them added em-

phasis. The woman in love is the principal concern of the playwright, and therefore this quality is most apparent throughout the act, even when Don Pedro is not present. Perhaps it is approached more forcefully during his absences. The third facet of the woman is her historical face. As previously stated, this is made subordinate to the central sculpture by the playwright but Lorca gives the right evocation of it during Mariana's conflict with Pedrosa. There, her heoric nature is given its most ardent voice. Mariana emerges from the second act as a heroine of love not yet fulfilled but promising to consecrate herself to Don Pedro, even to the death.

That treachery and lust hinted at in the first act are given positiveness here. The betrayal of Torrijos is a moving account which typifies the peril within which the revolution was posed. Pedrosa's attempts to seduce Mariana give evidence of his evil reputation and form another *agon* that extends plot complications and eventually will become the primary or most obvious cause of Mariana's downfall.

The two novices who open the third act are young and curious, much like those in Martinez Sierra's *Cancion de cuna*. They run through a garden in the convent of Santa Maria Egipciaca in Granada between their moments of watching through a keyhole in the gate. As they watch, they describe a woman who prays on the other side; a woman whose paleness is alarming. One of the novices explains the circumstances of the woman's imprisonment in the convent. It is Mariana of whom they speak. The fragrance of death which the woman carries with her reaches even the protected senses of the young novices:

> "Ay, Marianita Pineda!
> The flowers are already blooming
> which will go with you when you're dead."

Not even the comical situation of the older nun discovering their eavesdropping and then taking their place at the key-

hole can disperse the dankish odor brought on by Mariana's
incarceration.

Mariana's entrance into the garden marks the second
scene. She speaks to Sor Carmen:

> " . . . . If only I could
> stay here in the Convent,
> always."

Mariana's paleness and ill health are emphasized by the flowing white gown she wears; her attitude—one of recognition of
the inevitability of her fate—likewise marks the strain her
seclusion has brought. Sor Carmen's comforting words fail
to touch Mariana, who replies soulfully:

> "Sister, I'm greatly wounded
> by the things of the world!"

Afflicted by her sadness, the nun retires to her duties. Once
alone, Mariana runs to the end of the garden where Alegrito,
an old gardener, enters. The grinning man is appropriately
named. Mariana, impatient for any news he may have, questions him, seeking an answer to the errand she had entrusted
to him. But his message is that Don Luis and her friends cannot even attempt a rescue because they would all be killed
by the heavy guard around the convent. Mariana receives
the news valiantly, but when she is told that Don Pedro,
her lover, is leaving Spain her uncertain smile can hardly
hide the realization that she has been deserted:

> "Whoever told you that desires
> to kindle my suffering.
> Alegrito, don't believe it!
> You don't believe it, do you?"

Alegrito accepts her assurance to please her, knowing that
she is indeed alone. Mariana explains how Don Pedro will
come to her rescue, and the narration has the tinge of a
child's fantasy:

> "Don Pedro will come on horseback
> like a crazed man when he hears

> that I have been imprisoned
> for embroidering his flag.
> And, if they kill me, he'll come
> to die by my side
> as he told me one night
> while kissing my hair."

And then, as if to show her disbelief of his report, Mariana asks Alegrito to thank the other conspirators for their forthcoming aid; the gardener leaves, no longer wearing the happy smile which occasioned his name.

Alone in the garden, Mariana intones a lament which shows that her confident words to Alegrito were not securely based. She does not really believe in her rescue; but the hope of it has not yet left her:

> "Run faster! Come for me!
> I already feel very near
> fingers of bone and moss
> caressing my head."

The only response is a soft voice which, accompanied by a guitar, sings a further sigh:

> "My hope died
> by the edge of the water
> without anyone seeing it."

Mariana repeats the lines as if she were expressing vocally a sudden thought. Her meditations, however, are interrupted by the entrance of two nuns. Startled, Mariana receives Pedrosa—the visitor the nuns escort. Having performed their duty, the sisters leave in spite of Mariana's pleading look.

Pedrosa still expects Mariana to accept his offer and his assured attitude, cold and correct, seems to demand that she acknowledge his victory. But Mariana, too, adopts a pose of satisfaction:

> ". . . . . You forget
> that for me to die all
> Granada must die. And that
> great gentlemen will come to save me."

Her belief is half-real and Pedrosa destroys it with a simple
statement, no doubt based on his experience with human
nature:

> "There won't be anyone in Granada
> to see you pass with your retinue.
> Andalucians talk, but afterwards . . ."

Still, Mariana clings to the hope of Don Pedro's devotion.
In a moment of passion, Pedrosa faces Mariana with determination. His words show the dual desire to possess her and
to obtain the names of the conspirators. But to no avail.
With equal fury, Mariana heroically throws down his offer.
And Pedrosa resumes his masked stance, flatly declaring that
her death has been decreed for that same afternoon. The
desperation which the announcement brings to her face
pleases Pedrosa who tries once more to convert her to his
proposal. But Mariana is too deeply committed to her love
for Don Pedro to betray him. As an act of finality, she calls
to the nuns. When they appear, Pedrosa leaves.

Aware for the first time of the closeness of death, Mariana
sits limply on a bench recalling a song of her youthful days.
Then, as if instantly called back to reality, she cries out:

> "Pedro, mount your horse
> or come riding on the day.
> But quickly! They're now coming
> to take away my life!"

Her anguished cries usher in two nuns—the same novices
previously seen. They do not see Mariana being led out by
two other nuns. They speak of her misfortune, almost crying at the thought of her death. As they prepare to leave
Mariana re-enters. The novices depart reluctantly as Mariana
sits on the lonesome bench, her head bowed with grief, her
hands crossed in resignation.

Sor Carmen, entering with purpose, approaches Mariana.
Her announcement that a visitor has arrived causes a ra-
diant renewal of Mariana's spirits. "Let him enter! At last,

my God!" Believing him to be Don Pedro, she arranges her dress and hair. She sits on the bench with her back to the gate. The rustle of the nun's garments as she precedes the visitor, however, makes Mariana turn around. But as suddenly as it came, her smile disappears. It is Fernando and not Don Pedro.

> "Pedro! Where's Pedro?
> Let him enter, for God's sake!
> He's below, at the door!
> He has to be! Let him come up!"

Crazed by the disappointment, Mariana asks Fernando for Don Pedro's whereabouts. The youth replies strongly, aware that his rival is powerful even in his absence:

> "He won't be coming because he never loved you,
>   Marianita.
> By now he's in England, with the other Liberals.
> All your old friends have deserted you.
> Only my young heart accompanies you.
> Mariana! Understand and see how I'm loving you!"

And Mariana, who is finally forced to recognize the truth, admits openly that she knew of Pedro's greater devotion to liberty. Then, in the two most important lines of the play for they contain the clue to Lorca's interpretation of Mariana Pineda, she unites her love for Don Pedro with his cause:

> "Do you love Liberty more than your Marianita?
> Then I will become that same Liberty which you adore!"

It is an almost revengeful phrase because in admitting Pedro's real love and in being willing to die to become the symbol of liberty, Mariana seeks to become the unattainable goal itself. She will become Liberty in Pedro's eyes and he will have to love her equally, but in loving her he will suffer her loss.

> "Pedro, see to what your love has brought me!
> You'll love me so much, dead, that you won't live."

Knowing that his affinity for liberty will make Don Pedro recognize her death as the supreme human sacrifice for the cause, she is content that he will never forgive himself the desertion. It is not a culpable revenge that possesses Mariana, but rather a way of justifying her death. She has given herself a reason and a cause for which to die:

> "Pedro, I want to die for what you do not,
> for the pure ideal that shone in your eyes."

At her command, Fernando leaves. His attempt to make her save herself for her children and himself never presenting a challenge to the greater fabrication of her love, he exits with bowed head. The nuns enter silently and accompany Mariana. The last farewells spoken and felt, Mariana exits with her dreams: "I am Liberty because love demanded it!" The act ends with a distant sound of bells tolling mournfully and with the same song which was first heard in the "Prologo":

> "Oh, what a sad day it was in Granada,
> that even the stones were crying,
> on seeing Marianita was dying
> on the scaffold for not testifying!"

The act, begun feebly, proceeds to the enlivening events of Pedrosa's visit and Fernando's attempt to save Mariana from herself, and thus justifies itself in these final scenes. It is particularly in the last two french scenes that Lorca's poetry is most brilliant and provocative, rising to magnificence in Mariana's self-discovery and final sacrifice.

As a play, *Mariana Pineda* does not always achieve theatrical success. It is highly talkative, at times repetitive, and often static. The best scenes are those which combine forceful poetry and stage movement. Following the tradition of Greek classical drama, the play reserves all violent action for off-stage use. Not that this is a fault. But, because of the wordy nature of the play, such action is missed.

As a character, Mariana is the only personage who

achieves any change whatsoever. The supporting roles are generally no different at the end of the play than they were at the start. That, too, may be a reason for the heavy aspects of it. Mariana, however, develops accordingly as the events which envelop her change. Her character builds constantly through these events, until it reaches its climax in the final scene with Fernando. Since she is the most important element in the play, this scene is, of course, the climactic point.

Although the merits of *Mariana Pineda* far outweigh its deficiencies, the play's appeal is necessarily limited by its strongly nationalistic character. It would undoubtedly fare badly outside Spain, even in other Spanish-speaking countries, where an identification with the characters, the historical setting and the reason for their actions would not be possible to obtain. Believability would be impaired. There is in the play an attempt to capture the flavor of the romantic Granada of legend. The Granada of mystery, of danger, of love, of mysticism, all make their small appearances in the play. But none of them are fully grasped. Nor can they be completely contained and remain attractive in their original guises. It is perhaps for this reason that the play, though advancing constantly, never reaches the saturation of understanding. Mariana's sacrifice—romantic, heroic, inspirational—never rises above the melodramatic. As in melodrama, it serves a purpose. But once the purpose is disposed of, once hysterics are eliminated, once the mind returns to its normal functions, the flimsiness of the sacrifice is revealed.

Were the idea behind the drama bad or worthless, Lorca's later work in the theatre would not have reached its commanding pinnacle. Essentially and basically, the play is interesting. But apparently this is not sufficient recommendation. The same themes of Honor, Sacrifice, Frustration and Death are most ably treated by the playwright in a later maturity. It is that maturity, not of outlook because that is not missing, which encompasses experience and technique that is required most evidently. In spite of its shortcomings, *Mariana Pineda* is the play which most ably foreshadows Lorca's future tragic offerings—*Bodas de sangre, Yerma* and *La casa de Bernarda Alba.*

V. LA ZAPATERA PRODIGIOSA

COMMENCED IN 1926, shortly after *Mariana Pineda*, and written largely during Lorca's stay in New York (1929-1930), *La Zapatera Prodigiosa* received its first showing before a private audience. Thereafter, on December 24, 1930, it opened at Madrid's "Teatro Español." Margarita Xirgu portrayed the heroine under the direction of Cipriano Rivas Cherif. The costumes were designed by Picasso.

This earlier version was later amplified and the real premiere of the play as it exists today took place in Buenos Aires on November 30, 1933. Lola Membrives and her company, under Lorca's direction, presented the work there, later taking it to Spain where, on March 18, 1935, it was produced at the "Teatro Coliseum" in Madrid. Lorca also prepared a ballet version of the play.

LORCA'S FIRST FARCE, *La Zapatera Prodigiosa*, is subtitled: "Farsa violenta en dos actos y un prologo." Considering the humorous ending of the piece, it is obvious that the violence referred to is not in the usual category defined by the term, but rather a violence which has as its principal attributes vitality, strong characters and conflict of emotions. These are the strokes that individualize the play, separating it from predecessors of similar subject-matter.

The well-known plot of classical comedy—the young and beautiful girl married to the old and colorless man—is presented again by Lorca who embellishes the traditions of the form with music and dance in the folk idiom. Deserting poetry as such, though it is always present in some form in all his plays, Lorca achieved the most vibrant theatrical expression to this point in *La Zapatera Prodigiosa*.

> The *Shoemaker's Prodigious Wife* is a simple farce, in the pure classic manner, describing the spirit of a woman who is like all other women. At the same time— and with tenderness—it is an apologia of the human soul.

120

Thus, the shoemaker's wife is both a type and an archetype; she is a primal creature and a myth of our pure unsated illusion. . . .

In my *Shoemaker's Wife* I sought to express—within the limits of ordinary farce, and without laying hands on the elements of poetry within my reach —the struggle of reality with fantasy that exists within every human being. (By fantasy I mean everything that is unrealizable).[1]

The theme has been established. Much the same idea is conveyed in the "Prologo":

"The poetic creature which the author has dressed as the shoewife throbs and is enlivened everywhere with an air of refrain or simple ballad, and let not the audience feel strange if she seems violent or adopts sour attitudes because she is always fighting, fighting with the reality which creates her and with fantasy when it becomes visible reality."[2]

It is therefore the exchange between the real world and the world of fantasy that forms the basis for the play. As Lorca says:

The shoemaker's wife fights constantly with ideas and real objects because she lives in her own world, in which every idea and object has a mysterious meaning which she herself does not know. She has only lived and had suitors on the other bank of the river, which she cannot and will not ever be able to reach.[3]

Because the accent is on this conflict between reality and fantasy, the only two characters who are important are the wife and her husband, the shoemaker. In a broader sense the *agon* is represented in these very persons: the shoemaker is the symbol of reality and the young, hardly initiated, Zapatera is the symbol of fantasy. The other characters—

---

1. Federico Garcia Lorca, interview in *La Nacion,* Buenos Aires (Nov. 30, 1933); in Toby Cole, *Playwrights on Playwriting,* (New York, Hill and Wang, 1960), pp. 231-232.
2. *Obras Completas, op. cit.,* p. 822.
3. Toby Cole, *op. cit.,* p. 232.

Don Mirlo, Vecinas, Alcalde, Beatas, etc., are only a part of the crowd, even when they act singly. The child, alone, seems apart from the crowd. As La Zapatera's only friend, he seems to belong to her fantasy world.

> The most characteristic thing about the shoemaker's crazy little wife is that her only friend is a small child, tenderness personified and symbol of things in bloom, yet still very far from blossoming forth as a flower.[4]

In this early relationship between woman and child can be seen the promise of one of the central themes that would characterize Lorca's later work in the theatre. The bond of woman and child, more fully explored in *Yerma*, is given its first variation in this play.

La Zapatera Prodigiosa is completely conceived in the popular vein. Its language, though Castilian, contains many Andalusion expressions and constructions:

> The language is popular, spoken with a Castilian accent; but it contains Andalusian forms and expressions, enabling me at times—such as when the shoemaker preaches—to produce a slightly caricatural effect in the manner of Cervantes.[5]

The story itself belongs to a popular tradition which can be traced back to the "chansons de mal mariées," French songs which had become known in Spain because of the intellectual closeness of the two nations. Though the French "chansons" concentrated on the wife's infidelity flaunted in the face of the husband, Spain took a very different tack, ennobling the hurt husband and discrediting the adulterous wife.[6] Lorca approaches the situation with a novel twist, however, when he creates sympathy for both parties. He is able to do this because in his plot neither character is guilty of adultery;

4. *Ibid.*
5. *Ibid.*
6. Ramon Menendez Pidal, *Flor Nueva de Romances Viejos* (Buenos Aires, Espasa-Calpe, 1943); the book traces the development and usage of old songs—ballads, etc.—in newer versions.

their sins, respectively, are of questionable badness—he, the shoemaker, is too old for her and she is too much a dreamer to be tied down to his real world. Although La Zapatera causes her husband's desertion, he becomes equally liable for the blame when he stays away for so many months. The wrong-doing of one is cancelled by the other's mistake. In this manner both elicit the sympathy of the audience, earned not by mere contrivance but by the traditional elements in the play which, being understandable, arouse the desired effect.

The "Prologo," which opens the play, is spoken by El Autor, the figure who represents the playwright. In this prefatory section, Lorca avails himself of the opportunity to jab at an adversary who had previously disrupted two of his plays—*El maleficio de la mariposa* and *Mariana Pineda*. The opponent he now faced with bravado: the audience.

"The poet does not ask for benevolence, only for attention, since he long ago hurdled the thorny fence of fear which authors have for the house. Because of this absurd fear, and because very often the theatre is all finances, poetry retires from the stage in search of other locales where people will not be afraid that a tree, for example, may be turned into a puff of smoke or that three fishes, through the agency of a hand and a word, may be turned into three million fishes to appease the hunger of the multitude."[7]

As the speaker, often played by Lorca, prepares to leave the stage, he lifts his top hat in a salute to the public. Mysteriously, the inside of the hat begins to glow with an eerie green light. When El Autor, concerned over the strange occurrence, looks up to examine the contents a torrent of water pours down on him from within the hat. The unflinching face of the recipient, coupled with the picture of his sad appearance, recalls the hilarious episodes of Buster Keaton whom Lorca admired profoundly.

---

7. All textual quotations, unless otherwise specified, are from *Obras Completas,* pp. 821-888.

But the "Prologo" serves as more than a mood-setting piece, a laugh-getting device, or a subdued sermon:

> ... be mocks the devices of the conventional drama, insisting instead on the place of fantasy and imagination in the theatre, which will be a miracle to the eyes and spirit.[8]

This note by Honig applies to most of Lorca's theatre as well. Even in his most realistic plays, for example, can be found circumstances or events of a supernatural or fantastic nature. Yet, they never seem out of place so carefully are they handled through mood and dialogue as well as through a plotted expectancy. The best example of this facet of Lorca's drama presents itself in the Forest Scene in *Bodas de sangre*.[9] Though Lorca's interpretation of the hidden forces that surround Spanish life takes many forms, mostly dark and mysterious, in *La Zapatera Prodigiosa* his goal is to impress upon the audience that the most important, most beautiful, most intricate details in life arise in the imaginations of simple human beings whose makeup is free from the subtleties of sophistication or the adherence to artificial values. La Zapatera and her husband survive the gossip and malice of the town's population in an almost allegorical triumph of virtue over evil, though they are, at best, tinted examples of the former. The subordinate theme that no one is all good or all bad can be derived from this victory.

Structurally, the farce is divided simply into two acts, there are no further sub-divisions. Lorca's preference for this style in the physical construction of the play provides greater continuity possibilities than if he had chosen to separate the action through scenes. The play, being a fantasy, requires above all that credibility be established quickly and maintained. Where dialogue can support the first objective, the physical aspects of the play must be carefully managed so as to preserve the illusion. By allowing for

8. Edwin Honig, *op. cit.*, p. 130.
9. See Chapter VIII.

only one interruption, the problem is greatly minimized. The
state of belief is more easily maintained.

The first act is set in the shoemaker's house. The principal room, its white walls interrupted by several doors and a
window, serves as workshop and parlor. La Zapatera's entrance from the street is accompanied by angry shouts, de-
risive laughter and biting comments hurled at her by the
neighbors. She enters angrily, pausing by the door to return
their sarcastic remarks with equal gusto. But once inside,
she begins to cry over the misfortune of being married to an
old man:

> "Who could have told me that I'd marry such a . . . me
> with black eyes and such golden hair—and that is
> something—with this figure and this lovely coloring . . ."

These are the first important echoes of the narcissistic element in Lorca's plays. Stronger, more involved aspects of this
topic are dealt with in *Asi que pasen cinco años* and *Yerma*,[10]
but it is here that there is a preliminary statement. *La Zapatera Prodigiosa* is based largely on this premise, though it
is obvious that Lorca had not yet begun to explore the large
possibilities of the theme. The treatment is light and comical,
concentrating on the difference in age between La Zapatera
and her husband, as well as on the opposition of her beauty
and charm to his plainness and coarseness.

But La Zapatera's tears of self-pity are halted by the entrance of a small child, Niño, who brings his sister's shoes to
be repaired. With him she is tender and generously gives him
a doll. The child, however, innocently cruel as only children
can be, accepts the gift with the remark: "I'll take it because
I know you'll never have children." He has repeated the
words his mother had spoken in their house, not realizing
their effect on the young wife. Alternating her attitude, La
Zapatera now becomes angry at the insult. Frightened, El
Niño returns the doll. When El Zapatero, her husband, en-

---

10. See chapters VII and IX respectively.

ters, the child leaves. The two principal characters face each other. A ridiculous contrast in their clothing—she wears a bright green dress, he a velvet suit with short pants and a red tie—serves to give a physical setting to their vastly different personalities. The shrewish woman begins her torment of the shoemaker:

> ". . . remember that I'm only eighteen years old. . . . Curse the day, curse the day in which I listened to my godfather, Manuel. . . . With all the good suitors I've had."

Trying to calm her, El Zapatero listens to her complaints. She recalls other suitors, taunting him with one in particular:

> "But the one I liked most was Emiliano . . ., you knew him . . . Emiliano, who could come on a black horse with tassels and little mirrors, with shining copper spurs and carrying a willow branch. And what a cape he wore in winter! What folds of blue velvet and silk trimmings!"

As if dreaming, El Zapatero reveals that he had also owned a cape with the style and elegance she describes. But she brushes aside his words with disbelief. Her taunts are spoken with a casual venom and with a calculated abandon. Less patiently now, El Zapatero pounds his shoes mercilessly. His efforts, however, are no stronger than her avoidance of constant reference to the differences in their ages. The fifty-three year old shoemaker responds to her idolization of an eighteen year old suitor with: "I was once eighteen." Her retort is a conscious attempt to irritate the shoemaker and is full of sting and implications: "You've never been eighteen years old in your whole life." The pitch of the argument rises until El Zapatero, realizing that the neighbors can hear their shouts, pleads with her to be serene. She finally leaves the room. El Zapatero looks in the mirror counting the wrinkles on his brow. The shrewish wife no doubt caused many of them through her scandalous behavior. It is such conduct that upsets the shoemaker most, that makes him blame his sister for his plight:

"My sister, my sister is to blame, my sister who insisted!
. . . This is my downfall. The devil take my sister, may
she rest in peace!"

The mixed blessing which ends his brief meditation is typical
of the attitude in the entire play, mixing the two poles—
love and hate—to achieve a comical hybrid.

A neighbor, Vecina Roja, and her daughters appear at the
large window. All three are dressed in red. The daughters
are crying loudly and it is this that attracts El Zapatero's
attention to the window. Vecina Roja, the same woman
whom La Zapatera had stood up to at the start of the play,
has come to face the shoemaker's wife:

"Tell your wife to come out. . . . Let her come out and
we'll see if she barks as much in front of me as behind
me!"

The scene is comically exaggerated: the neighbor with her
aroused temper, the two crying daughters, the upset Zapatero trying desperately to prevent a scandal. But El Zapatero, prompted by the woman's sympathy, confides his pitiable episodes, looking every moment to make sure that his
wife will not hear:

"The day before yesterday . . . she butchered the ham
we had been saving for Christmas and we ate it all. Yesterday the only thing we ate all day was egg and parsley
soup; then, because I protested, she made me drink three
glasses of unboiled milk one after the other."

Dreading another fight between Vecina Roja and La Zapatera
or a scandal which would bring the entire village to his door,
the shoemaker ushers the trio beyond the window, accepting
even one tenth of the price for the repaired shoes so that
they may leave quickly. But La Zapatera, who had been
listening to the conversation from behind a curtain, enters
and faces Vecina Roja:

"Thief! You dare to rob this man so openly? And you,
to let yourself be robbed? Give me those shoes. They'll
stay here until you pay ten pesetas for them."

Frightened, the three women exit rapidly; La Zapatera fumes over the woman's words until she is interrupted by her husband. El Zapatero calmly, but with urgency, explains that she must not cause a scandal. La Zapatera defends her actions, but El Zapatero becomes more potent in his new voice of protest, announcing with finality that she will have to change because he is tired of her irresponsible ways:

> "Have I made myself clear? This is my last word. . . .
> We've been married for three months—I, loving you, and
> you driving me crazy. Can't you see I'm tired of jokes?
> . . . I'm up to here with them!"

She exits in a huff, declaring that he will not get his dinner that day. The shoemaker, now smiling with satisfaction after his strong demonstration of authority, adds an epilogue to her words: "Perhaps tomorrow you'll have to look for yours, too."

With these thoughts, which hint at what is to follow, El Zapatero returns to his workbench. The main door opens slowly as he works and the imposing figure of El Alcalde, the town's mayor, enters ceremoniously. He is a flamboyant character, caricature of the politician known in every country, who adopts an attitude of concern over his constituents. El Zapatero's forlorn look does not escape El Alcalde who guesses it to be occasioned by the young wife. Already the survivor of four wives, El Alcalde is somewhat of an authority on women in the eyes of the shoemaker. El Zapatero listens with attention as the politician provides his theory on wives:

> "Wives must be given strong hugs around the waist,
> stepped on quickly and spoken to in a voice of authority,
> and if they still dare to cackle, there's only one remedy—
> the rod."

But El Zapatero's trouble lies not in being unable to act boldly towards his wife but in another type of predicament. He confesses to the astonished Alcalde that he is not in love with La Zapatera, having married her only at the insistence of his sister who did not want him to be alone in his old age.

The once happy and wealthy bachelor thus found himself led out of his blissful existence into a foreign life. He has found misery and unrest in the three months of his marriage with the promise of more of the same before him. Very opportunely, as if underlining what El Zapatero has said, the voice of his young wife is heard singing briefly:

> "Ay, hooting and hooting,
> the riot has ended
> and now starts the shooting!"

La Zapatera's entrance is deliberately coquettish. El Alcalde's admiring eyes devour her beauty as he becomes very gallant and complimentary. When La Zapatera sits apart from them at the window, El Alcalde adds:

> "A little unpolished, but a most handsome woman. What an ideal waist! . . . And those ripples in her hair!"

He exits majestically, his eyes focussed on La Zapatera. She has enjoyed the brief flirtation with the mayor, but now that he is gone she sits plotting what further mischief she can inflict upon her much harassed husband. El Zapatero sings a quartet of lines as he works on the shoes, but his eyes never leave La Zapatera. With the most innocent of looks on her young face, she begins to spin a chair knowing that to be one of her husband's superstitions. El Zapatero rushes to the nearest chair and begins to spin it in the opposite direction to counteract the evil spell:

> "Why do you do that when you know it's a superstition of mine and it's like shooting me?"

When she stops for a moment, he tries to leave the room, but the mischievous wife begins once more. El Zapatero is forced to run to the chair to renew his antidotic action. The sound of a street band captures La Zapatera's attention and her husband flees. Alone, La Zapatera begins to dance to the comic tune played by a flute and a guitar. As she whirls through the room she recalls amorous meetings with imagined lovers—Emiliano and Jose Maria. It is the daydream of a lusty girl, a technicolor sigh that quickly ends when the music comes to an abrupt end at the appearance of Don Mirlo at the window.

Like El Alcalde, Don Mirlo is a caricature rather than a character. Dressed in black evening jacket and short pants, his voice trembling like that of an inexperienced lover, his head moving jerkily as if controlled by marionette wires, Don Mirlo is the perfect laughing stock. There is no subtlety in his behavior or in his speech. Both are full of the baroque, superfluous and ridiculous elements that usually are equated with such situations. Where El Alcalde's pompousness is derived from his office with its false tones of dignity and majesty, Don Mirlo's flamboyance is the result of an overwrought donjuanism, made even more ridiculous by his decrepit state. Amused at his antics, La Zapatera replies:

> "How funny, Don Mirlo; and I thought buzzards never spoke. But there is a grave blackbird fluttering around, black and old."

La Zapatera has defined him as a blackbird and her definition is borne out by his name. Don Mirlo can only attempt to counter the embarrassment by resorting to his snuff box; in so doing, however, he commits a "faux pas"—he sneezes on La Zapatera's exposed neck. Her anger is unreserved as she strikes him. Shaking from fright, Don Mirlo manages to escape her wrath.

As he exits, another suitor takes his place at the window. The young man, El Mozo, is the exact opposite of Don Mirlo in all but his goal. The saddened lover grieves because he cannot possess La Zapatera. His feverish speech is cast in the triteness of all such love words. El Zapatero enters but stops suddenly when he sees his wife at the window. His fears of scandal revitalized by her obvious flirtations, he exits sullenly. Meanwhile, La Zapatera has been enjoying the fervor of El Mozo—his words are more direct and less ornate

than those of Don Mirlo—but after their effect has worn off
she treats him as shabbily as she did his older counterpart:

> "Really, all that talk of "I love you, I love you" makes
> me feel as if my ears were being tickled by a feather.
> "I love you, I love you! . . ."

When her words do not calm his passion, La Zapatera resorts
to other more indignant attitudes:

> "Be quiet. I listen to you because I like it and it's
> pretty, but that's all, do you hear me? A fine thing. . . .
> Look, go away."

When El Mozo refuses to leave without a promise of her
faithfulness to him, La Zapatera pushes him away and closes
the shutters violently:

> "How impertinent, how crazy! . . . If I've hurt you, too
> bad. . . . As if I were here only to, to . . . Can't I speak
> to anyone in this town? It seems there are only two ex-
> tremes here: either you're a nun or a dishrag."

Her resentment is comical, particularly because of her right-
eousness. To her, the advances are wholly unwarranted; it
seems a surprise that her friendliness and flirtation can be
interpreted as wantonness. But typically enough she does
not dwell on the problem long enough to reach a conclusion
and rushes into the kitchen as she smells the dinner which
earlier she had resolved not to prepare.

As the light of day begins its decline, El Zapatero enters.
He is wearing a broad cape and carries a bundle of clothes.
These are to be his sole companions on his retreat to search
for his lost peace. After a last look at his shop, he opens the
door. But his attempted exit is retarded by two women returning from church, appropriately named Beatas, who pause
a moment to speak with him. True to his code of preventing
scandal, El Zapatero halts his plan until they are gone. Then,
realizing that they had been watching through the keyhole
and that his action will be known by all within a few hours,
he exits.

After his departure, La Zapatera calls her husband to dinner. Not hearing his reply, she appears. Seeing the open door, she thinks that he has gone to the tavern and begins to complain in a soliloquy characterized by much movement and nervousness. Her thoughts are interrupted by the child who stands framed in the open doorway. Intrigued by his mysterious hesitation, La Zapatera entreats him to reveal the message he is supposed to bear from the townspeople. But as he is about to do so a butterfly enters the room and El Niño chases after it. Finally, La Zapatera gives in and helps him. Together they attempt to capture the butterfly, but it escapes through the door. The child returns, having remembered his mission:

"Ay, well, you see . . . your husband, the shoemaker, has gone forever. . . . that's what he said in my house before he took the stagecoach. . . . and he said to tell you and now all the town knows."

At first totally shocked by his news, La Zapatera then becomes furious. El Niño runs out as her shouts bring the neighbors to the window and door. When they take the side of her husband, La Zapatera defends herself:

"Yes, I loved him, I loved him so much that I never paid attention to any of the wealthy suitors I've had."

Then, adopting El Zapatero as her real love for the benefit of the neighbors, she exclaims: "Oh, my poor darling, what things they must have told you!"

Suddenly, women begin to run in and out of the room, carrying various refreshments for the weeping Zapatera. They are dressed in gaudy yellows, reds, greens, and purples, moving through the room in dance patterns. The scene becomes a ballet of rapid movement, a color wheel spinning madly, with La Zapatera as its center. The whole procedure has evolved quickly from reality to a fantasy of color and dance. The reality of the act is suddenly transformed into a grotesque caricature. Within a few seconds the action becomes oppressive, unbearable. The curtain descends charitably on the mad sequence.

There is both a trace of courage and cowardice that marks El Zapatero's decision to desert his wife of three months. Courage is demonstrated in the decision to leave his work, his home and the town where he had lived all of his life; it took great resolution also to break the bonds which his unfortunate marriage had created. On the other hand, cowardice was the leading force in the decision. El Zapatero, who put great emphasis on human respect and all the trimmings such dependence manifests, could not stand up to the jeers, the whispers and the general scandal of the townspeople over the behavior of La Zapatera. In his cowardice he fled. It is this diversity of adjectives defining his actions that makes El Zapatero a believable human being. His is the complexity of humanity at a single instance.

La Zapatera, too, has in her character conflicting traits which make her actions interesting, even appealing at times. She endears herself by her cuteness, vivacity and beauty; however, her less complimentary aspects—a temper and shrewishness—clash vigorously with her better points. While her young age and inexperience excuse her, her selfishness and disregard for others condemn her. And, not unlike Lorca's other heroines, La Zapatera is alone at the end of the act, though physically surrounded by the screeching mob. Her husband has left her. But the comparison hangs only on a thin strand since the selfishness of Lorca's other women is primarily centered on the necessity to love and be loved. With La Zapatera, however, the selfish attitude has no such laudable end; it exists merely for her own convenience for without her husband she cannot understand how she will survive. But the solution to her problem is clarified in the second and final act.

The room has hardly changed in decor, but the addition of a bar, two tables and a sink have caused the shoemaker's bench to be pushed aside. La Zapatera has turned the workshop into a tavern to support herself. The clientele is composed of her many admirers—Don Mirlo, El Alcalde, El Mozo and other young men of the town. They avail themselves of the refreshments only to have an excuse for dedicating their eyes to the vision before them. This situation has not helped La Zapatera's standing in the community. The gossip about her increases with every day of her husband's absence, no doubt fanned by the unbased boasts of her clientele. Her temper aroused by the loud sighs of the men and by their searching looks, La Zapatera denounces them:

> "What is this, a tavern or a hospital? Abusers! How could I put up with this if it weren't that I have to earn my living with these wines and these trappings because I'm alone since my poor darling husband left on your account?"

Don Mirlo, trying to gain her good graces, agrees with her but is ignored. He begins his exit, but as La Zapatera speaks he acts as if there were intimate relations between them. His smile and apparent duplicity contrast with her confession of devotion for El Zapatero:

> ". . . it's been four months since my husband left me and I'll never yield to anyone because a married woman must remain in her place as God ordains. . . . I was decent and I will remain decent. I bound myself to my husband. Then, until death."

El Mozo, who notices Don Mirlo's lecherous actions, chases after him and La Zapatera is left alone in the tavern.

El Niño, re-entering playfully, tells her of a fight he had to defend her from an indecent song that another boy was singing. The devotion of La Zapatera for El Niño shows the extent of feeling which she can achieve. This love has been transferred also to the imaginary figure in which La Zapatera has ennobled the old shoemaker. With the child on her lap, she tells him of the courtship. The child listens, fascinated by her fairy-tale for it is no more than that:

" . . . I would see him mounted on his white horse. . . .
He would wear a sculptured black suit, a fine red silk
tie and four gold rings which shone like four suns. . . .
He looked at me and I looked at him. I lay on the grass.
. . . He stopped his horse and the horse's tail was white
and so long that it touched the water of the stream."

But the spell of the tale is broken by a murmur which becomes a song. La Zapatera recognizes the song as that which
was being dedicated to her misfortune. She asks the child
to sing it. El Niño hesitates, but at her insistence picks up
the melody:

> "Zapatera, who regales you
> with the cloth for all your dresses
> and those jackets of batiste
> with embroideries of lace?
> Now she's courted by the Mayor,
> now she's courted by Don Mirlo.
> Zapatera, Zapatera,
> Zapatera, you've done well!"

Cruel, though comic in its content, this ballad is typical of
the Spanish genre and, in no sense, is it unique. It does,
however, capture the desired effect, conveying as it does the
Spanish usage of such forms to comment on a special
situation.

As La Zapatera prepares to meet the balladeers with her
irate temper, El Alcalde enters, preventing her exit. He claims
that he has arrested "two or three" of her defamers and
looks for a thankful smile from her. But La Zapatera, wise
with that touch known as "picardia"—a mixture of common
sense, wit, earthiness and knowledge imparted by hard
knocks—forcefully rejects all his amorous advances. Not
even the offer of a mansion wherein she would reign as queen
can obscure her devotion to El Zapatero:

> "I'm not used to those luxuries. You sit in the drawing-
> room, you get into the bed, you look at yourself in the
> mirrors and you lie under the palms with your mouth
> open waiting for the dates to fall, because I will not
> budge from being a shoewife."

Her lashing tongue has knocked down another suitor. When she calls him an old man, El Alcalde threatens to put her in jail because of the affront to his dignity (but it is his pride which has been hurt). His irritation is answered by trumpet flourishes, resounding comically in the street. The child and the neighbors running through the streets announce the important arrival of a troubador. As La Zapatera prepares to leave the tavern, however, the minstrel enters followed by the crowd.

His disguise being perfect, no one recognizes El Zapatero. La Zapatera welcomes him to the tavern, the townspeople sit around him expectantly and El Alcalde is only too glad to pay for his wine. The child alone seems to recognize something in the voice of the disguised Zapatero and he spends the rest of the time trying to recall its familiarity.

El Zapatero holds the interest of the public by declaring that he comes from the Philippines where all the inhabitants are shoemakers. Sipping his wine while looking at La Zapatera, he exclaims:

"What a delicious wine! How very, very delicious! Wine from grapes as black as the souls of some women I know."

All the neighbors' eyes are fixed on La Zapatera. The shoemaker begins a tale of a patient husband and his blond wife as she listens guiltily:

"She was a wife who was surly,
he was a man of great patience,
she was coursing towards twenty
and he had passed beyond fifty.
Holy God, how they would quarrel!
Imagine the woman, ferocious,
mocking the feeble old husband,
lashing with eyes and with tongue."

As if to defend herself from the accusing eyes of the townspeople, La Zapatera interrupts to condemn the woman in the story. But as she listens to her own story, La Zapatera becomes uneasy. She begins to cry loudly. The neighbors, gloating over her exposure, remark bitingly: "Those who cry are those who have reason to be quiet!" After these several interruptions, El Zapatero continues with his tale, introducing the unfaithfulness of the woman:

> "Her friend arrived on the gallop
> upon a Cordovan horse
> and said to her between sighs:
> 'Girl, if only you wished it,
> tomorrow we could dine
> alone, we too, at your table."

The audience is intrigued as El Zapatero tells of the plot to kill the husband with a barber's razor. He details every moment of the plot. La Zapatera, meanwhile, sits with the child on her lap. She holds him strongly as if seeking his protection; with the other arm she covers her face. The tenseness of the moment, as El Zapatero outlines the sinister plot of the wife and her lover, is climaxed suddenly by a woman's shouts:

> "They're fighting with knives! ... They're killing each other! They're stabbing each other because of that woman!"

The woman, who has appeared suddenly in the doorway points accusingly at La Zapatera as the reason for the knife duel in the street. All run out of the tavern, but not before casting hateful looks at La Zapatera. She and her husband, still in disguise, are left alone.

In between her tears, La Zapatera swears her allegiance to her missing husband, but tells a fictional story of her great love and devotion for him, of his wisdom she had respected so faithfully, of her dependence upon him for all her needs. Indignant at her lies, El Zapatero faces her:

> "Your husband was right about you. Those tales are pure lies, only fantasy."

As La Zapatera tries to defend herself from the sudden onslaught, El Zapatero adds further:

"In my village lived a woman . . . whose heart was sufficiently bad to allow her to speak with her admirers at the window while her husband made boots and shoes from morning to night."

But La Zapatera realizes that his comments are directed at her and begins to counterattack. In turn, he calms down. When she cries once more, El Zapatero becomes very sympathetic to her cause. Though he cannot believe that his absence has made her change so radically, he gives her the benefit of the doubt. Her devotion becomes more believable with each word she utters but El Zapatero tests her by pretending to be interested in her for other than friendly reasons. La Zapatera reacts immediately:

"What do you think I am? I keep my whole heart for that man who roams the world, for the man I should, for my husband!"

The shoemaker is very content with her response. La Zapatera, in turn, is astonished at his changing moods and decides that the man is crazy.

A knocking at the door, a desperate knocking, halts their exchanges. El Niño, entering out of breath, announces that the young men who had fought over her had been injured and that the townspeople were on their way to eject her from the town. El Zapatero becomes maddened at this and prepares to defend his wife. She and the child enter her room to see the approaching crowd. As she leaves, he blames himself for not having seen the goodness in his wife:

"How wrong I was not to realize that my wife is pure gold, the purest on earth! I almost feel like crying!"

Two of the women enter hurriedly, inviting El Zapatero to leave the house before the others arrive. After listening to their accusations of La Zapatera, the shoemaker forces the jealous women out of the house. He is suddenly transformed into her defender, as vociferous as La Zapatera had been in the opening sequence of the play. The mob stopped at El

Alcalde's residence, La Zapatera and El Niño return. La
Zapatera is calm but resolved to face her adversaries. Again
testing her truthfulness, El Zapatero plans to leave the tavern. But La Zapatera's concern over his plight, her kindness
and good-will weaken his resolution until, moved by his renewed love for her, he asks:

> "Then, would you accept him back kindly? . . . If, by
> chance, he should arrive right now? . . . Would you for-
> give his folly?

Overjoyed at her answers, El Zapatero discloses his true
identity. The unbelieving Zapatera cannot speak as El Zapatero embraces her madly. Outside, a voice sings the ballad
of her infidelity. Finally reacting to the unexpected encounter, La Zapatera resumes her former character as she insults
her husband and throws chairs around the room in a fit:

> "Playboy! Ay, how glad I am that you've returned! What
> a life you're going to lead! Not even the Inquisition . . .!
> Not even the Roman crusaders . . .!"

But El Zapatero picks up his beloved bench and looks
pleased at being home again: "House of my happiness!"
La Zapatera, hearing the approach of the mob singing the
derogatory ballad opens her door and shouts triumphantly:
"Now there are two to defend my house, two. Two! My husband and I." The mixed chorus of voice and bells floods the
scene as the curtain descends on the final act.

This farce is the only play in Lorca's repertory, excluding
the puppet plays, which ends happily. At least, it is a relative happiness or a philosophic resignation to life that punctuates the plot, and not the heavier, more tragic aspects
that occur in his other dramas. Though all of his plays contain elements of humor and music, nowhere in Lorca's
theatre are these quantities better integrated than in *La
Zapatera Prodigiosa*. It is a nearly perfect play—both in
conception and actualization—containing characterizations
and caricatures worthy of the old masters of the farce, Lope

de Vega and Moliere. As such, the play is the best indication of Lorca's growth as a dramatist. It is as far ahead of his previous theatre works as *Mariana Pineda* was from *El maleficio de la mariposa*.

VI. EL AMOR DE DON PERLIMPLIN CON BELISA
EN SU JARDIN

UPON ITS completion on June 15, 1928, *El amor de don Perlimplin* was promised to Cipriano Rivas Cherif, director of the theatrical group "El Caracol." Plans were announced for a Madrid production in 1929 at the "Sala Rex." But these preparations were unsuccessful, and it was not until April 5, 1933 that the play was presented. Under Lorca's direction, the "Club Teatral de Cultura" of Madrid produced the drama at the "Teatro España." The decor was by Santiago Ontañon.

THE RECEPTION ACCORDED *El amor de don Perlimplin* was even more turbulent than that which greeted *El maleficio de la mariposa* upon its opening. Where the latter play had been subjected to public animosity, Lorca's latest play was opposed, even before its presentation, by stronger and more emphatic forces. There are two versions of why the play did not reach the stage in 1929, one by Rivas Cherif and the other by Lorca. Both, however, agree that political pressure was the unmovable obstacle.

Rivas Cherif, in an article published in 1957,[1] explains that the play had been in rehearsal for some weeks and the premiere date decided on when he received word from the military authorities that the "Sala Rex" was to be indefinitely closed. The reason given for this apparently unfounded action was that the theatrical group had not observed the formalities of mourning for the recently deceased Queen Mother, Christina of Hapsburg-Lorraine. As flimsy as this excuse was, when taken along with Lorca's account it achieves more sinister aspects.

Garcia Lorca disclosed earlier[2] that the play had drowned in a sea of military censure under the direct order of General Severiano Martinez Anido, who, upon learning that the role

1. C. Rivas Cherif, *Excelsior, op. cit.*
2. Angel del Rio, *Revista Hispanica Moderna, op. cit.,* p. 203.

of Don Perlimplin was to be interpreted by a leading military personality of the day, threatened incarceration of the author, the officer and the director. Though the entire content of the play did not possess anything which might be considered politically or militarily objectionable, governmental contrariness was founded on the ridiculous point that the officer's participation would be degrading to the career of arms. The officer, whose name is not available, was reprimanded according to Lorca's account, and the author was forced to submit his manuscript to the official censor where it was detained without approval in spite of the changes made. It was this office that during Primo de Rivera's dictatorship ordered the closing of the venture. As a result of these pressures the entire group had to disband, forsaking its name "El Caracol."

It was perhaps the disillusionment with that production that prevented Lorca from ever expanding the one-act play into a full-length drama as he had done with *La Zapatera Prodigiosa*. But the intention was there, even as late as 1933 when the play was to be presented by the "Club Teatral" of Madrid:

> "*El amor de don Perlimplin con Belisa en su jardin* is the sketch for a longer drama. I have placed in it only the precise words needed to draw the characters. . . . I call it 'a chamber version' because I intend later on to develop the theme more fully in all its complexity."[3]

The single act is divided into four scenes wherein the six characters—Don Perlimplin, Belisa, Marcolfa, Madre and two sprites (Duendes)— create an atmosphere intermixing realism and surrealism. Where the first touches of this technique appeared inadequately in *El maleficio de la mariposa*, were experimentally handled and excused in the puppet plays, and showed themselves faintly through La Zapatera's daydreams, it is in this play that surrealistic tendencies become impor-

---

3. "Una interesante iniciativa," interview in *El Sol,* Madrid (April 5, 1933).

tant. Not that they are fully developed or integrated into the action, but they are well-handled as will be seen in the discussion of the text.

Having overlapped each other in the writing, *El amor de don Perlimplin* and *La Zapatera Prodigiosa* are very similar. They complement one another in the development of the basic plot: the old man married to the young wife. But where the previous play relies heavily on folk traditions and dialogue, on a simple approach to the marital quarrels, on a more physical level of activity, in *Don Perlimplin* Lorca prefers to treat more poetic sides of the basic plot.

> To the student of "pure" theatre nothing would be more rewarding than a close study of this play of changing moods and identities as a man of fifty, married to a voluptuous girl, invents a lover for her and kills himself for her, in order to teach her the meaning of love.[4]

Thus, this play takes an entirely different route from that travelled in *La Zapatera Prodigiosa*. Perlimplin's unselfishness contrasts with the self-interest that prevails in the characters of La Zapatera and her husband; furthermore, Belisa's final recognition of Perlimplin's sacrifice lifts her well above La Zapatera whose last words show that she has not changed. The similarity between the two men lies in that both are resigned, towards the end of each respective play, to the situations which confront them; but their solutions are vastly different: El Zapatero merely returns to his shop and accepts his wife's taunts philosophically, while Perlimplin, less stoically but more poetically, kills himself so that Belisa may understand love and live a worthwhile life in that knowledge. Belisa and La Zapatera also have a basic premise that unites them: both are young, earthy and contemptuous. But as their respective husbands differ so, too, do they. Where La Zapatera rejects all advances of her many suitors, Belisa accepts all of them joyfully. She is the

---

4. John Gassner, *The Theatre in Our Times,* (New York, Crown Publishers, 1960), p. 224.

exaggeration of physical love while La Zapatera represents the extreme of ideal or romantic love. Belisa cannot love, during the pre-climax moments of the play, except in sensual terms; her love being narcissistic, centered on her own body and the pleasures it can give her, Belisa can find satisfaction only in physical love. She rejects the lovers whose attitudes are more poetic, but characteristically falls in love with an unknown admirer whose letters reveal his intense love of her body. The secretiveness of this suitor, who is the disguised Don Perlimplin, mixed with his passionate understanding of her, make Belisa rise a little above her usual interest. This rise continues as the play reaches a climax in the garden scene where Don Perlimplin is revealed to her as the secret lover. In these final moments Belisa's passion turns to love and the climax is sustained to the last moment of the play.

Perlimplin and Belisa are the principal characters, but Marcolfa—Perlimplin's housekeeper—plays an important part as the instrument through which the action is sparked. In her, Lorca has placed many of the qualities of Harlequin, the sometimes too-bright servant in the commedia dell'arte. Thus, it is at Marcolfa's suggestion and prodding that Perlimplin arranges to marry Belisa; the idea of marriage had not seriously presented itself in all of his fifty years. Again, the resemblance of incident to El Zapatero's plight. The joint scheming of Belisa's mother and Marcolfa has the planned result. Like the ancient Arlecchino, Marcolfa is always present when plans are being made but is conspicuously missing at moments when her presence could prevent a crisis. Her derivation is also celestinesque.

The "Prologo" takes place in Perlimplin's house where he and Marcolfa are having a conversation on marriage: she, trying to convince him that his old age makes it imperative that he have someone to look after him; he, resisting this suggestion weakly. As a defense of his single state, Perlimplin interjects:

"When I was a child, a woman strangled her husband.

He was a shoemaker. I can't forget it. I have always intended not to get married."[5]

His words refer back to *La Zapatera Prodigiosa*, recalling the days when he was a child, possibly El Niño who had befriended La Zapatera. In a sense, then, this revelation of relationship to those characters could provide the real ending for the previous play.

But in spite of his protests, Marcolfa continues to woo his interest for the revolutionary proposal. Her cause is aided unexpectedly by Belisa's sweet voice coming from the balcony across the way.

> "Love, love.
> The sun swims like a fish
> enclosed within my thighs.
> Warm water among the rushes,
> love.
> Rooster, the night is going!
> Don't let it depart, no!"

Sensing the advantage she has gained as Perlimplin listens raptly to the sensuous song, Marcolfa declares that Belisa is the one best suited to be his wife. Perlimplin can hardly argue before he is pushed to his balcony and instructed to call her name. Hardly the master of his fate, he complies with Marcolfa's command. When the lovely and young Belisa appears at her balcony, voluptuously dressed, Marcolfa hides behind the drapes. Perlimplin, trembling and weak, faces Belisa and after much hesitation, during which he has to be prompted, succeeds in declaring his intention of marrying her. Shocked by the sudden and almost indecent overture, Belisa calls her mother. La Madre appears and Marcolfa, who is enjoying the turn of events, grins happily. Belisa announces Perlimplin's intentions. La Madre becomes very complimentary to the old man who stands before her once again nervously committing himself to the formalities

---

5. All textual quotations, unless otherwise specified, are from *Obras Completas, op. cit.*, pp. 889-928.

of the proposal. While he and Marcolfa converse out of sight
of La Madre, Belisa listens to her mother's arguments in
favor of the marriage:

> "Don Perlimplin has much land. On the land there are
> geese and sheep. The sheep are taken to market. At the
> market they are bought with money. Money gives
> beauty. And beauty is coveted by other men."

The mother has the eye of a money-changer and sees the
advantageous side of the marriage. Her objections overcome
by the prospect of wealth through which pleasure would
later follow, Belisa retires while her shrewd mother converses
with Perlimplin over the wedding arrangements.

But Perlimplin does not realize the gravity of the discussion until after she re-enters her house. Frightened by the
idea, he looks at Marcolfa:

> "Ay, Marcolfa, Marcolfa! What kind of a world are you
> getting me into?"

His words are echoes of the misguided Zapatero who had
heeded the advice of his sister under similar circumstances.
But as Marcolfa whispers in his ear, his eyes grow brighter.
Belisa re-appears on her balcony singing her song. Perlimplin begins to look at her differently and Marcolfa's words inspire his growing admiration as the "Prologo" closes.

The business of the marriage ceremony has been accomplished as the first scene opens upon Don Perlimplin's bedroom. It is a large room. At its center is a magnificent bed
with a feathery canopy; its walls are interrupted by six
doors, five of which lead to balconies. The sixth leads into
the house proper. It is this last door that Marcolfa closes
as she bids her master goodnight. Alone in the bedroom
while Belisa prepares herself for bed, Perlimplin seems nervous. He exits after first peeking through the door where
Belisa is undressing:

> "Belisa, with all your lace you seem like a wave and you
> frighten me as the sea did when I was a child."

Belisa then enters in a flowing nightgown, her hair loose, complaining of Marcolfa's ineptitude in following her orders for the room's decoration. But Belisa's feelings arise from a restlessness which soft guitar music enhances:

"Ay! Whoever looks for me with passion will find me. My thirst is never quenched."

As it started, suddenly, so the music ends. In its place are heard five different whistles. Belisa, recognizing them as the calls of her lovers, tingles with the delight of expectation. Before she can answer them, however, Perlimplin re-enters. Almost a mockery to her anxiety, he declares his love for her, seriously retelling of the moment when he discovered this new feeling:

"I married you for whatever the reason, but I didn't love you. I couldn't have imagined your body until I saw it through the keyhole while you dressed for the bridal night. It was then that I felt love."

He confesses that she is the first woman in his romantic life and Belisa is astonished at the revelation. The whistling is again heard but Belisa tells Perlimplin that it is the clock. He accepts her explanation and turns out the light. The whistling continues, growing stronger each time. As Perlimplin and Belisa approach the bed, two sprites, Duendes, enter from opposite sides of the stage pulling grey curtains that hide the room from view. Lorca says these two figures should be children. As they perform their task, they speak somewhat shrewdly of the reason for their action:

Duende 2: ". . . It's always nice to cover the faults of others."
Duende 1: "The audience can uncover them later."
Duende 2: "Because if things are not covered with all kinds of precautions . . ."
Duende 1: "They can never be discovered."

The night passes quickly during their conversation and upon feeling the chill of morning entering through the curtains, the sprites prepare to allow the spectators to view the scene once more. As they draw back the curtain, Perlimplin is sitting on the bed. Two large gilded horns decorate his head. Belisa lies beside him, feigning sleep, while the five open doors that lead to balconies inspire suspicions in her husband. Awakening her, he demands to know why they are open. When he discovers five ladders and five hats, one at each balcony, Perlimplin becomes furious. But Belisa explains away his suspicions by telling him that such is the custom in her mother's town, and that the hats belong to: ". . . the little drunkards who come and go, darling Perlimplin." Totally seduced by her beauty, Perlimplin believes every lie she tells him:

> "You explain everything so well. I'm satisfied. Why shouldn't it be as you say?"

His doubts return, but they are momentary only as Belisa reassures him that he alone has kissed her during the night. But Belisa's active night with her five lovers has depleted her energies. She returns to bed and falls asleep immediately. Perlimplin is left alone with the dawn, murmuring the sad words:

> "Love, love
> which is wounded.
> Wounded by fleeting love;
> wounded,
> dying with love.
> Tell everyone it was
> the nightingale."

The curtain closes on the first scene as Perlimplin tenderly covers Belisa's sleeping figure. But the question remains, advanced further by his closing words: did Perlimplin know of his wife's night of infidelity?

> The story is old, lewd and rather savage: that of the old man married to a lusty young wife, one of the standard situations of neoclassic farce. But Lorca, without losing

sight of the farce, lifts it to poetry also, and poetry of power and freshness.[6]

The second scene, a few days later, gives the answer to the question. Not only Perlimplin but also Marcolfa saw the night-time visitations of Belisa's lovers. Marcolfa tearfully describes the event:

"On the wedding night five persons came in through the balconies. Five! Representatives of the five races of the earth. The European, with his beard; the Indian, the Negro, the Oriental, the North-American. . . . Imagine, yesterday I saw her with another."

But Perlimplin seems undisturbed by her words, commenting happily:

"But I'm happy, Marcolfa. . . . You have no idea how happy. I have learned many things, and, above all, I can imagine them."

These are keys to the transformed character of Don Perlimplin. He has changed almost completely from the ignorant and suspicious old man of the first scene into a man who has learned to love. But more importantly, as he says, he has learned to use his imagination. All this has been achieved through Belisa, though she is not aware of the deep effect she has had on him. So, there are no more serious accusations of infidelity even though Perlimplin is fully aware of her deceptions. Puzzled by her master's attitude, Marcolfa exits with exasperation on her face as Belisa approaches from the garden. Perlimplin himself hides in a solitary corner from which he can observe Belisa secretly.

The lovely but unfaithful wife shows her concern over a new lover whom she has not been able to meet. She soliloquizes:

"I haven't even seen him. On my walk through the park, they all followed me except him. He must have dark

---

6. Francis Fergusson, *The Human Image in Dramatic Literature* (N. Y., Doubleday & Co., 1957), p. 86.

skin and his kisses must perfume and burn like saffron and clove. Sometimes, he passes underneath my balcony and waves his hand in a greeting that makes my breasts tremble."

When Perlimplin interrupts her with a feigned cough, Belisa turns irritatedly. But her husband does not reproach her. Instead, he teases her by withholding a note that has been thrown through the window. The anxious Belisa implores him to give her the letter. In an unexpected gallantry he entrusts the paper to her:

"I give you this piece of paper which means so much to you because I understand your state of mind. I'm aware of things. And although they wound me profoundly, I know that you're living in a drama. . . . I know everything! I was aware of it immediately. You're young and I am old."

His new outlook surprises her, but she does not doubt his sincerity. She speaks freely of the young man whom she has never seen except in the shadows beneath her balcony and who writes passionate letters:

"The letters I've received from other men . . . spoke of ideal countries, of dreams, and of wounded hearts; but these letters from him . . . speak of me, of my body."

In her excitement she shows the letters to Perlimplin who grins knowingly as he scans them.

"Belisa, it isn't your soul which I desire, but your soft and white trembling body!"

Her new admirer knows that the things which please her are sensuous things. Knowing that her body is the most important thing to her because it gives her pleasure, he dedicates his love to it. This understanding of her assures Belisa: "There's no doubt that he loves me as I want to be loved." Perlimplin listens contentedly to these confessions but he teases Belisa further by saying that he knows the young lover. Then, as he looks out the window, he claims to have seen him in the garden. But when Belisa looks for him the garden is empty. Perlimplin enigmatically proclaiming:

"Since I am old, I want to sacrifice myself for you. . . . What I am doing, no one else has done. But I am already beyond the world and the ridiculous morality of people. Goodbye."

His exit marks the end of the second scene. It is a grandiose movement during which he tells Belisa that she will know everything later.

The final scene frames a garden with large cypress and orange trees. Perlimplin and Marcolfa are again in deep discussion. Don Perlimplin's change is again accentuated in his conversation; his exuberance is communicated to Marcolfa in a touching speech which expands on the topic first seen in the second scene:

"It seems as if a hundred years had passed. Before, I was unable to think on the extraordinary things of the world. I stayed at the doorways. . . . But now! Belisa's love has given me a precious treasure of which I had been ignorant. . . . You see? Now I can close my eyes and see what I want to see."

Marcolfa, however, is preoccupied with plans her master has confided to her. Between sobs, she reports that Belisa has been informed, as he requested, that the secret lover would meet her that night, at ten, in the garden. Marcolfa describes Belisa's reception of the news:

"She became as fiery as a geranium, grasped her heart with her hands and passionately kissed her beautiful tresses. . . . She only sighed. But what sighs!"

Marcolfa's puzzlement grows as Perlimplin receives the report happily. His explanation shows the dedication of his careful plan to a change in Belisa's outlook on love:

"I want her to love that young man more than her own body. And there's no doubt she loves him."

By loving someone, Belisa will be freed from her narcissism.

Perlimplin knows that she cannot love him as he is, so in his plan he has created the unknown lover. The meeting in the garden will be the climax of his involved episode, the moment when Belisa will be converted. But his voice still has the ring of mystery, hinting that there is more to his plan than seems evident. To Marcolfa's protests, he replies:

> "Don Perlimplin has no honor and wants only to amuse himself. . . . What should I do but sing? . . . Tomorrow you'll be free as a bird."

She exits, this time offended by his lack of honor, to do his bidding. Evening turns night as Perlimplin hides himself in the cover of some rose-bushes to await Belisa's appearance for the tryst. A sweet serenade accompanies his vigil at first, but it gives way to a group of voices singing of Belisa in erotic stanzas:

> "On the shores of the river
> night is becoming moist.
> And on the breasts of Belisa
> branches are dying of love.
>
> "The night is singing naked
> over the bridges of March,
> Belisa is washing her body
> with water of brine and spikenards.
>
> "The night of anise and silver
> is gleaming over the roofs.
> Silver from brooks and from mirrors,
> anise from your thighs of white."

Each stanza is concluded by Perlimplin's chant of love: "The branches are dying of love!" Perlimplin is a branch on the tree which is Belisa. While she grows from the generous earth, he draws life from her; but her self-love is killing him, the branch, because its nourishment is withheld for herself. Only in the sharing of the nourishment, love, with another will the tree sustain the branch. The metaphor is implied in Perlimplin's anguished chant. Content to be loved by Be-

lisa in this bizarre manner of transference, Perlimplin waits
patiently.

The moon guides Belisa to the appointed place as the
real farce begins. The rosebush where Perlimplin is hiding
trembles as a figure in a red cape emerges suddenly. Belisa
rushes to her lover but he crosses quickly, indicating he will
return. Belisa sighs with anticipation. Perlimplin enters,
then, from the same place where the figure had disappeared.
Eager to tell him of this new sensation—love—Belisa seems
like a different person in her radiance:

> "The scent of his flesh passes through his clothing. I
> love him! Perlimplin, I love him! I seem to be another
> woman!"

It is a sensual love, but nonetheless it achieves the purpose
which Perlimplin had intended. In his eyes, her love for another person is a great accomplishment: "That is my triumph . . . The triumph of my imagination." Belisa does not
grasp the meaning of his triumph. She understands even less
the words that follow:

> ". . . Now I will help you to mourn him. . . . Since you
> love him so much, I don't want him to leave you. And
> so that he can be yours completely, it has occurred to
> me that the best thing is to stick this dagger into his
> gallant heart."

At that moment, Belisa feels true love for the unknown
lover whose death sentence Don Perlimplin has pronounced
while brandishing a large dagger. She pleads for his life, but
Perlimplin remains resolute:

> "He'll love you with the infinite love of the dead and
> I'll be free of the dark nightmare of your magnificent
> body . . . Your body! . . . Which I've never been able to
> fathom! ! !"

He runs out quickly, tearing away from Belisa's hold. Frightened, Belisa calls for Marcolfa to bring her a sword to kill
Perlimplin. But the servant does not answer.

The shrubbery again parts and the red-caped figure stumbles into the garden with the dagger centered in his chest. His features are completely hidden by the huge cape. Belisa takes him in her arms and only then does the man reveal his face to her. It is Don Perlimplin who lies dying within the crescent of her arms. The revelatory scene recalls Cyrano de Bergerac's death sequence in Edmond Rostand's famous play.

The fantastic affair holds Belisa in a tight grip, tearing into her comprehension. Perlimplin, no longer speaking as the old man but as her lover, explains the fantasy:

> "Your husband has just killed me with this dagger of emeralds. . . . He ran through the field and you'll never see him again. He killed me because he knew I loved you like no one else. As he killed me he shouted: 'Now Belisa has a soul!' "

Belisa cannot grasp immediately what he is saying, though she begins to recognize aspects of his completed plan. Perlimplin draws her closer to him as his life ebbs away:

> "I am my soul and you are your body. . . . Since you have loved me so much, let me die embracing it in this last moment."

Belisa finally realizes the truth, but Perlimplin has died in her arms. To Marcolfa, who has entered after Perlimplin's farewell, Belisa cries out: "I would never have thought that he was so complex!" In her changed personality, strongly shadowed by what Lorca calls "a magical light," Belisa expresses her love for Don Perlimplin:

> "Yes, yes, Marcolfa, I love him, I love him with all the strength of my flesh and soul."

Belisa's voice reveals the sense of real loss Perlimplin's sacrificial death has caused. She no longer sees him as the quaint old man who had first been the naive husband and later the fatherly confidant. Perlimplin has now become the fictitious young lover. Wishing him back to express her new-found love, Belisa speaks her final words in desperation: "But where is the young man in the red cape? ... My God, where is he?" Marcolfa's words to the body of Don Perlimplin indicate that the metamorphosis is complete: "Sleep peacefully, Don Perlimplin ... Do you hear her?" Distant churchbells accompany the closing curtain, mixing with Belisa's cries in a symphony of laments. Yet, the note of triumph is ever present through Marcolfa's words, echoes of Perlimplin's victory over Belisa's narcissistic love.

It is this achievement which makes Perlimplin's act of self-extinction much more than merely a poetic "tour de force" or a ridiculous undertaking. His is the greatest sacrifice which human love can make. It is an act completely free from selfishness. Devoted to the redemption of a human spirit and apart from any taint as it transcends the normal values of everyday life, it reaches the heights of magnificence. Through his charade and subsequent death, Perlimplin turns the vain and wanton Belisa into a woman capable of truly loving someone other than herself. Through his tragic act he gives her real life. But it is more than this renewal that Perlimplin accomplishes, as his dying words attest: "I am my soul and you are your body." His greatest gift to Belisa is a soul—his own. Theirs is now the perfect union. So, in that sense, Perlimplin reaches the only plateau he could have inhabited once his love for Belisa was kindled, and she attains a stature she could never have reached alone.

El amor de don Perlimplin is the culmination of a particular set of dramatic and poetic values especially expressed in the earlier puppet plays and *La Zapatera Prodigiosa*. These ideas, which simply consist in the integration of the lyric and the grotesque within a farcical framework, are here endowed most completely. The grotesque character of Lorca's Don Cristobal is now refined, poetically imbued with an ideal, and transferred into the soul of Don Perlimplin. There, it grows through love and emerges as a miniature tragic figure once the selected sacrificial act is consummated and the recognition scene is played. The lyric element, though always on an equal plane with the grotesque, is subtle and haunting. It wends its way through Belisa's distorted view of love as well as through Perlimplin's fanatical complexity, and is movingly fused with the grotesque in the final sequence, causing the dramatic eruption.

El amor de don Perlimplin, derived generally from the traditional Spanish *Aleluyas* (eighteenth century colored sheets which contained brief stories in caricature and poetry), is admittedly "a sketch" for a longer play. It contains the most advanced ideas on a subject-matter briefly explored in *El retablillo de don Cristobal*, *Tragicomedia de don Cristobal y la seña Rosita*, and *La Zapatera Prodigiosa*. It is a climactic point in Garcia Lorca's theatre for this reason, though it does not divert from the larger pattern which unites all his plays in content, outlook and expression.

VII. ASI QUE PASEN CINCO AÑOS

Asi que pasen cinco años was conceived in New York and a large part of it written there between 1929 and 1930. Left inedited by Lorca, it was never produced during his lifetime although plans had been made to present the play at Madrid's "Club Anfistora" in 1936. The historic events of that year prevented the premiere. New York saw the first presentation of the drama in an English version, on April 5, 1945, at the Provincetown Playhouse under the auspices of the Jane Street Cooperative Association. The production was directed by Joann Strauss. Prior to this, on September 13, 1937, the Maniquin scene was enacted in Paris; it was published thereafter.[1] The Spanish language premiere occurred on November 22, 1954 at the University of Puerto Rico.[2] Mexico saw an impressive television production under the direction of Salvador Novo on October 1, 1956.[3]

IF THERE IS a drama within Lorca's repertory which is intellectually, rather than emotionally, motivated, it is *Asi que pasen cinco años*. That is not to say that intellect and emotion are divorced here, but that the play's appeal is certainly to the former. Within the play's fluid framework Lorca has woven a strange and exotic fabric with the threads of psychology and poetic symbolism. Though both these factors are well represented in the greater part of Lorca's poetry and drama, seldom have they led to such intriguing disembarkment of relationships as occurs in this surrealistic drama.

The entire outlook of the play is subjective; that is, it is centered on the "experiences" of the young man, El Joven. The approach to his problem, therefore, is principally lacking in objectivity; the symbolism cannot be marshalled into a phraseable pattern; the situations are always disguised by a web of intrigue. Lorca has drawn everything in pastel layers which become progressively harder to penetrate. The elusive-

---

1. *Hora de España,* Valencia (November, 1937), pp. 67-74.
2. *La Torre,* vol. III, No. 9, Rio Piedras (1955).
3. Vazquez Ocaña, *op. cit.,* p. 283 (footnote).

ness of the play is never allowed to wander into shallow streams where it may be grasped.

Asi que pasen cinco años is a monologue. What makes it less recognizable as such is Lorca's technique—surrealistic and symbolic—which disguises effectively the origin of the characters who appear on the stage. The "reality" of the action takes place in the amorphous mind of El Joven. He is the only real person in the play. All the personages are no more than physical representations of his varied thoughts, his personalities, his desires. The work, then, develops as a monologue in which the speaker is El Joven, be he as himself or as a mental projection of his inner self. These images of El Joven exist physically because of the demands of the stage as well as the credo which influenced the conception of the play, namely, surrealism. Because of these imperatives, the characters are visible; in their physical aspects they require treatment equal to that given real characters. Lorca attacks the problem masterfully, giving credibility and roundness to each of these images. Therein lies the perplexity which the play presents. At one moment there is apparent reality, at the next there is surrealism, then poetic symbolism and finally an irrevocable and exotic entwining of these elements.

To this seeming confusion of ideas Lorca adds an outward conservativeness of form. The play is cast in the mold of more traditional fare—three acts divided into five scenes— and encased in the trappings of reality. That this point of departure is misleading for the spectator becomes obvious almost immediately; these "trimmings" belong only to the facade of the drama and not to the core.

Developed dramatically as an investigation of psychological behavior, *Asi que pasen cinco años* lacks a plot of any magnitude and depends for its action on the intricacies of El Joven's behavior pattern. Plot pre-supposes the expiration of time within which incidents may be related to each other. By this relationship of incidents in time a plot is compounded. But there is no such passage of time in this play. Everything that occurs is not in the realm of time, but somewhere beyond it in an expanse reached only through the deviations of the human mind. So, the time at the beginning and at the end of the play is the same and the action, which did not even occupy one second of time, took many years to develop in another area of existence where measurements are unimpaired by mere physical standards.

The non-existence of time for the subconscious mind becomes Lorca's principal thesis in *Asi que pasen cinco años*. And within that secret chamber lie the experiences, dreams, fears and other unrealized aspects which have shaped that being whose mental agony is displayed, El Joven. He has lost the reality of time in the surrealistic world of the mind. To him, in his attempt to flee the reality which surrounds him, the past, the present and the future are as one—irreconcilable, yet co-existing in an unholy trinity.

> . . . a type of suspension which annuls the passage of time, which concentrates the past in a present that does not occur, immovable and static. The miracle of the impossible made real.[4]

In its abstraction of ideas through reality, the play recalls the paintings of Salvador Dali wherein every day objects and landscapes are brought together in an atmosphere of insinuation, subtlety and mystery. Dali's earlier influence on Lorca is most obvious in this drama. Like the surrealist painter, Lorca uses apparently unrelated settings, personages and symbols to create that middle ground in which El Joven is suspended. The drama is an exciting and intriguing account of the workings of a complicated mind, lost in the chaotic existence of mental twilight.

In his exploration of surrealist principles and in their application to his theatre, Lorca severed many of the cords that had maintained a relationship between his drama and

---

4. Morla Lynch, *op. cit.*, p. 107.

the traditional drama which had preceded him. He did this in two ways. First, and most important, Lorca took a well-known theme of the Spanish theatre—the frustration of love—and placed it in an abstract setting, adding to it a modern theme—the oneness of time. Integrated through poetic symbolism, the two themes became united in an impressive variation. Second, in *Asi que pasen cinco años* Lorca designates his characters without recourse to proper names; instead he uses descriptive nouns—Joven, Mecanografa, Viejo, Gato, Niño, Novia, Jugador de Rugby, etc. Though Lorca follows this practice to some extent in all of his plays, it is in this one that he completely abandons the traditional manner of individualizing characters. Again he is following the practice instituted by earlier surrealists,[5] and adhering to the general anti-realism that was prevalent. To equip these doubly fictitious figures with proper names would be to give them an individuality which does not pertain as they are no more than embodiments of confused thoughts and are more effective in their near anonymity.

As the first instance of a full-length drama along surrealistic lines, *Asi que pasen cinco años* is the only survivor of the genre in Lorca's writings.[6] The failure of other dramas to materialize in the pattern of this advanced play has led to views that Lorca was merely satisfying a whim temporarily succumbed to and that the work is entirely beyond the path of his dramatic line. No view could be more incorrect for had the playwright lost interest in such means of expression he would never have allowed the proposed production in 1936, nor repeatedly said, as he did in an interview:

"I have followed a well-defined trajectory in the theatre. My first comedies are unpresentable. Now I believe that one of them, *Asi que pasen cinco años*, will be produced

5. Gomez de la Serna, Lenormand, Cocteau and others.
6. Lorca's three brief sketches—*El paseo de Buster Keaton, La doncella, el marinero y el estudiante,* and *Quimera*—were playlets in the surrealistic vein. *El Publico,* of which only scenes remain, is the only other drama-at-length so inspired.

by the 'Club Anfistora.' My real goal is in these impossible comedies. But in order to demonstrate a personality and be worthy of respect, I have done other things."[7]

Therefore, the opposite of the general view, so inappropriately held by critics such as Garcia Luengo,[8] is true; the evidence is in Lorca's own words. Of course, the furtherance of this idea could not find relief as the playwright's sudden execution in 1936 cut short all such aspirations.

The criticism that the play stands by itself, that it does not belong in the society of Lorca's other drama, can also be destroyed by a presentation of the facts. Thematically, *Asi que pasen cinco años* has strong kinship to the rest of Lorca's theatre. Its principal themes are related effortlessly to those in *Bodas de sangre, Yerma, Doña Rosita la soltera* and *La casa de Bernarda Alba*. Lorca's preoccupation with time and frustration are likewise found in his earliest plays—*El maleficio de la mariposa* and *Mariana Pineda*. Thus, *Asi que pasen cinco años* is connected directly to the mainstream of Garcia Lorca's drama.

As another point of emphasis, this play contains antecedents to characters in later works, acting as a focusing element also for the creations which preceded it. Thus La Novia in *Asi que pasen cinco años* is related to Belisa and La Zapatera; her lineage extends directly to the tempestuous Novia of *Bodas de sangre* and to the youngest of Bernarda Alba's daughters. Yerma, too, has her counterpart in the surrealistic drama in the figure of El Maniqui. In El Jugador de Rugby can be found a preliminary sketch of Leonardo, the sensual lover who runs away with the bride in *Bodas de sangre*. El Padre in *Asi que pasen cinco años* is the first notable model in Lorca's theatre and serves as a pattern for the father in *Bodas de sangre*. El Joven himself bears a great

7. Felipe Morales, "Declaraciones de Garcia Lorca sobre teatro," *Heraldo de Madrid* (April 8, 1936).
8. E. Garcia Luengo, *Revision del teatro de F. Garcia Lorca* (Madrid, "Politica y Literatura," 1951), pp. 32-33.

resemblance to both Yerma and Doña Rosita in the withering wait for fulfillment which he shares with them.

The first act of the play, subtitled "Leyenda del tiempo,"
is set in El Joven's library. He and El Viejo are sitting, in
conversation begun long before the parting of the curtain.
The young man wears blue pajamas, the old one a cut away
coat in grey. The dialogue between these opposite persons,
one of interrupted phrases, initiates the action. Its tone is
intimate, confession-like, as El Joven haltingly recalls his
earlier youth: "I remember that . . . I kept the candies for
later."[9] But El Viejo's idea of memories is sharply different.
He abhors the past and any connection with it. Instead, he
proposes:

"That is, one must remember, but remember beforehand.
. . . . Yes, one must remember towards tomorrow."

His words absorb El Joven as the clock signals that it is
six o'clock. Unobserved by El Joven or his companion, La
Mecanografa crosses crying and disappears. The moment is
like that in which a Swiss clock strikes the hour and a figure
appears to accentuate the event. The more it occurs, the less
important it becomes until the duality of action passes unnoticed. Such is the significance of the secretary's passage
through the room.

After the pause during which the clock strikes, their conversation resumes centering on El Joven's love affair with
La Novia. He reveals the reason for his sadness as her absence of five years:

"I know her only slightly. But that is not important. I
believe she loves me. . . . They went on a long trip. . . .
for reasons that cannot be explained. Until five years
have passed."

El Viejo listens to his story, somewhat incredulous that the
departure of La Novia, the young man's fiancee, has not

9. All textual quotations, unless otherwise specified, are from *Obras
Completas, op. cit.,* pp. 955-1054.

stirred resentment or anguish. But in reality it has because El Viejo is the personification of the idea of "remembering towards tomorrow." Through him El Joven's real thoughts— of abstinence, of hopelessness, of solitary old age—are made clear. El Joven sees himself as El Viejo, "remembering towards tomorrow," and realizing that La Novia's long journey will prevent their union. His fear of never possessing that which he loves inflicts El Joven with this forward remembrance, giving reason for calling up the image of himself as an old man. Thus El Viejo's resentment of the past. The early presence of El Viejo in the play indicates the young man's great preoccupation with this idea.

The noise in the street interrupts El Joven. Outside the house exists a real world which the young man does not want to face and which he tries to shut out by the closing of windows and doors:

> "Noise, noise, dust, heat, bad smells. It bothers me that the things of the street enter my house. Juan, close the window."

Juan, the servant, closes the window after first entering on tiptoe. Of necessity he bears a name as he is the only figure spoken to in a manner requiring a name. He exits as unobtrusively as he came.

Renewing the discussion of the romance, El Viejo speaks of La Novia. Sometimes his statements show a desire to deplete time:

> "She has lived fifteen years, which are herself. But why not say that she has lived fifteen snowfalls, fifteen airs, fifteen dawns? Don't you dare to flee, to fly, to extend your love through the whole sky?"

It is becoming clear to El Joven that the plan is to separate him from her. The recognition that the love fantasy which he has detailed around La Novia may soon give way to the cynicism of his frustrated self, personified by El Viejo, arouses an angry indignation:

"You want to keep me from her. But I know your method. . . . I am in love. . . . and so I can wait five years in the hope of lying with her, with all the world in darkness, with her tresses of light around my neck.

Once more the cynic, El Viejo reminds him that La Novia cut her hair and El Joven recalls that she did so without his permission. His momentary happiness fades in the recollection. Yet, for all the love he professes, El Joven cannot face the idea of calling her his fiancee:

"Then, if I begin to think of her, I draw her, I make her move—tender and alive; but suddenly, who changes her nose or smashes her teeth or turns her into someone else covered with rags? . . ."

At that moment when he thinks of her as his fiancee, as his completely, he sees her thus deformed. That is why he prefers to think of La Novia as his little girl, deluding himself entirely. But El Viejo does not leave him to proceed on that course:

"But if in that precise instant she confesses she has deceived you, that she does not love you, wouldn't her wrinkles become the most delicate of roses? . . . And wouldn't you love her more for that very reason?"

El Viejo has made El Joven confess the truth by making him face the reality of life, if only for an instant, a reality of relative values based entirely on circumstance:

"That's why one must fly from one thing to the next until one is lost . . . To do otherwise is to die instantly . . ."

El Joven responds to his awakening by heartily thanking El Viejo for his dissertation. Preparing to leave, El Viejo encounters La Mecanografa who is still in tears. Hopelessly in love with El Joven while he is indifferent to her, she announces that she is leaving. La Mecanografa is unwilling to wait for him. Having loved him since childhood, she has received only empty words from him. El Viejo takes the part of El Joven in his opinion: "And why not? To wait is to believe and live." Though her hope of receiving his life and love is gone, she cannot give him up. Only when he reminds her that his life belongs to La Novia does she leave, retreating to her room. She represents another aspect of frustrated love in El Joven, a memory which haunts him for having denied a childhood love that was real. He becomes very sad, again confessing to El Viejo:

> "I want to love her as I want to be thirsty in front of the fountains. I want . . ."

But the consolation is not there for El Viejo reminds him only of tomorrow. Would it not be as it is with La Novia in the horrid dream? Distracted by the entrance of Amigo, a young friend, El Joven does not notice the exit of his other companion. El Viejo's calm exit is in contrast to the boisterous entrance of Amigo.

El Amigo—lively, passionate and manly—represents El Joven's reality before his withdrawal into an enigmatic existence. In a sense, then, he is the embodiment of the present and the recent past with its memories of drinking bouts, boisterousness, laughter and romantic entanglements—always too many to be accommodated properly into the shortness of a day. But even in that happy past there was the preoccupation with time which now haunts El Joven; in Amigo's words:

> "I don't have time, I don't have time for anything, everything is confused. You can imagine. . . . I'm already late; it's awful, the same thing always happens. I don't have sufficient time and I regret it."

Though El Joven's present state, however, borders on disilluionment, El Amigo merely resents the passage of time because it prohibits his further activities. In a moment of surrender to his old ways, El Joven adopts his friend's carefree manner as they wrestle playfully. An indicative moment.

The moment is short-lived, however. As if to remind El Joven of his problem, El Viejo re-appears to retrieve the hat he had left upon a table, saying pointedly: "I shall forget my hat." El Amigo is confused at the future indication of an act already committed, but El Joven realizes the subtle stab at the past which El Viejo has delivered. El Joven loses the joy he had inherited from Amigo and returns to his fearful and edgy self. His struggle resumes, characterized and underlined by a sudden storm which blows open the windows. Frightened, El Joven orders the servant to close the shutters. El Amigo and he argue, the former trying to convince El Joven that he must accept life as it is and must listen to the storms that surround his secluded existence. El Viejo becoming stronger at El Joven's hesitation, defends him from the reality which Amigo desperately proposes. El Joven does not listen to Amigo's words, again fearful of the reality which is just beyond his windows and which is emphasized by the loud thunder. After a tremendous clap of thunder, the three run to the apparent safety of a black screen decorated with stars. There, they hide as the bright lights diminish into an eery blue glow, the darkness of the storm.

The swift silence ushers a child and a cat into the scene. El Niño leads the cat, El Gato, into the room. They walk slowly and painfully. El Niño is dressed in a white communion suit with a garland of white roses on his head; his face is a white wax mask from which eyes and lips seem to portrude. El Gato, blue with a grey chest, has two bloody wounds—one on his head, the other on the chest. Their pace is the ceremonious step of death, complemented by El Gato's lamentations over his wounds. Their conversation is completely in poetry, a simple and striking pattern which is well-suited to the "play-within-a-mind" atmosphere. Through it are revealed the respective deaths of the new occupants of the stage. El Gato cries painfully:

> "My wounds hurt,
> the wounds the children made on my back. . . .
> Ten stones
> the children threw at me."

El Niño too, has his great sorrow as he tells the story of his
death. Like El Gato, he also died "yesterday":

> "My heart is also pained. . . .
> Because it stopped.
> Yesterday it stopped very slowly. . . .
> They placed me
> in front of the window with these roses."

The awareness of their deaths and the thought of burial becomes a terror to the child and his companion. As the thunder increases, crashing mercilessly outside the house, El Niño
fears the inevitable arrival of his pall bearers: "I don't want
to be buried." El Gato, the least afraid of the two because of
his lesser knowledge, now becomes agitated by El Niño's tale
of the burial:

> ". . . in dark holes,
> everyone cries. Everyone is silent.
> But they leave. I saw it. . . .
> They come to eat us . . .
> the lizard and his wife
> with all their little children, many of them.
> . . . Cat!
> they'll eat your legs and mustache."

Their panic grows as they try to leave the house and find
all the doors locked. Every noise frightens them as terror
takes hold. The small song they sing, overcome by the thunder outside, does not prevent the gnawing. The light diminishes further and in the darkness El Gato tries to open one
of the doors. Suddenly, a hand grabs it and El Gato disappears through the door, crying anguishingly. The low-voiced
soliloquy of El Niño exposes his resignation:

> "She sank.
> A hand grabbed her!
> It must be God's hand.
> Don't bury me. Wait a few minutes
> while I depetal this flower.
> I'll go alone, very slowly . . ."

The child slowly depetals a rose he has plucked from his

crown. He depetals the flower of Time plucked from the crown of Hope. He walks towards the door. The same hand appears again and takes hold of El Niño, dragging him into the deeper shadows beyond the door—the darkness of death. Upon his disappearance, the light returns to its normal level.

A beautiful and powerful scene in every aspect, it is a triumph of underscoring of emotions and basic human feelings in a poetic tonality consonant with dramatic impact. The inevitability of death is the theme thus introduced and, although the scene and its "message" may appear superfluous at first, inspection verifies Lorca's idea of designating a possible result of the struggle which was slowly consuming the mind of El Joven. This assertion seems well founded in the light of the dialogue which follows immediately upon that scene as the three figures emerge from their hiding place:

> Viejo: "It will be still worse."
> Joven: "Yes, afterwards."
> Amigo: "It's been bad enough. I don't think you can escape the storm."

Anguished shouts from outside the house attract the attention of El Joven. Answering his query, Juan, the servant, enters the room:

> "The gatekeeper's child died and now they're taking him to be buried. His mother is crying."

Having been returned to his coffin by the unexpected hand, El Niño's body is now being carried in procession to the cemetery. Giving an ending of definiteness to the affair, the adversaries proclaim:

> Amigo: "Naturally!"
> Viejo: "Yes, yes; but what's past is past."
> Amigo: "But it's happening now."

The servant adds further verification to the event as he requests the keys to the roof to remove the carcass of a dead cat which street urchins had just killed.

But these events serve to rekindle the animosity between El Viejo and Amigo as they vie for El Joven's mind. Amigo tries to convince him that he should not sacrifice himself by waiting for La Novia, that he should, instead, live in the present and be aware of his past. El Viejo, however, seems to hold the better grasp in the contest as El Joven again gravitates towards his pole: "Blessed be hunger!" El Joven speaks as a fanatic sponsoring a cause of great importance. The hunger which he calls blessed is the apetite of the flesh which he is suppressing in the period of celibacy dictated by La Novia's absence. Amigo can only scoff at him for his monk-like existence. And El Viejo supplies cowardly courage in the promise of a future devoid of any connection with the present or the past. El Joven does not see the impossibility in this but accepts the easier path offered by El Viejo. The embodiment of the present and the recent past in Amigo holds no attraction for him any longer. El Viejo has succeeded, for the moment, in his goal:

> The intention of the divining Viejo is evident: to destroy the importance of the immediate, of "what is to arrive right now," to show that the present is always painful and, therefore, should be avoided while the eyes focus on the unforeseen beauty of what is to come, of the distant future. . . . El Joven debates between waiting and the vehement desire of "having," of possessing what he loves.[10]

Though he has defeated El Amigo, El Viejo's victory is tasteless because the appearance of a new personage, Amigo Segundo, presents a new foe. He is very young, completely dressed in white—suit, shoes and gloves. The suit is cut in an exaggerated manner and adorned simply with enormous blue buttons and a large lace bowtie. His entrance startles the others for Amigo Segundo represents El Joven's deep past, his childhood. The three aspects of time are now united in El Joven's mind, and the struggle to gain possession of it

---

10. Maria Teresa Babin, *El mundo poetico de F.G.L.*, op. cit., p. 225.

begins anew. El Joven remains silent throughout most of the
ensuing conversation in which the newcomer talks of his earliest memories:

> ". . . what was really beautiful was the rainfall a year
> ago. There was so little light that my hands turned
> yellow. Remember?"

But El Viejo does not remember anything. His antagonism
toward the new adversary growing, he listens uneasily to his
description of the rain:

> "The rain is beautiful. At school it came in through the
> patios and burst on the walls revealing very small nude
> women which it carried inside it. . . . one year I caught
> one of these little rain women and kept her in a fishbowl
> for two days. . . . She became smaller and smaller, child-
> like, as it should be, as is right, until only a drop of
> water remained."

And this little rain fairy, symbolically elusive in captivity
until she disappeared, had sung a haunting tune which remained with him:

> "I come back for my wings,
> let me return.
> I wish to die becoming dawn,
> I wish to die becoming
> yesterday.
> I come back for my wings,
> let me return.
> I wish to die being a spring.
> I wish to die outside the sea."

Irritated by the sentimentality, El Viejo denounces Amigo
Segundo as crazy. But the past is not so easily put down;
seeing his opportunity to counterattack, Amigo Segundo
reproaches El Viejo:

> "Crazy? Because I don't want to be full of wrinkles and
> pains like you. Because I want to live my life and you
> rob me of it. I don't know you. I don't want to know
> people like you."

Finally, El Amigo adds his own comment, unexpectedly turning on the past by saying that his sentiments show only a fear of death. Again, Amigo Segundo defends his stand nobly, citing the burial of the child as his idea of a perfect end. Yet, El Viejo remains his principal obstacle:

"My countenance is mine but you're stealing it. I was tender and sang, and now there's a man, a man like you, who roams inside me with two or three masks ready."

El Viejo continues his cynical comments on the past, trying to disillusion El Joven's nagging desire to seek refuge in it. Only the future should prevail as El Viejo sees it. Amigo Segundo, heartened by El Viejo's lack of arguments, thrusts deeply with a remark:

"Behind us, everything is tranquil. How is it possible you don't know it? All you have to do is carefully awaken things. On the other hand, all that exists in four or five years is a well into which we'll all fall."

Infuriated by the reminder of old age, of that reality "into which we will all fall in four or five years," El Viejo exits hastily. Only El Joven is affected by his sudden departure. He has been left to contend with the present and the past. Desperately, El Joven follows El Viejo. El Amigo, noting his strength over both future and past, quietly derogates his companion. This done, El Amigo finishes his drink and rapidly exits as if remembering something.

Amigo Segundo sits unobtrusively, alone, his head inclined. The rain resumes. Juan re-enters on tiptoe, crossing the room and leaving. Half-asleep, Amigo Segundo looks at his hands in the light of the storm as El Joven returns to the room. Sitting near his companion, El Joven thinks of El Viejo: "He'll return tomorrow. I need him." He, too, closes his eyes. La Mecanografa enters slowly carrying a suitcase. She crosses to the door and in a final gesture—hopeless and pitiable—she speaks to El Joven: "Did you call me? ... Do you need me?" Sadly, she leaves the house. Her exit is the last hope of love in El Joven, this time cut off from reality by the strong memories Amigo Segundo has evoked.

> We feel he has surrendered not to the present of living memory, whose illusions he hopes to sustain forever, but rather to his Second Friend's past suicidally cut off from the present by dead memory.[11]

And this view is strengthened by the fairy's song which Amigo Segundo repeats in his sleep, the last two lines interpreting El Joven's desire to fly from reality:

> "I wish to die outside
> the sea."

The act ends thus, after Juan has announced significantly that it is six o'clock in the evening. Not a moment has elapsed and yet a great struggle has been experienced.

Supposedly five years, the waiting period decided upon by La Novia, have elapsed between acts and the day in which El Joven will claim his fiancee has arrived. But the action follows directly from the first act in such a manner that it is inconsistent to consider it outside the dream into which El Joven succumbed. It is in this dream, very deep within his subconcious mind, that El Joven "remembers towards tomorrow" as El Viejo has suggested. The action of this second act, therefore, is the visualization of this mental process. Where in the first act El Joven achieved a psychological regression (physically reconstructed through the exits of characters in the order of their most recent existence, i.e., El Viejo, the future; El Amigo, the present and recent past; La Mecanografa, an earlier past of adolescence; until he remained only with Amigo Segundo, his childhood), the process is reversed in the second act through the bridging of time. Thus the five years of waiting for La Novia's return have been abolished mentally by El Joven. The complication of time elements is portaged by the regression series

---

11. Edwin Honig, *op. cit.,* p. 139.

in the first act. His regression, in fact, becomes prognostica-
tion through the complex working of his fevered mind.

Throughout the second act the pace is quicker and more
turbulent; La Novia, mainly, is responsible for the life in
the act through her passionate behaviour—first romantic,
then cruel and finally indifferent—which makes her glow
surpass that of the other characters. She is revealed lying
on an impressive bed decorated in grandiose taste expressed
in plummage and lace. Echoes of Belisa's bed in *El amor de
don Perlimplin*. La Novia is awake, herself patronizing daydreams. The stillness of the setting is interrupted by the repeated call of an automobile horn approaching from a distance, making itself heard through La Novia's open balcony.
As if her dream had suddenly materialized, she runs to the
veranda:

> "Come up. It's important. My fiancee is coming, the old
> one, the lyric one, and I need your strength. Come in-
> side. I haven't seen you for two days."

In answer to her plea the impatient horn-blower, El Jugador
de Rugby, enters in full regalia—helmet, kneepads and a
bag. The last contains a large quantity of cigars which he
incessantly lights, smokes and crushes underfoot. Though
he never once speaks during his stay with La Novia, El Jugador shows great vitality in his actions towards her. He
embraces her with much impetus, looks at her devouringly,
blows smoke in her face when she calls him "my dragon" and
always kisses her in a different manner. She, in turn, is like
a girl with a large doll; her hands never leave his body, caress-
ing his hair or his chest. If she stops kissing him occasionally it is to tell him of her love and dependence on him.

> "But you're handsomer. You're like a dragon. I feel as
> if you're going to crush me in your arms because I'm
> weak and small . . ."

Obviously, La Novia has long since forgotten El Joven. The
decision to run away with El Jugador is made after a rapid
comparison between the two suitors:

"Oh, What a white coal, what an ivory fire flows from your teeth! My fiancee had frozen teeth; when he kissed me his lips would be covered with small withered leaves; they were like dry lips. I cut my tresses because he liked them and now I go barefoot for you. . . . We must leave."

The excited voice of a servant woman as she knocks on the bedroom doors separates the lovers. El Jugador leaves as silently as he came, but not before a final embrace. La Novia guardedly opens the door and La Criada enters to announce the arrival of El Joven, her father, and El Viejo. Cynical about the visit, La Novia orders his flowers thrown out the balcony and then grabs her most drab dress. But La Criada knows of La Novia's betrayal with El Jugador. She warns her mistress and defends El Joven's goodness. But like Belisa who refused those who loved her poetically rather than physically, La Novia has turned from El Joven in disgust at his tenderness. She can only accept passionate love, such as that manifested by El Jugador. Even the sound of his car's horn excites her as she orders all her clothing packed for her elopement with him.

El Padre, a myopic old man in black, enters distractedly to escort La Novia to El Joven. Without preliminaries, La Novia declares her disinterest in her suitor. El Padre objects to her sudden attitude for she had written faithfully during their journey and never had shown interest in another man. He grows more nervous and upset as she makes her excuses:

"I didn't exist before either! The earth and the sea existed. But I slept sweetly on the train's cushions."

Her casual disregard of honor and feelings disturbs him greatly. The shock of her disclosure prevents his will from forcing her to complete the agreement and El Padre becomes a silly old man as he says:

"Don't I have a right to rest? There's an eclipse of the moon tonight. Now I won't be able to see it from the

terrace. Whenever I'm irritated the blood goes to my
eyes and I can't see."

In a curious mixture of self-pity and concern for the deserted
young man, El Padre tries to convince his daughter to mend
her ways and perform her duty. But she remains unmoved
by his plight.

Unable to restrain himself from seeing her, El Joven
rushes into the room. His reception is cold, and only after a
long pause of embarrassment does the conversation resume.
El Joven again introduces the theme of time as he explains
his agitation:

"Excuse me, but I'm out of breath from running up the
stairs. And, then, in the streets I had to hit some children who were stoning a cat to death."

It is as if it were six o'clock anew, as if the first act were
again present. The episode of the cat stoned by street urchins shatters the apparent reality which had pervaded the
scene up to this point. The phrase is a reminder that the
action is all at once and conclusively in the mind of El Joven.
The technique is Brechtian in quality, less forceful, perhaps,
than a piece of discordant music or another such interruption, but just as effective in alienating emotional response
and involvement. Lorca uses the scene between El Niño and
El Gato as the reference point for the unreality of the play,
choosing it whenever the surrealist tendencies become hidden
by necessary references to life, order and reality.

But Lorca's technique of variation is employed for further reasons than alienation, unlike Brecht's. The latter's
plays have a realistic basis, as have Lorca's, yet the ideas of
each playwright in employing techniques clearly at variance
with the reality of the plays are vastly different. The use
of discordant elements or extraneous material was resorted
to by Brecht in an attempt to destroy a play's illusory
power. In this way he could unbalance his audience, making
them sit apart from the action. By permitting a minimum

of emotional involvement in the play, Brecht hoped to make his audiences more intellectually aware of it. In such a state they would be more receptive to the play's ideas. The result was an intellectual rather than an emotional understanding of the play. This was Brecht's principal goal.

Lorca, on the other hand, though calling upon similar techniques throughout many of his plays, never desired such separation of emotion and intellect. To him the play had to be observed on its various levels if it was to be fully understood. Lorca had no thesis to expound, at least no thesis of his ever made itself more important than his poetic drama. In using the techniques made famous by Brecht, Lorca has only one purpose: uniting the play through a communion of emotion and intellect. Quite the opposite of Brechtian ideals. However, this union results in an intriguingly believable atmosphere. To Lorca that is the important aspect of a play. It is behaviour, human complexity made rampant by life—a mixture of reality and Fate—that interests Lorca.

It is so in this play. Lorca weaves a strange pattern with El Joven's mind as the place of departure. Everything comes from deep within his tortured mind which harbors aspects of youth and old age, restlessness and despair, indifference and love. Thus La Novia does not see him as a young man but as a wasted and ancient man:

> "A cold hand. A chapped hand of wax. . . . And an ancient look. A look that breaks like the dried up wing of a butterfly."

The symbol of the butterfly again serves the playwright's theme. Then, in a cruel and exacting interrogation, La Novia mocks El Joven by bringing up the image of El Jugador de Rugby:

> "And weren't you taller? . . . Didn't you have a violent smile which was like a mushroom on your face? . . . And didn't you play rugby?"

To each of these questions El Joven responds in the nega-

tive. Quite typically, the situation becomes unfathomable, as
Morla Lynch states upon having heard Lorca read this part
of the play:

> And here I become lost, as I am uncertain whether the
> slender and pale fiancee and the robust sportsman are
> "one person" in two different aspects—a "as you are"
> united to an "as I would like to see you"— or really two
> diametrically opposed persons.[12]

La Novia's questions unearth the interesting proposition that
El Jugador is the figure of El Joven as he imagines La
Novia wishes him to be. Attempting to emulate his creation,
El Joven embraces La Novia passionately, revealing the frus-
tration of his long wait. But her protests disclose the truth:

> "I'm the one who wants to be consumed by another fire!
> . . . How can I allow you to enter my bedroom when
> another has already been here? . . . I already hear the
> cry of a pursuing child in the mirrors and in the lace
> of the bed. . . . A mirror, even a table, would be closer
> to you than I."

Her satisfaction had been found in El Jugador. But El Joven
is above being hurt by such disclosures. His sorrow proceeds
from a love without meaning:

> "It's not your deception that hurts me. You're not bad.
> You signify nothing. It's my lost treasure. It's my love
> without object."

Their shouts bring the servant and El Padre into the room;
the scene is quickly dissolved as La Novia orders that all his
gifts be returned to El Joven, and especially the wedding
dress which hangs on a mannequin in another room. Upon
making his embarrassed excuses El Padre returns to the
balcony and his first preoccupation—the lunar eclipse—which
he was able to see after all. La Novia and La Criada exit.
El Joven is left alone with a dream eclipsed like the moon.
"What will I do with this coming hour which I do not
know?"

---

12. *op. cit.,* p. 110.

The light in the room diminishes steadily as he speaks. Only the moon's light, as it comes into eclipse, falls upon El Joven. But the door opens once more. A sobbing announces the strange figure of El Maniqui, who, wearing the wedding gown over its golden frame, enters the bedroom solemnly. Its voice is plaintive: "Who shall wear my dress? Who shall wear it?" As in the scene with El Niño and El Gato, the dialogue is entirely in poetry. The chant-like quality of the meter, coupled with the chimerical nature of the event, give an aura of mystery to this extended scene between El Joven and another of his mental images, El Maniqui. This figure resolves itself into conscience as its voice drags El Joven into the darkness of reproach. First, it laments the unused wedding dress:

> "I sing
> of death never mine,
> the pain of an unused veil,
> with lament of silk and feather.
> The underclothing which stays
> frozen by darkest snow,
> without the lace competing
> ably with the foam."

Then, as El Joven tries to excuse himself, El Maniqui haunts him with the accusation:

> "You lie. You're to blame.
> You could have been for me
> a colt of lead and foam,
> the wind torn in the bridle
> and the sea tied to the rump.
> You could have been a neighing
> but you're only a sleeping lagoon,
> with leaves that are dried and moss,
> on which this dress will rot.
> ....
> Why did you not come sooner?
> She waited for you, denuded."

El Joven cannot contain his concience's voice. His attempts not to listen are without fruition as El Maniqui continues by showing him the clothing for the child which was to be his:

> "My son. I long for my son.
> He is traced on my skirt
> by these ribbons which joy
> makes me burst on my waist.
> And he is your son."

El Joven acknowledges his lost son, but suddenly brightens at the thought of La Mecanografa who still loves him. El Maniqui spurs on his hopes:

> "She's always waiting, remember?
> Once she was hid in your house.
> She loved you so much and she left.
> Your child hums in her cradle
> and being a child of the snow
> it waits for the blood you will give.
> Run quickly to find her,
> deliver her naked to me
> and let the silks which I own,
> thread by thread and one by one,
> open the rose which is hiding
> her womb of fairest skin."

El Maniqui speaks as hope rather than conscience and El Joven is elated over the new object for his love. La Mecanografa is the bearer of his child. His elation is turned into action:

> "Before the reddish moon
> can wipe with blood of eclipse
> her curve's very perfection,
> I will bring my own naked woman
> trembling with love to you."

As he speaks, La Criada enters with a candelabrum which she places on a table. She exits silently as the light in the room returns to normal. During this interim El Maniqui assumes a rigid pose maintained until the end of the act. It is as unshakeable as El Joven's new-found hope. But El Viejo now returns to the astonishment of El Joven, who no longer has a need for him. Holding his chest, El Viejo explains wearily:

"Oh, you've wounded me! . . . A wound, but . . . the blood dries and what is past is past."

El Joven begins to walk away, anxious to begin his search for La Mecanografa. El Viejo calls to him, tries to hold him, but the renewed hope in El Joven proves stronger than the bony hands of despair. He runs out of the room as La Criada's voice marks another flight—that of La Novia. Grasping for life, El Viejo, too, exits. El Maniqui, resuming life briefly, adds the disturbing words:

"Who shall wear my dress? Who shall wear it?
The river delta shall wear it in its marriage with the sea."

El Maniqui faints and remains hunched over a sofa as the shouts of El Viejo bring a swift curtain on the second act.

The final act is divided into two scenes. In the first, the setting is a forest of large trees surrounding a platform stage. The baroque curtains of the "stage-within-a-stage" are closed. A set of stairs unites the two. As the scene opens, two figures in black cross the stage; their hands and faces are brilliantly white. As they walk solemnly out of sight in a funeral gait, another figure enters through the trees. It is Arlequin, a harlequin in green and black whose walk and manner are those of a dancer. The plasticity of his movements underscores his song:

"The dream moves over time,
floating along like a sailboat.
No one can hope to grow seeds
in the very heart of the dream."

His words serve as a prologue to the act and as a warning of what is to come in El Joven's search for La Mecanografa. "No one can plant seeds in the heart of a dream." His two masks, carried behind his back unless they alternate with his face during the song, are of different expressions. One

is very gay, the other represents sleep. This duality of dream
and time is represented in his song as well, paralleled with
the images of the weeping child and the old man. For both
aspects are as one in El Joven:

> "On the same column entwine,
> with the dream and time embracing,
> the child's whimpering cry,
> the old man's broken tongue."

Throughout the rest of the scene muted hunting horns
can be heard, plaintively symbolic of El Joven's search for
fruition. Another symbol is evident in the person of La
Muchacha, a young girl in a Grecian tunic. She is gay, skip-
ping rope as she recites her simple words:

> "Who can say it,
> who will say?
> My lover is waiting
> on the trough of the sea."

Searching for her lover, she is the embodiment of El Joven's
hope; it is cast in the figure of a girl to indicate the idea of
fulfillment in La Mecanografa. Although the lover has not
been found, Hope is in command. But what La Muchacha
does not realize until Arlequin promises jestingly to give
her what she desires is that:

> "You will deny me.
> We can never reach
> the trough of the sea."

This realization has the bitter-sweet taste that also marked
El Maniqui's words at the closing of the second act. Even El
Payaso, a clown whom Arlequin calls upon to help him in
delivering her lover from the sea-depths, cannot stem her
awakened fears. She exits, crying. A circus skit between
Payaso and Arlequin follows after which they also exit, ready
to face a new challenge or entangle another situation.

As these two descendants of the *commedia dell'arte* depart, La Mecanografa appears. She is accompanied by an-

other woman, La Mascara. Their vestiture is very dissimilar. La Mecanografa wears a tennis suit supplemented by a large cape and a brightly colored beret. La Mascara, glaringly attired in yellow, has on a dress circa 1900 which is too generously endowed with gold sequins. Her face, in pale contrast, is framed by a white mask. Against the somber blues and greens of the forest, she stands out like a light.

Their conversation is almost as curious as their clothes. La Mascara listens attentively as La Mecanografa retells the story of her frustrated love with a flair which would make it seem she had deserted El Joven against his wishes: "Because he loved me too much." But La Mascara, with a story of her own, no doubt as fictitious as La Mecanografa's, exclaims affectedly in her Italian accent: "O mio Dio! He's exactly like Count Arturo of Italy." It is the other's turn to listen to the tale. It is a story of La Mascara's desertion of Arturo and his son. In her fanciful tale, however, she is discovered as an aspect of La Mecanografa's personality—old age in the presence of her youth. Just as El Amigo has El Viejo to accompany his dreams, so, too, La Mecanografa has this preposterous creature to represent her future years. This facet is made more clear as their dialogue continues.

> Mecanografa: "As a small girl I kept the candies for later."
> Mascara: "Yes, they do taste better."

Now it is clear. La Mecanografa has adopted the words of El Joven while her companion has responded as El Viejo did in the first scene of the play. These echoes complete the pattern of El Joven's intricate personality. As if in warning of someone's approach, the trumpets are again heard. The two women retire to a secluded section of the forest.

Followed by Arlequin, El Joven enters. He does not see the figures huddled secretively nearby. El Payaso likewise enters, but not until Arlequin has succeeded in making El Joven stray from his planned road. His tale of the circus blocking several roads has forced El Joven to return by the same path. But before he can leave, La Mecanografa's voice reaches him; El Payaso and Arlequin depart, executing a dance step, as the new lovers face each other. They embrace:

> Joven: "I'll carry you naked,
>   flower spiced and clean body,
>   to the place where the silks
>   are trembling with cold."
>   ....
> Mecanografa: "Leave me, my love, on the mountain
>   surrounded by cloud and by dew,
>   so, though sad and large, I'll see you
>   covering a full dormant sky.
>   ....Wait!"
> Joven: "Love does not wait.

Anxious to take her away, El Joven tries to overcome her hesitation. But she separates herself from him. As she goes up the steps to the platform, the baroque curtains part revealing a miniature of the study in the first act. La Mascara re-enters momentarily to announce:

> "I have just left the Count forever. He remained back there with his child. I'm certain that he'll die."

She disappears into the forest crying strongly while protesting that she never loved Arturo. Her words are indicative of what will take place between La Mecanografa and El Joven. The tension of the scene begins to mount as their dialogue continues:

> Mecanografa: "I have loved you, darling! I will always
>   love you."
> Joven: "Now . . ."
> Mecanografa: "Why do you say now?"

She has loved him and she will love him, but there is no promise for the present. As his fears are renewed, El Joven becomes less and less the hopeful young man whose heart beat fast at the thought of La Mecanografa's love. El Viejo reappears and stands mute nearby nursing the wound in his chest. The apparition of the dead child crossing the setting upsets El Joven further:

> "Yes, my child. He runs inside me like an ant alone in a closed box. A little light for my son. Please."

La Mascara and two other similar figures enter and watch with concern. But La Mecanografa adopts El Joven's detached attitude in the first act. She begins to withdraw from him, punishing him for his cruelty to her until she finally declares timidly: "I'll go with you! When five years pass!" El Joven descends the small stage while La Mecanografa remains ecstatically transfixed. Juan, the servant, crosses to her and places the white cape on her shoulders. The dejected Joven is suddenly surrounded by moving figures—El Payaso, Arlequin, La Mascara and her companions, as well as El Viejo. Their movements become a mockery to El Joven's grief. Crazed by lost love, infuriated by the antics of the figures, El Joven seeks a path back to his previous existence of despair. El Viejo leads him away as the first scene ends.

The last tableau is set in the Joven's library. The wedding dress hangs on a decapitated mannequin—a symbol of all the shattered hopes of love and fatherhood which had been El Joven's. Several open suitcases are lying unattended on chairs and tables. Juan and La Criada are immersed in conversation, discussing the gate-keeper whose little boy has just been buried:

> "She's a gatekeeper now, but once she was a great lady. She lived with a rich Italian count for many years, the father of the child they just buried."

It is La Mascara of whom they speak. The timelessness of the action is again re-asserted through the incident of the dead child. The denouement has begun with the integration of figures into a closer bond with El Joven. Thus La Mascara is no longer just an aspect of La Mecanografa's life, but a symbol of frustration and decay in relation to El Joven's own life.

As La Criada—the same servant woman in La Novia's household—begins to leave, El Joven enters. He appears worn and physically exhausted. His manner also reflects his degradation for he finds fault with his surroundings, and even the air he breathes seems rank. He recalls his days as a child, especially the hours spent on his small bed watching the moon. Juan, however, reminds him that the bed was given to La Mecanografa many years before. Only the doorbell interrupts El Joven's regression. While Juan opens the door to admit the caller, El Joven retires to change his clothes.

Three men, striking figures in evening clothes and long capes, appear in the doorway. Settling themselves at a card table, they reveal that they are card players. But their games are for the highest possible stakes—the lives of those who play with them.

> "We play and we win; but how difficult it is! The cards drink savory blood while they're held and it is hard to cut the thread which unites them."

As they speak, they form a plot against their latest victim, El Joven. They must be careful with him, however, because he holds a powerful ace: "A young heart where arrows will probably be deflected." Their cunning will draw out this life-saving card and destroy him unless either La Novia or La Mecanografa decides to return before the expiration of five years.

When El Joven returns, shakily greeting his three visitors, the game of life begins. Promptly, the sinister players prepare their cards. They are eager to achieve their purpose. But El Joven stalls their fervor with repeated interruptions for wine. Los Jugadores, the three players, impatiently call for El Joven's card: "It is imperative that you deliver your ace." The words recall a similar scene in Cocteau's *Blood of A Poet* and like that script's "hero," El Joven is unable to resist the call of death, so impressively sounded by the three players. El Joven finally realizes he must give his "as de couer," the symbol of his life. As he places his last card on the table, a look of satisfaction crosses the faces of the three men. Then, the ace of hearts is seen enlarged upon the library wall. Instantly one of the players draws a pistol and fires an arrow which silently shatters the illuminated card. El Joven falls, his hands clutching his heart. After cutting an invisible string which is the tread of life, the dark figures disappear hurriedly.

El Joven is alone. His last desperate words are answered only by a strong echo which repeats every syllable distinctly. A second echo joins in as El Joven dies. Juan crosses the room with a candelabrum as the clock chimes six times. The echo repeats the six strokes. The time is the same as at the start of the play and nothing has changed except one life which has become death. The final curtain shrouds the scene.

> Knowing all of Lorca's work well, a laberynthian intertwining of images and themes resplendently Lorquian can be seen in this mixed but always balanced drama, and within that complexity of movement reigns a firm expressive unity. But the case is that this expressive unity reiterates with pathetic insistence the feeling of general frustration, but especially the frustration of love in time. The brevity of transition, the exact feeling of "now" does not exist because the concept is hardly pronounced before it passes.[13]

Whatever problems the play may awaken, it cannot be dismissed as inconsequential. It is a powerful theatrical drama, the product of intense feelings on the absurd and mysterious in human existence, and important in the catalogue of Spanish drama as both an erudite and passionate study of psychological behavior. It is possibly Lorca's most important single work and, although it has only received grudging attention in the past, the modern theatre may soon adopt it as the earliest example of the Spanish prototype of the "theatre of the absurd," placing it alongside the already accepted works of Beckett, Pinter, Ionesco and Genet.

---

13. Jose Mora Guarnido, *op. cit.,* p. 175.

Lorca's own "theatre of the absurd" began with the three short sketches usually referred to as the "brief theatre"— *El paseo de Buster Keaton, Quimera,* and *La doncella, el marinero y el estudiante.* These pieces, written in 1928, are the cornerstone upon which *El Publico* and *Asi que pasen cinco años* are built. They established the tradition in Lorca's theatre of examining man's foibles in his attempts to conquer Fate, be it implemented by natural laws or by the artificial codes which mankind has imposed on itself. Sometimes, as in the playlets and in the puppet farces, man's predicament is treated with a peasant humor; their grotesque overstatement hides the sense of impotence in the presence of Fate that these characters, as representatives of the human race, have inherited. Sometimes, as in the existing scenes of *El Publico,* man is viewed with sardonic laughter and made the object of all that is ridiculous in life. And in *Asi que pasen cinco años* he reaches what must be, of necessity, the climactic point—his withdrawal into the subconscious, his negation of the values of reality and his subsequent death. Thus, man's world is absurd because he has become absurd, and so on in the paradoxical circling of causation.

It is this existence which Lorca has transferred to the theatre. Man's absurdity, based on the overwhelming complexity of life, is crowned by his mock heroic stance. And, as in *Asi que pasen cinco años,* the sad moment arrives when the realization of life's futility strikes man the blow of despair. This is the panorama Lorca has deciphered with great lucidity, in spite of the fog of man's circumscription which shrouds the process of full recognition, and which he has chosen to preserve.

VIII. BODAS DE SANGRE

GIVEN ITS FIRST presentation as a reading at Morla Lynch's residence on September 17, 1932, *Bodas de Sangre* was officially premiered on March 8, 1933 at the "Teatro Beatriz" in Madrid. Josefina Diaz de Artigas and her company were directed by Garcia Lorca.

BODAS DE SANGRE is the first play in the trilogy of folk tragedies written in Lorca's last years. Because of the separation in time of this and its companion pieces from the mainstream of his creations for the theatre, there has been a tendency among critics to separate these tragic dramas in other ways. Labels have been affixed—"early" and "late" production—to effect this separation. Thus, the plays prior to *Bodas de sangre*, the greater part of Lorca's theatre, are usually considered of lesser importance than the four plays in the final segment of his career. But what is forgotten in this stammering representation of the truth is that all of Lorca's plays, from the first fantasy to the last tragedy, are intricately related through plot, characterization and outlook.

Moreover, as is especially true with *Bodas de sangre*, Lorca never created a play within a given period; instead, the idea began many years prior to the commencement of the writing. Frequently the writting would go on for extended periods, sometimes put aside for similar periods. The process often took years.

> Before *Blood Wedding* was a play, it was a short newspaper account in *El Defensor de Granada*, one of the local papers. I remember Federico reading to me an account of a bride from Almeria who, on her wedding day, ran off with her former lover. The bridegroom followed them and the two men killed each other. . . . Apparently, after this, the newspaper account was forgotten; yet some time later Federico told me of an idea he had for a tragedy—it was based on the incident in Almeria. Then, for some time, the play would seem to have been forgotten again. This process of letting a play write itself

188

was my brother's method. He never consciously wrote down a play's outline.[1]

The attempted separation is annulled by the facts. Particularly impressive is the argument of time as it gives the lie to any further proposal which would destroy the unity of Lorca's theatre. The constant overlapping of ideas for plays, noted throughout these chapters, serves to accentuate most definitely the viewpoint that to Garcia Lorca there was no such break as that proposed by his critics.

What can be evidenced in *Bodas de sangre*, however, is a heightened power of expression, more powerfully dramatic than in any of Lorca's previous works. Part of the reason for this lies in the greater experience and maturity which was the playwright's after his many "awakenings" through his travels with "La Barraca" in Spain and his excursions to the Americas. *Asi que pasen cinco años* and the unfinished *El Publico* gave light to one aspect of his new maturity; *Bodas de sangre* and the plays which followed it are instances of his renewed interest in Spanish life as it exists. A second reason for the greater vigor of these last dramas is found in a more experienced technique which thoroughly integrated poetic and dramatic values. Lorca's growth as a dramatist is most obvious in his trilogy, but as a climax to his career as a dramatist, these tragedies are indebted to the plays which went before.

Bodas de sangre has been the recipient of many notions of comparison. One of the earliest, and decidedly the best known because of the many subscribers to it, is the thesis based on an identification with J. M. Synge's *Riders to the Sea*.[2] Another opinion offers precedents for Lorca's play in Shakespeare's *A Midsummer Night's Dream* and Valle In-

---

1. Francisco Garcia Lorca, "From Granada to Bleecker Street," *The New York Times*, (January 30, 1949), p. 1.
2. Patrick O. Dudgeon, "Lo universal en la poesia popular europea: J. M. Synge y Federico Garcia Lorca," *Cursos y Conferencias*, XV, Buenos Aires, (1939), pp. 765-791.

clan's *Tragedia de Ensueño*.[3] As theories they have their
flaws, grasping at hazy conjectures and expanding them sug-
gestively. Mention of their existence suffices as it is the play
itself that is important.

The story of *Bodas de sangre* is simple and direct, emotionally appealing in its torrent of passions, and purgative
in its idiom of folk tragedy. The principal characters of this
drama live within the confines of an ancient moral and social
code based on the unshaking tenets of Honor and Death. La
Madre is a strong-willed woman, ancestor of Bernarda, and
possessed by a despairing fear that her son, El Novio, will
die as did her husband and another son. Her love for El
Novio is cast in this emotional mold. Her hatreds are as
powerful as her love; it is the name of Felix that evokes both
hatred and fear for the two dead men had been crushed in
the traditional feud between the families. These passions are
again aroused as El Novio prepares to marry the woman who
had been Leonardo Felix's fiancee. La Madre still suspects
their mutual devotion and fears that her son will suffer thereby. It is La Madre who holds the tragedy together; it is her
sense of love and hatred, honor and vengeance that directs
the physical action of the play. Therefore, it is her tragedy.

Basically, the plot develops as a triangle situation but
Lorca builds intricate patterns around it—tradition, codification, and mysticism—which give life and interest to the simple
newspaper report. First, there is an obvious concern with
Spanish conscience as reflected in everyday existence. As
Lorca portrays it, this conscience in turn mirrors the many
years of Catholic and Oriental influence imposed upon it.
This is the tradition. Next, Lorca places his characters within
the embrace of strict codes—the barbaric "an eye for an eye"
exists at the same moment as the patient lessons of Chris-
tianity—and these mixed concepts produce the strange and
demanding laws of Honor so prevalent in Spain. And these

3. De La Guardia, *op. cit.*, p. 356.

already awkward people, regulated by tradition and codification, are finally pawns in the hands of the very mysticism which they have guarded faithfully through the years. Fate is their master and Fate always leads them to Death. Then, too, there is belief in marriage, not so much because of the mutuality of love, but because through it a man can create a life which will carry on his memory and the family name.

> This moral conviction that men and women must be fecund and that the man and husband is the master because he is the instrument of fecundation has the deepest possible psychological and social roots.[4]

Finding herself with only one son, La Madre sees the rich fields and her own hopes lying barren unless El Novio gives her many grandsons. These will not only serve to make the land yield its wealth, but will also fulfill the desires of La Madre for the extension of the family. This hope remains strong:

> kept alive in its ancient form by a powerful economic fact: there must be sons to work the land and to defend the property. In Spain this law was reinforced by the rules of the Moorish harem . . . It was adjusted, exalted, and perpetuated in the stern teachings of the Church, which made it sinful for husband and wife to enjoy each other, but righteous to multiply.[5]

The first act, divided into three scenes, opens on a fittingly barren room in the home of La Madre and El Novio. It is a room in a pale yellow color whose starkness is further accentuated by the clipped speech of its two occupants. The emphasis of the dialogue shifts to the great fear which is evident in La Madre's eyes whenever El Novio has to travel to the fields. It was in those fields that her husband and other son were killed by the feuding knives. The knife is the most evil of human inventions in her eyes:

"The knife, the knife . . . Damn them all and the evil

4. Arturo Barea, *op. cit.,* p. 36.
5. *Ibid.,* p. 37.

man who invented them. . . . Anything that can cut a
man's body. A handsome man with his flower on his lips
. . . I don't know how you can carry a knife on you . . ."[6]

El Novio listens uneasily, having heard her lament many
times before. He cannot make her forget the bitter memories,
thoughts of not possessing her husband in his passionate
ways, of having had him for only three years. She recalls, in
transitions from bitterness to happiness, how he had loved
her, taking her to the wheat fields to consummate this love:

> "Your father would take me there. That's a sign of good
> breeding. Blood. Your grandfather left a son on every
> corner. I like that. Men, men; wheat, wheat."

To her the wheat fields are a sign of fertility, hence of men;
all men must be as productive as the wheat, as her husband
who in three years gave her two strong sons.

> The major metaphor of this scene is the comparison of
> men to yellow wheat. The Mother makes explicit the as-
> sociation of her son, the Bridegroom, with the color
> yellow.[7]

Diverting her attention, El Novio discusses his plans to
marry La Novia, daughter of another land-owner, whom he
has courted for three years. La Madre is happy to the extent that her son resembles his father in his impatience, but
her fears return as she intuitively feels:

> ". . . when I speak her name, it's as if someone hit me
> on the brow with a stone."

Noticing that her anguish is caused also by the realization
that her last son is about to leave her, El Novio assures her
that she will live with them after the marriage. But La Madre
declares:

> "No, I can't desert your father and brother. I must go

---

6. All textual quotations, unless otherwise specified, are from *Obras
Completas, op. cit.,* pp. 1081-1182.
7. Robert Barnes, "The Fusion of Poetry and Drama in *Blood Wedding,*" *Modern Drama* (Spring, 1960), p. 397.

to them every morning; for if I leave one of the Felix
could easily die, one of that family of killers, and be
buried next to them. . . . And I won't allow that! Because I would dig him up with my nails and I alone
would smash him against the wall."

At her son's insistence, however, she deserts these dark
thoughts, returning to his plans for the marriage. She instructs him as to what gifts he must buy for La Novia, gifts
to be given on Sunday when the long journey to her house
would be theirs jointly. Before he leaves, she adds:

". . . and let's see if you can make me happy with six
grandchildren, or as many as you want. . . . but girls
also. I want to sew and make lace and live in peace."

At his departure, a neighbor—La Vecina—enters and La
Madre is not given time to re-arrange her thoughts into their
former somberness. However, she manages to ask La Vecina
about La Novia's mother, long deceased; La Vecina replies:

"I knew her mother. Beautiful. Her face shone like a
saint's; but I never did like her. She didn't love her husband. . . . Now, whether she was decent or not nobody
knew. No one ever discussed it."

The neighbor also reveals another unknown fact in La Novia's background: her previous romance with Leonardo Felix
at the age of fifteen. But he later married her cousin. The
hated name renews La Madre's anger in spite of the fact that
it had been many years since the feud had taken the lives
of her husband and son. La Vecina calms her and then entreats:

"Don't oppose your son's happiness. Don't say anything
to him. You're old. So am I. You and I must now be
quiet."

Assured that La Madre will not uncover La Novia's earlier
romance with Leonardo, La Vecina returns to her own duties.
As the first scene ends, La Madre pauses to cross herself.
    This opening sequence is entirely in prose and reflects

Lorca's attitude in all his drama of reserving poetry and song
for more auspicious circumstances:

> In the dramatic works, verse obeys theatrical necessity
> when the lyric or musical element must prevail to high-
> light a sentiment, to give relief from the tragic tension
> or to transmit the magic of a precise setting.[8]

Lorca adheres to this plan purposefully. Thus, the scenes in
which poetry replaces prose as dialogue are unusual or above
the norm of everyday life. Such instances as the appearance
of the Moon, the Woodcutters and the Beggar Woman in the
forest scene are particularly enhanced by poetry. The second
scene of the first act, too, contains excellent poetry and songs
expressed in lullabies:

> "Nana, baby, nana
> of the horse so big
> who did not want water.
> The water was so black
> inside of the branches.
> And when it reached the bridge
> it stopped and sang romances."

The setting is a rose-colored room in Leonardo's house where
copper fixtures and decorations alternate with flowers of many
varieties. There, at either side of a central table, sit two
women—La Suegra and La Mujer. Leonardo's mother-in-law
and his wife chant softly to the small child in the former's
arms. It is a sad and bloody ballad containing repeated
rhythms which will enforce sleep. By presenting a harsh and
fearful picture through its story, the lullaby touches the
child's sensibilities. In sleep he finds safety. Lorca was very
concerned about the usage of these songs:

> I wanted to know how the women of my country put
> their children to sleep and, after a certain time, I got the
> impression that Spain makes use of its melodies of most
> marked sadness and its texts of most melancholy expres-
> sion to tinge the first sleep of their children. This does

8. Maria Teresa Babin, *op. cit.*, p. 8.

not only concern a model or an isolated song in some region, by any means; all regions accentuate their poetic character and background of sadness in this type of song.[9]

The blackness of the themes in these songs, Lorca explains in his lecture, proceeds from the hard life of the peasant, a toilsome, weary and impoverished existence:

> We should not forget that cradle songs were invented (and this is shown by their texts) by the poor women to whom their children are a burden, a heavy cross which they very often cannot bear. Each child, instead of being a matter of joy, is a sorrow, and, naturally, they cannot refrain from singing to them even in the midst of their love, their disgust towards life.[10]

When Leonardo makes his initial entrance at the end of the song, La Suegra is already returning the child to its bed. When he enters, the memory of the conversation in the first scene is revived. The descendant of the feuding line seems to impregnate the rose colored room with earthiness and strength. It now becomes obvious that the various gradations of red in the house—the rose of the walls, the reds in the flowers, the tinted glow reflected in the copperware—are symbolic of the Felix name. The blood in the lullaby completes the tonality representing the household. Leonardo has returned from the farrier's shop where once again the horse was shod. His wife listens to his complaints, but she senses yet another reason for the constant unshodding:

> "Couldn't it be that you abuse him? . . . Yesterday, the neighbors told me they had seen you on the border of the plain. . . . Was it you?"

Guardedly, Leonardo denies having strayed so far on his horse. Yet, he is forced into further denial, guiltily conceal-

---

9. Fed. Garcia Lorca, "Children's Cradle Songs," *Zero Anthology No. 8* (N.Y., Zero Press, 1956), pp. 64-65, trans. by R. Artesani-Lyons; Spanish text: *Obras Completas, op. cit.*, p. 50.
10. *Ibid,* p. 66.

ing some deviation from the expected behavior of a married man, when La Suegra exclaims as she appears:

"Who's been galloping the horse that way? He's below, broken, his eyes rolling, as if he'd come from the end of the world."

The poor condition of his horse has alarmed her but Leonardo offers only a lame explanation. Sensing the tension, La Mujer takes a different tack:

"Did you know that they're asking for my cousin's hand? . . . Tomorrow. The wedding will be in a month. I hope they'll come to invite us."

Leonardo exhibits no interest in the announcement except to state that La Novia bears watching. La Suegra, pointedly and with intention, corroborates his statement:

"When he says that it's because he knows her. Didn't he court her for three years?"

When La Mujer begins to cry, Leonardo quickly takes her away with the excuse of seeing the child. They exit in an embrace, leaving La Suegra in the room.

In the next moment a young girl, Muchacha, hurries into the room to report, half out of breath, that El Novio and his mother had bought beautiful and impressive things for La Novia. Cynically, having listened to the list of expensive gifts, La Suegra comments on the wealth of the two families. Leonardo and La Mujer re-appear; more cross than before, he frightens La Muchacha away. She exits, crying. La Suegra's intervention is likewise silenced. The nagging of his wife becomes too much for him and Leonardo goes into the fields. The scene ends with the same lullaby with which it opened, sung to the child whose sleep was interrupted by Leonardo's angry shouts. The two women begin to cry as they sing, anticipating the final moments of the play.

Three of the major characters in the drama have thus far been introduced: La Madre, El Novio and Leonardo. The fourth, La Novia, is to appear in the final frame of the first act, set in her cave home. The white cavern walls make it a luxurious retreat from the hot and arid fields which surround the hill. The heat makes such domiciles imperative. On the far wall hangs a large cross of roses, and throughout niches in the stone stand other colorful objects—small mirrors, blue jars, round fans. A servant, full of humble hypocrisy, leads El Novio and La Madre into the quaint quarters. La Madre, surveying the unfamiliar scene with a woman's critical eye, never utters a word as she and her son await La Novia's father. Both sit rigidly, elegant in their finery. Finally, as if seeking a pretext to break the silence, La Madre asks El Novio to keep in mind the length of the journey:

> "We must return early. How far these people live! . . .
> Four hours on the road and not a house or a tree. . . .
> Your father would have covered the wasteland with trees."

His father would have made these dry lands productive, just ` as he had enriched everything he touched, including La Madre.

When El Padre, La Novia's elderly father, greets his guests it is with a ceremonial handshake uninterrupted by words. All three sit and, after the usual formal politeness, begin to discuss the anticipated union; El Padre adds wishfully:

> "What I regret is that the lands are . . . so separated.
> I like everything together. . . . If we could only bring your vineyards here with twenty pairs of oxen and place them on the hillside. . . . What's mine is hers and what's yours is his. That is why. To see it all together."

It is La Madre, however, who brings up the matter of the wedding itself, knowing of her son's desire for an early date. His wishes for the following Thursday, the date of La Novia's twenty second birthday, appeal to the parents. But the mention of her age upsets La Madre for her older son would have been that age had he lived. It is part of her tragedy that she can never cleanse her thoughts of the agony of that loss.

The arrangements completed, El Padre orders the entrance of La Novia. The final member of the plot's hierarchy enters hesitantly, eyes downcast, her manner serious. La Madre contemplates her with interest and some suspicion, defining for her the strictness of marriage:

"One man, some children and a wall two yards thick for everything else."

La Novia responds, acknowledging the obligations she is to assume, but her voice sounds uncertain and lacks conviction. But it passes unnoticed as the gifts are presented to her. She receives them coldly and places them aside. Always self-conscious before her, El Novio tells her that he will see her on the following day at five o'clock. Again, her response shows resignation rather than the enthusiasm it should possess. El Novio and La Madre exit with El Padre, wishing to avoid travelling at night.

No sooner are they outside than La Criada rushes to the gifts, eager to satisfy the curiosity which the town's gossip had inflamed. But La Novia prevents her from looking, bitterly opposing even the servant's playful insistence. Her strong hands force La Criada to loosen her hold on the packages. Puzzled, the servant changes the conversation:

"Did you hear a horse last night? . . . At three. . . . There was a rider on him. . . . He stopped by your window. It was very odd. It was Leonardo."

No longer able to restrain herself, La Novia becomes furious at the insinuations of La Criada. But at the height of her denials, the sounds of a galloping horse near her window makes her admit that it was Leonardo. The first act ends on this promising development.

Thus the first act shifts within a dark and light motif: hard imagistic language, natural and colloquial, when

people converse together; and symbolic, aerated language·
when feeling passes into the anonymity of the scene and
is translated into poetry. But throughout, the atmosphere is stark, devoid of desire, and the human will is
left out. This is the proper emotional setting to a play
which turns more and more on a passionate release of the
instincts.[11]

La Criada, like Marcolfa in *El amor de don Perlimplin*
and all other female servants in Lorca's plays, is an important
agent in the plot complications. In this last scene of the act
she serves as the instrument through which the playwright
uncovers the strange relationship between La Novia and Leonardo, her past lover. But there are only hints so far. Later
as will be observed in the second act, the situation is amplified through La Novia's conversations with La Criada. She
becomes a "confident" who tries to remedy the illicit wan-
derings of La Novia by awakening in her a sense of responsibility as well as an acceptance of her good fortune. The
result of the intervention, however, as in *Don Perlimplin,* is
tragic and directed in the direction opposite to the intended
goal, serving only to inflame the rebellion already exhibited
in La Novia.

When the first scene of the second act continues the
action, it is several days later, the early morning hours of
the wedding day. The pre-dawn darkness reveals La Criada
and La Novia, still in their nightclothes, as they enter the
patio of the house. The wedding preparations begin as La
Criada combs her mistress' hair. La Novia is still serious
and pensive; the oppressive heat of day, already beginning,
makes her even more uncomfortable. She speaks porten-
tuously:

"My mother wasted away here. . . . Like we all waste
away. The walls are like fire."

The only enthusiasm over the wedding is expressed by La
Criada as she prepares La Novia:

---

11. Edwin Honig, *op. cit.,* p. 155.

> "Lucky you who will embrace a man, and kiss him, and feel his weight! . . . And the best part is when you awaken and feel him by your side and he caresses your shoulders with his breath."

But La Novia cannot bear the thought of a nuptial which she knows will cause only sorrow. La Criada continues, emphasizing the physical attractiveness of marriage:

> "What is a wedding? A wedding is this and nothing more. . . . It's a resplendent bed and a man and a woman."

Torn by as yet undisclosed tensions, La Novia fluctuates between despair and acceptance, between the secret desire for Leonardo and the duty towards El Novio. Finally, she becomes less sad as La Criada recites a wedding canticle. As La Novia enters into the house, a knock at the outside door calls La Criada.

Framed in the doorway as La Criada opens the gate, Leonardo stands alone. He has raced ahead of his wife on his abused horse to speak to La Novia. La Criada treats him coldly, surprised by his unhonorable visit. To divert his attention from the passion his eyes reveal, she asks after his child. This reminder hardly dents his boldness. His sole interest is La Novia and the wedding preparations. His questions are answered by La Novia herself who re-enters in the same sleeveless petticoat. Shocked at her appearance La Criada reprimands her, but the bride answers wantonly: "Does it matter? . . . Why did you come?" Drawing nearer to her while La Criada looks on fearfully, Leonardo begins to expose the torment that is in his heart because she had refused to marry him:

> "Since my marriage, I've thought night and day about whose fault it was, and every time I think a new fault appears to devour the other; but blame is always there!"

As accusingly, La Novia returns her own indictment of his previous acts which had forced her decision:

"A man with his horse knows many things and has the strength to crush a girl stuck away in a desert."

Then, in a righteous mood, she declares her intention of maintaining her pride and fulfilling her obligations to El Novio:

> "But I have pride. That's why I'm getting married. And I'll lock myself up with my husband whom I have to love above all else."

Leonardo moves even closer to her. La Criada's face shows her concern but her intervention in the conversation is unheeded. Leonardo commands all of La Novia's attention as he describes the torture of his feelings:

> "To be quiet and burn is the greatest punishment we can inflict on ourselves. What good was my pride and not looking at you and letting you lie awake nights and nights. All for nothing! All it did was consume me with fire! You think that time heals and walls hide things, and it isn't true, it isn't true. When things are rooted so deeply, no one can tear them out!"

It is in these words that the crux of the situation is contained, that the existence of the plot is justified. La Novia trembles, for these are the very things she fears in him—the suppressed desires which torture and disrupt. But these are also her torment. Each's pride no longer points out the other as guilty for the negation. Time has worn such subjectiveness thin and what remains is the unresolved and unsatisfied passion which Leonardo and La Novia feel burning within them. Fate has worked mightily against the lovers, depriving their souls even of the comfort of resignation. Now they stand close to each other, La Novia almost ready to succumb to that spell which surrounds them:

> "Don't come closer! . . . I can't listen to you. I can't listen to your voice. It's as if I had drunk a bottle of anise and fallen asleep on a quilt of roses. And it drags me, and I know I'm drowning, but I follow. . . . And I'm crazy and I know my breasts are rotting with desire, and

I am tranquil now to hear him, to see him move his arms."

Only the voices of the approaching guests, singing nearby, give La Novia a chance to regain her senses. She flees into the security of her room to dress for the wedding. Leonardo, too, exits, promising La Criada not to speak to La Novia again.

The night is slowly replaced by the light of early morning as the guests enter into the patio. All are singing, having come to awaken the bride in the traditional manner. The festive strains clear the air of the heaviness imposed by the recent episode. Even La Criada joins the revelers and soon the patio is filled with the innocent dancing of relatives and guests.

In response to the song, La Novia enters in a splendid black dress with a train of rich lace. Her hair is adorned with a wreath of fragrant orange blossoms. Upon her entrance all rush to her with their congratulations. When El Novio appears, he is escorted to her side as La Madre and El Padre look upon the scene with joy. But La Madre's smile subsides when Leonardo and his wife enter. La Novia, too, is concerned about Leonardo's presence and urges El Novio to take her to the church quickly:

"I want to be your wife now and be alone with you and hear no voice but yours. . . . and see nothing but your eyes. And I want you to embrace me so strongly that even if my mother, who is dead, called me I couldn't break away from you."

It is a strange and passionate confession of love inspired by the fear of Leonardo's presence. His eyes are focused on her. Everyone begins to leave for the church and La Criada cries softly. But Leonardo hesitates, remaining in the courtyard with his wife. La Criada follows, her last words echoing in the nearly empty patio:

"Dark air is the lace
of her mantilla."

Alone, Leonardo and La Mujer face each other. She senses their distance and, as if driving together in the carriage could be a remedy, she convinces Leonardo to drive her to the church. He escorts her resentfully as her words fall on his deaf ears:

> "I don't know what's happening. But I think and I don't want to think. I do know one thing. I'm already cast off. But I have a son. And another on the way."

As they exit, the now distant voices repeat the wedding refrain.

Act two, scene two, returns the action to the home of the bride. The exterior of the house is being prepared for the celebration; La Criada excitedly sets the table with fine dishes and glassware, singing in the meantime. Yet, the spicy quality of her song cannot dispel the feeling of trouble inspired by Leonardo's restlessness in the previous scene. This feeling is enhanced when, upon the return of La Madre and El Padre, La Criada announces that Leonardo and his wife were the first to return from the church:

> "They drove like demons. His wife arrived frightened to death. They made the trip as if they had come on horseback."

La Madre is not surprised, adding vitriolically after La Criada's account:

> "What blood could he have? That of the whole family,
> It comes from his great grandfather, who began killing,
> and continues in the whole evil breed, knife-wielding
> men and people of false smiles."

And again the deep hatred of the Felix name shows itself, this time gaining the allegiance of La Criada who realizes the danger of Leonardo's presence in the house. But El Padre succeeds in directing La Madre's thoughts to brighter things —a future of grandchildren:

> "I want them to have many. This land needs arms that

are not paid. . . . Many sons are needed. . . . I only wish it were a matter of a day, that they could have two or three men right away. . . . Now you must wait. My daughter is broad and your son is strong."

La Madre, however, remembers the fate of sons and wishes also for girls; they never leave the house and never cause a mother the sorrow of seeing their blood spilled on the earth.

The wedding guests begin to enter, interrupting the seriousness of their words with their laughter and good spirits. El Novio and La Novia, now husband and wife, walk together commenting on the many guests and relatives at the ceremony. Leonardo, too, has entered the patio. He sits apart, sullenly, while his wife watches intently. Whenever Leonardo is present, La Novia's face reflects her concern. It is so now as her reserved attitude contrasts with the gayety of the others. La Madre notices this continuing moroseness, but she is distracted by El Padre who begins to observe the dancing. With Leonardo in the background, La Novia and El Novio are by themselves. As they speak, however, Leonardo is seen leaving. La Novia retires with her friends and El Novio speaks first with La Mujer who is looking for Leonardo and then with La Criada, until he is also taken away by friends.

When La Novia returns, she is even more nervous. Her condition is enhanced by Leonardo's silent but ominous appearance as he again crosses. Her friends run off and for a moment La Novia is alone. El Novio gamefully approaches his bride without being seen and embraces her. But she, her thoughts on Leonardo, pushes him away forcefully not realizing it is El Novio. El Novio accepts her nervousness without question, accepting likewise her excuse that people might be watching them. She convinces him that it is best for her to rest. Before she retires, La Mujer re-appears:

"Did my husband come by here? . . . It's just that I can't find him, and his horse isn't in the stable either."

In her martyr role, La Mujer resembles Ferenc Molnar's

heroine, Julie, in *Liliom*. Like her she senses the evil intentions of her husband and tries desperately to prevent what she knows will have a grave consequence. But like Julie, La Mujer is unable to cope adequately with the secret forces working within her man. The constant worrying, the loss of love, the futile efforts at reform characterize both situations. The outcome, also, will be similar.

The pace of the scene begins to quicken with La Mujer's exit. Its intensity has been building constantly since the exchange of glances between Leonardo and La Novia earlier. Now La Novia retires to her room, promising to be fresh for her husband by evening. As she enters, La Madre approaches her son to give him the advice his father could have delivered had he lived:

> "Be loving to your wife, and if you find her selfish or cross give her a caress that will hurt a little, a strong embrace, a bite and then a tender kiss. Not so she'll become angry, but so she'll know that you're the man, the master, the one who gives orders."

Throughout their dialogue, La Criada is seen rushing in and out in a state of agitation as if searching for someone. El Padre enters and inquires as to his daughter's whereabouts. After much searching by El Novio, El Padre and La Criada there are no results. La Criada already has the worst presentiments though she does not express them. The mystery is suddenly uncovered as La Mujer, Leonardo's wife, rushes into the patio, screaming:

> "They've run off! They've run off! She and Leonardo. On the horse. They rode off like lightning, embracing each other."

The irony is that it had to be Leonardo's wife who discovered the flight of the tormented lovers. Her news shocks El Padre, he stands unbelieving:

> "It's not true! Not my daughter, no! . . . It couldn't be her. . . . Maybe she threw herself in the pool."

In his eyes it would have been better, more desirable, if she had drowned herself in the reservoir. But La Madre, whose instincts had warned her of danger from the beginning, finds no excuse for her action. With hatred in her voice, she takes immediate charge and orders her son and his kinsmen to follow Leonardo and La Novia. The patio is now filled with men anxious to pursue the lovers. La Madre again dictates:

> "There are two groups here. My family and yours. Let's all set out. Shake the dust from our shoes. Let us help my son. For he has clan, his cousins from the sea and all who come from inland. Away from here! Take all the roads. The hour of bloodshed is here again. Two groups. You with yours, and I with mine. After them! After them!"

The curtain descends rapidly on the angry scene as La Madre and El Padre take their particular groups in search of the two whose passion broke all rules of Honor and Tradition. The second act ends.

> Two struggles, two diverse resistances, but equally persuasive. Two equities and two truths which unmercifully torture the body and the conscience of the same being. On the one hand, the healthy promise of an honest life, without shadows, in a peaceful home. Home. Family. Fields. A husband and a wealth of children. But, on the other hand, a scaring love, an exalting passion. Two truths and two equities, one logical and prudent; the other brutal and blind; but between them, the second is the stronger. The one which almost always wins.[12]

With the struggle of choice resolved in favor of passion, the final act concerns itself with two other aspects of the conflict—the spiritual and the physical. The latter gives rise to the climactic point in the drama, but it is the other which creates and sustains suspense and mystery. This interest is maintained even after the tragedy has reached its physical level of impact. Within this spiritual conflict rage two fur-

---

12. Carlos Morla Lynch, *op. cit.,* p. 286.

ther controversies—that of Leonardo and La Novia in their forest retreat, and that of La Novia and La Madre in the last scene. In both, Lorca makes effective use of poetry, conveying not only the powers expended but also the many-faceted reasonings that forge the situations in the minds of the characters concerned. Throughout this last act there is an aura of unreality which touches the physical truth of the play so effectively that the result is a middle ground where Fate is in full control.

The first scene of the third act is set in a forest of large trees whose trunks are covered with the damp moss of swamps. The lush and extensive vegetation seems impenetrable, magnificently foiled by the aridity of previous settings. There are no human regulations here which prevent fulfillment. Nature is rampant and productive. The forest itself becomes a symbol of contrast—unspoiled Nature as opposed to the man-hindered world which the lovers fled.

The forest is very dark as the moon has yet to make its appearance. The eeriness of the setting is increased by two distant violins and the crackling of the underbrush. Three figures are discernible in a small clearing. These are the Woodcutters, Leñadores, chorus types who comment on the flight of Leonardo and La Novia much in the manner of their ancient counterparts in Greek tragedy.

"They look for them everywhere. . . . They seem to be closing in from all the roads at once. . . . They should leave them alone. . . . One must follow impulse; they did right in running off. . . . Her body for him and his body for her. . . . There are knives and guns for ten leagues around."

In the Woodcutters, the lovers find unknown sympathizers. But their understanding of the demands of passion cannot help the persecuted. The revenge of the world is too strong. The forest is surrounded by hunters tracking a human prey. As the Woodcutters speak, the light of the moon becomes evident. It increases steadily and, when the Woodcutters exit, becomes full. The setting takes on a resplendent blue glow which seems to emanate from the figure of a young woodcutter with a white face. This is the personification of La Luna, the moon. La Luna introduces itself with three beautiful images:

> "Round swan on the river,
> eye of the cathedrals,
> deceitful dawn on the leaves,
> I am."

But the beauty of the imagery is quickly enveloped by the sinister lines which follow, detailing the vain attempt of the lovers to hide from the knife of moonlight which cuts the night. Then, as if the thought of the warmth of blood had stirred it, La Luna intones desperately:

> "Let me enter! Frozen,
> I come by walls and windows!
> Open roofs and breasts
> where I may warm myself!"

The Moon retires into the forest and its light deserts the setting; it repossesses its ominous darkness. Thus Lorca has introduced into the seemingly realistic drama a personage from a realm beyond the real. The Moon has lent realization to that feeling of the supranatural which has been hinted at during the course of the action. But the incarnation of the Moon does not become obstructive or problematical because Lorca prepared the mind of the spectator for this scene through the subtle suggestions of dialogue and plot. This has been primarily achieved through the identification of Man with Nature. The alliance suggests that Man is not in complete control of his acts, that a force beyond him dictates his mode of behavior. That force is Fate and Nature is its messenger. Thus, when La Luna is introduced there is no antagonism to its appearance in a drama populated with real people because of the previously established liaison between Man and Nature.

Another figure from that other "reality" which Lorca has
created, Death, appears in the guise of La Mendiga, an old
beggar-woman. She, too, is preceded by an air of mystery,
but, where La Luna was ushered in by its radiance, La
Mendiga is announced only by a silent and dark figure, La
Anciana. This old woman in green rags and bare feet crosses
the setting and departs. She is, as Lorca points out, excluded
from the cast of characters.

La Mendiga, Death, has seen the Moon disappear behind
the trees and curses its poor timing. The hunted lovers are
approaching and there is little light for the pursuers to de-
tect and kill them.

> "The moon is waning, and they approach.
> They shall not pass. The river murmur
> and the murmuring trees shall deaden
> the shameless flight of their screams.
> It must be here and soon. I tire."

In answer to La Mendiga's impatient shouts, La Luna returns and again floods the clearing with its light. La Mendiga instructs:

> "Shine on the vest and spread apart buttons,
> as knives, afterwards, know well their path."

As all else, La Luna must bend to the majesty of Death. Before it departs to carry out her instructions, it requests:

> "But let death come slowly upon them. So blood,
> in its delicate ebbing, will course through my hands."

As La Mendiga hears the adjacent underbrush moving,
she covers herself with the cape and seems to blend into the
forest. El Novio and another young man enter, still searching for Leonardo and La Novia. After they chose different
paths, El Novio sees La Mendiga, not knowing she has heard
his vengeful words:

> "Do you see this arm? Well, it isn't my arm. It's the
> arm of my brother and my father and of all the dead in
> my family. And it is so powerful that it can pull out
> this tree by its roots if it wished."

Through this chance meeting, or so it would seem to El Novio, he finds a guide who will lead him to Leonardo. El Novio eagerly follows La Mendiga unaware of the irony in the act. Death is already with him.

The Woodcutters re-enter briefly as the two violins "which express the forest" resume. Upon their exit, two other figures cautiously approach the clearing. Leonardo and La Novia's speech becomes violently sensual as passion struggles with reason for supremacy:

> Novia: "With teeth, with hands, as you can,
>   remove from my chaste neck
>   the metal of this chain,
>   leaving me forsaken
>   back in my earthen house."
> Leonardo: "We've taken the step; be quiet!
>   because they're close to us now
>   and I will take you with me."

But the hold of passion is too great for La Novia to think of Honor. The scene grows more and more significantly erotic as Leonardo's attraction for her increases. The strange mixture of hatred and love is expressed in La Novia's words to Leonardo:

> "I love you! I love you! But leave me!
> If I were able to kill you
> I would wrap you up in a shroud
> with the borders done in violets.
> Oh, what a moan, what a fire
> Is sweeping through my head!"

Leonardo, too, is in agony—the thoughts of his years of self-denial now made dishonorable by a passion which subdued his reason—and feels unsure and afraid of the forces which have driven him to this act:

> "What splinters of glass pierce my tongue!
> Because I tried to forget
> and placed a wall of stone
> between your house and mine.
> It is so. Don't you remember?

> And beholding you from afar
> I threw the sand in my eyes.
> But I rode upon my horse
> and the horse went to your gate.
> Like silver pins
> my blood turned black,
> and the dream began to prick
> my flesh with poisoned weeds.
> And the blame lies not with me,
> for the blame belongs to the earth
> and to that scent which exudes
> from your breasts and from your hair."

The blame lies with the earth; the lovers embrace, seeking that same earth to support their weight. The scene acquires a heightened sensual tone as words and physical passion blend:

> "Moon nails are forging
> my waist and your hips."

But their love is not consummated though the point of resistance has been passed. The sounds of their pursuers bring them back to the principal instinct—survival. They flee together in a final affirmation of their love:

Leonardo: "If they separate us, it shall be because I am dead."
Novia:　　"And I also dead."

The Moon returns with its bluish light of Death's command. The same two violins play in the otherwise absolute silence. Suddenly piercing screams destroy the false calm. Death, in the person of La Mendiga, enters on the second cry and facing the forest centers itself on the setting. La Mendiga's cape is spread on its outstretched arms—the triumphant gesture of the condor poised for flight after the conquest of its prey. The violins are silenced. The Moon remains constant as the curtain falls on a deadly silence.

One of the most important, certainly the most impressive, of the scenes in this turbulent drama, its power is concentrated in a poetry which is movingly human, yet, cynically mystical. Lorca depicts the basic human passions of love and hatred with the conviction that nothing is all one color. The reason he cites for this truth is the existence of secret forces—Nature as the agent of Fate—which handle man's destiny. Love, therefore, is not the idealistic state which creates felicity; hatred is not a simple matter of satisfying an appetite. These passions have many guises, all complex, all predictably different. If La Mujer loves Leonardo in the context of their married life centering on their child, La Madre loves her son, El Novio, as the last of their line; if El Padre cannot see any wrong in his daughter, La Novia, La Criada can love her for an entirely different reason—to prevent the fruition of the desires she discerns behind La Novia's secretive facade. If El Novio loves the bride blindly, Leonardo loves her in all the awareness of passion. La Novia, of course, possesses the most complex of loves for it has two attractions at opposite poles. Though she longs for the peace and contentment of life with El Novio, she runs away with Leonardo because he alone can fulfill her as a woman. The dual aspect of La Novia's attraction to Leonardo is clearly explored in this forest scene.

Hatred, too, reaches an apex in the forest sequence as El Novio and Leonardo meet in the fated clash of opposing forces. They fight, each in his private terror, unable to do anything but continue the fierce struggle of passions. As they must, they kill each other. The dual deaths bring into quick focus all the forces of vengeance which had made themselves known earlier. La Madre's much discussed hatred of the Felix clan achieves recognition in the finality of clashing knives. La Criada's fear of Leonardo's actions towards La Novia, itself a form of hatred, is vindicated in the death of the two men. A third type of hatred, however, manifests itself in the physical struggle of the two rivals. Neither had expressed any explicit animosity towards the other; the sole basis for such reference is an implicit state created by La Madre. But the passivity of the two men towards each other is most evident prior to the forest scene. Only during it does El Novio show hatred. Still, as if driven to an unsought climax, the two men fought and died in the name of Honor.

The forces which dominate the actions of the characters, giving rise to the conflict of passions and Honor, are within the bondage of Fate. They are just beyond man's reach. Man feels the foreign impulses, fights them hopelessly and, in the end, is driven into a destiny which he has not consciously sought. Cynically, Fate handles the strings of puppet-men. Hence, Death is the beneficiary. Honor is the agency of Fate; it is in the name of Honor that man seeks to satisfy himself in this drama. But Honor can only be satisfied through the purification of Death for Fate allows no other cleansing process.

> The Spaniard, as Madariaga has said, is a man of honor, violence and death...and they are the things Lorca sees with such terrible lucidity ... Honor, for the Spaniard, is related to the cult of the virgin, to chastity, purity. In Lorca's poetry the theme of honor deals with unconsummated love or marriage, with the conflict between primitive innocence and "civilized" society. But the result of the conflict between innocence and "civilization" is death. ... Death is omnipresent in its horror, its anonymity, its finality.[13]

The last scene of the tragedy is set in a large and bare room wherein thick white walls are intermittently broken by impressive arches. The stairs which dominate each end of the room are also white. The floor glows magnificently in the reflection of the surrounding starkness. There are no signs of shadows and the perspective of the room remains undefined.

Two young women, dressed in dark blue, sit in the vast room unwinding a spool of red wool. A small child, La Niña, questions them about the wedding but as they haven't attended they continue to entertain themselves with the red

---

13. Warren Carrier, "Meaning in the Poetry of Lorca," *Accent*, vol. 10 (Spring, 1950), p. 159.

spool. The speech in these early moments is in poetry, again only subtly indicative of the reality of the deaths:

"Lover without words.
Bridegroom bright red.
On the muted shore
both lay quite dead."

After La Niña departs, La Mujer and La Suegra enter. The older woman, La Mujer's mother, comforts her in a matter-of-fact tone which divorces sentimentality from her words:

"You, to your house,
brave and alone in your house.
To grow old and to cry.
But keeping the door closed.

....

Cover your face with a veil.
Your children are yours,
only yours. Over the bed
place an ashen cross
where his pillow had been."

They exit promptly and La Niña enters anew, followed by La Mendiga. Her presence is menacing to the young women and they back away from her begging hands. To attract them, La Mendiga tells the girls of the death of Leonardo and El Novio:

"I saw them; soon they'll be here; two torrents
finally still among the great stones,
two men under horse's hoofs.
Dead in the splendor of night."

La Mendiga continues, her leering smile causing the protests of her listeners; there is pleasure in her tone:

"Their eyes were depetalled flowers, their teeth
two handfuls of calcified snow.
Both of them fell and the bride is returning
Her skirt and hair dyed with their blood."

She exists. The girls, relieved at her departure, repeat the last words playfully and they, too, pass from the scene.

The final moments of the play re-introduce La Madre. She is consoled by a neighbor. But La Madre does not cry; she speaks dryly to her sobbing companion:

> "Your tears are only from the eyes, but mine will come when I'm alone, from the soles of my feet, from my roots, and will be more ardent than blood."

Now there is nothing left to torment her, nothing that can make her face another tomorrow with the fear of death. Her last son is gone. Yet sorrow is not all black. In the losing of El Novio, La Madre has gained a spiritual peace and though that hardly seems like a worthy compensation it serves to distill what might otherwise be despair. All that remains is the physical sorrow.

La Novia, meanwhile, has entered in her mourning cloths. She approaches La Madre. La Vecina tries to stop her before La Madre sees her, but too late. La Madre crosses to her, all the hatred and fury showing in her tearless eyes. Unable to restrain herself, La Madre beats La Novia until La Vecina stops her. Lying on the ground, La Novia speaks penitently:

> "Let her; I came to be killed by her and to be taken with them. But not with the hands; with wire hooks, with a sickle, and with strength, until it breaks on my bones. Let her! I want her to know that I'm pure, that I may be crazy but that I can be buried without any man having seen himself in the whiteness of my breasts."

Again Honor is paramount for paradoxically her statements become pledges that her purity has not been blemished. Thus, in her mind, El Novio was never deceived. His honor, therefore, was not sullied except by the lesser act of her escape. It is as if with this disclosure she made expiation. And, in order to prove the truth of her claims, La Novia proposes:

> "Pure, pure as a new-born girl. And strong enough to show it. Light the fire. We'll place our hands in it; you for your son; I for my body. You'll pull yours out before I do mine."

It is a strange code which influences her words, or the necessity for them, at a moment when nothing matters except that two men are dead because of her. And yet, though nothing can replace them, though words cannot mitigate her guilt, La Novia is proud that in preserving her body from Leonardo's passion she observed the laws of Honor.

La Madre is not concerned with La Novia's honor nor desirous of her death. Nothing, now, can warm her, not even revenge. There is only the void of a solitary existence before her. But, where her grief is kept to herself, two other women —La Mujer and La Novia—sit apart in anguished silence suffering in their private hells. The triple lament of these women, though interlaced, is personal to each as they contemplate their lonely lives—three women without men. They speak as a chorus, brought together in a final irony.

The tragedy is that of La Madre. It was she who foresaw, as it were, the death of her only son; it was she who was instrumental in pleading his cause to El Padre in spite of the warnings that La Novia had been interested in Leonardo; finally, it was she who pushed her son into his death-duel with Leonardo to satisfy her sense of honor. Yet, somewhere above her, as with all the characters, there is the hand of Fate, implacable and selfish, so that she becomes a pawn in its grasp. La Madre, alone, is capable of recognizing the reason for the death of the two men. And she alone suffers deeply, from her innermost feelings, knowing with a finality that tears the heart that what she has really lost is Hope. Her state has become a quiet despair.

Certainly Lorca's most dramatic play, *Bodas de sangre* represents the most advanced cohesion between poetry and drama in all his theatre. It satisfies as a theatre experience, being powerful and unforgettable, and as a literary tour-de-force. It is, as Campbell has pointed out:

> . . . one of those plays that will satisfy those who think of Spain in terms of Bizet's *Carmen*.[14]

---

14. Roy Campbell, *op. cit.*, p. 89.

IX. YERMA

Yerma was premiered by Margarita Xirgu and her company on December of 1934 at the "Teatro Español" in Madrid. The decor was conceived by the painter Burmann. The play was directed by Cipriano Rivas Cherif.

YERMA follows immediately upon *Bodas de sangre*, being the second tragedy in the proposed trilogy. As such it bears an interesting relationship, particularly in that it continues the exploration of Spanish tradition. This time Lorca deals with the moral code which binds woman to the strict observance of her matrimonial vows, forcing her in this case to sacrifice her greatest need. Yerma, the heroine, is encased in a sarcophagus of moral inhibitions which frustrate her maternal instinct. As in *Bodas de sangre*, *Yerma's* plot is dependent on outside forces—here, the moral code interpreted tightly—which surround the characters and prevent the free exercise of their powers. It is a tragedy of frustrations.

As in all of Lorca's drama, irony plays an important part in the development of plot. In *Bodas de sangre* it appears frequently in the naive approach of the characters to their situation; in *Yerma*, the irony lies in that even the strict adherence to the moral code leads to death. It will be recalled that in *Bodas de sangre* the opposite course also leads to death. The result is equal in both cases, whether the code is wantonly broken or blindly preserved.

The principal theme in *Yerma* is that of sterility. The name Yerma itself is a fabrication of the playwright, borrowing from the masculine adjective, "yermo," which means barren, unfertile, unfulfilled. Lorca applies this term to his heroine, depicting her as a barren woman haunted by the inevitable loss of hope.

"*Yerma* will be the tragedy of the sterile woman. The theme, as you know, is classical. But I want to give it a

217

new development and intent. A tragedy with four principal characters and a chorus, as all tragedies should have."[1]

This sterility, however, is Yerma's only insofar as she is not made fertile. It is not the usual circumstance of a woman unable to bear children, but rather the situation of a woman deprived of a child through the selfishness of her husband, Juan. The blame for her privation is his.

This theme reaches its greatest manifestation in *Yerma*. Previously, it had been touched upon in much of Lorca's poetry and many of his plays. Although never a major theme in these works, the subject was ably treated as early as 1918 when it was conceived in *Elegia*:

> "In your white hands
> you bear the yarn of your illusions,
> forever dead, and in your soul
> the hungered passion of fiery kisses
> and your love of motherhood which dreams distant
> visions of cradles in quiet places,
> weaving with your lips the blue of lullaby."[2]

Other brief mentions of it occur in *Mariana Pineda*, where Fernando realizes that in losing Mariana he has lost the hope of children; in *La Zapatera Prodigiosa*, where La Zapatera speaks grandly of the children she will have; in *Asi que pasen cinco años*, where El Maniqui symbolizes sexual frustration; and also in *Bodas de sangre* where the theme embraces La Madre in her despair of shorn motherhood. The later dramas, *Doña Rosita la soltera* and *La casa de Bernarda Alba*, have such elements within their plot structures. But nowhere is it so fully exposed as in *Yerma* where the many aspects are studied in the framework of the vivid drama of a tortured woman.

The application of the theme in *Yerma* places two undeniable forces in conflict—the natural need of motherhood

1. Juan Chabas, "F.G.L. y la tragedia," *op. cit.*
2. *Obras Completas, op. cit.*, p. 129.

as opposed to a rigid morality which prevents satisfaction. This *agon* of abstracts occurs within Yerma, the lone participant in this intimate tragedy. The battlegrounds are the deepest caverns of her soul, mind and heart.

> While *Bodas de sangre* follows in the tradition of Lope de Vega, who insisted on the spectacular and collective conception of tragic action, *Yerma* follows in the tradition of Calderon de la Barca, who insisted on the individual conception of tragedy, formulated by a religious code setting certain moral bounds to action.[3]

Yet, though the tragedy is centered on Yerma, another person has an important role in the development and complication of the plot. Juan, Yerma's husband, is the cause of her pitiable condition. Through a selfish contradiction of his marital obligations, he denies Yerma the child of her innermost desire. It is because of this denial that the tragedy exists. And although the tragedy is Yerma's alone, the interest in Juan is maintained by following his actions and inactions, if somewhat more restrictedly than Yerma's. The situation develops, then, along two principal routes: the inward action as reflected in Yerma's self-repression, and the outward manifestations of Juan's selfishness. Each is important in the denouement of the plot, one, in turn, influencing the other. And the magnified image of these twisted impressions always reveals itself in Yerma. That is to say, Yerma is the only character in the play who changes as a result of these occurrences. Juan is untouched by her plight or her recriminations; but with each thrust against her hopes, Juan succeeds in affecting Yerma. He may be unaware of the effect of his selfish stance but that does not alter Yerma's tortured state which becomes progressively more unbearable.

Added to the physical conflict between Yerma and Juan in her search for satisfaction of the maternal instinct is an even greater struggle. This is the spiritual conflict in which

---

3. Edwin Honig, *op. cit.,* p. 163.

human need is pitted against its strongest adversary—morality. Being denied satisfaction by her husband, Yerma is faced with the prospect of existing without purpose. The choice is clear—life with Juan without fulfillment of her maternal needs or unsanctioned gratification outside of marriage. But the choice is not simple within the context of Spanish life. There exists one of the "hidden forces" which Lorca always discerns and which hinders, rather, prohibits, the natural outcome. Where in *Bodas de sangre* Fate was the instigator, through its henchmen—Honor, Passion and Death —Yerma has inherited all three but with the difference that it is Morality which governs their actions. Honor, Passion and Death are present, but not in the less defined manner of *Bodas de sangre*. In *Yerma* they exist under the regulation of an unflinching morality, their irrevocability sustained by a tradition of moral judgments whose origins are lost in antiquity. Supervised by this code, Yerma's actions are frustrated as are her desires.

Yerma is written principally in prose. Lorca reserves the use of poetry for those occasions which require a more vivid and concentrated lyricism than can be demanded of prose. However, the playwright underlines this drama with what must seem a curious subtitle: "Poema tragico en tres actos y seis cuadros." But he does so rightly because *Yerma* was conceived as a tragic poem. The greater part of the dialogue may be in the shape of prose, but its content, nuance and tonality is that of poetry. In short, it is poetic prose. Likewise, the subject matter and its concentrated treatment are considered in the light of poetry and music, though these elements may be less apparent than in other plays. As it stands, *Yerma* is a moving representation of the torture superimposed on human life, poignantly illustrated through masterful language and plot.

Act one, scene one, discloses Yerma asleep on a chair, her sewing basket on the floor. The half-light of the setting, the mental quiet and the physical silence usher in a dream se-

quence during which a shepherd crosses the stage leading
a small child dressed in white. As they cross, their eyes are
fixed on Yerma. Upon their exit, as a clock strikes, the light
becomes the extravagantly bright glow of a spring morning.
Yerma awakens to the false glory of another day while a
lullaby's last verse is heard in the background. The song is
very similar to that in *Bodas de sangre*, but there the child
to which it was sung was real. The need for a lullaby here
is mystical and the notes introduce the first touch of irony.
Thus, the theme of maternity is premiered.

Juan enters, intent on reaching the fields where he can
commence his day's labor, but Yerma detains him in an attempt to fathom his strange manner:

> "You were different when we got married. Now your
> face is white, as if the sun never shone on it. . . . We've
> been married twenty-four months and you only become
> sadder, thinner, as if you were growing backwards."[4]

But Juan seems indifferent to her worry over his attitude.
His work is hard and tiring, as she says, but it is worthwhile
to him:

> "I work hard. Every year I'll grow older. . . . Work is
> going well, we haven't any children to waste money."

At the mention of the children they do not have, Yerma becomes agitated. Her tragedy is slowly developing through
her attitudes. Juan, knowing her feelings, tries to leave. But
Yerma holds him in an impassioned embrace, declaring her
need for a child through the symbol of the hedge mustard
whose yellow flowers decry the plant's uselessness:

> ". . . people say that they're not good for anything. . . .
> but I see their yellow flowers sway in the breeze."

Uncomfortable, Juan departs, ironically asking if she needs
anything from the town's shops. But he shuts out the real

---

4. All textual quotations, unless otherwise specified, are from *Obras
Completas, op. cit.,* pp. 1183-1260.

demand which Yerma makes. Advising her not to leave the house, Juan exits.

Yerma returns to her sewing. In a significant pause before she sits, however, she passes her hand over her womb and sighs; then, as she sews, a song escapes her—a symbol of her as-yet-unconquered hope:

> "Where do you come from, my love, my child?
> ....
> I shall say, my child, that yes,
> for you I'll be severed and torn.
> How painful this waist can be
> where your first cradle will be!
> When will you come, my child?"

The song is an imagined dialogue with the child for which she longs. It is the first definite expression of her desire, the others having been indirect, as the source of her tragic attitude is glimpsed.

Maria, a neighbor who has recently married, comes into the room, almost immediately confiding in her friend that she is pregnant. The wonder of her revelation is apparent on Yerma's face as she compares the lengths of their respective married lives. Maria, married only five months, already possesses what Yerma has wanted for two years. She is genuinely happy for her friend but she cannot hide the sadness which the news has caused. Her own sterility pursues her constantly. Even her advice to Maria gives further notice of her anxiety:

> "Don't walk much and when you breathe do it as softly as if you had a rose between your teeth. . . . And that is when you love him most, when you can say: my child!"

It is an instinctive knowledge which Yerma imparts to Maria, the true feelings of a mother projected into a sterile being. And again, as all through the play, irony is present. It is Maria, who knows nothing of motherhood and seems disturbed by her pregnancy, that carries the child in her womb. Yerma tries to overcome the hopelessness of her own thoughts by recalling other women who waited many years before bearing a child. In spite of Maria's added encouragement, the moment is brief. She is again the bitter woman:

"Every woman has enough blood for four or five children, and when she doesn't bear them it turns to poison, as will happen to me."

Yerma's pathetic situation moves Maria into a state of awareness of, if not full appreciation for, the child which will soon be here. Before she starts out, Maria asks Yerma to make some garments for the child with the material she brought. Yerma consents readily, glad to be at least that close to the child she cannot have. Her hands hold the rich cloth lovingly.

As Maria exits, another figure crosses nearby. It is a familiar form in that its dress and manner, those of a shepherd, recall the apparition at the beginning of the scene. Yerma calls to him: ". . . Victor." In his reality, Victor is a strong type, healthy, and with a grave manner that shows his depth of character. To all appearances, he is the opposite of Yerma's husband, Juan. His visit is brief, but he does manage to comment on the need for a child in their house:

"This house needs a child. . . . Well, then. Tell your husband to think less about his work. He wants to save money and he will; but to whom will he leave it when he dies?"

The first scene closes with Yerma's song after Victor has left. She moves dreamily to the place where Victor has stood. Still in her trance-like attitude, Yerma breathes deeply of the air which had enveloped Victor. The movements become a fertility rite in which she seeks outside elements to make her fecund. As she returns to her sewing, eyes fixed on one point in an attempt to will into existence that which physical forces had failed to create, the curtain closes.

The several aspects which will give depth and insinuation to the theme of frustration have not as yet been introduced.

The first scene concerns itself mainly with the disclosure of the fundamental problem in the play, and, therefore, it is well that the complications and variations on the topic are reserved. But the scene does suggest two possible intrigues in the later plot: the role of Juan in Yerma's aridity, and the role of Victor in the outcome. Having introduced these characters with a certain vagueness, Lorca creates a stimulus to the mind; the possibilities are numerous as to what course each character will follow, how they will influence one another, and in what manner they will be involved in Yerma's plight. The elements for Yerma's choice are already delineated in Juan and Victor.

To this is added the second scene in which Yerma, some months later (it is now three years since her marriage), on her way to bring her husband his afternoon meal, meets an old woman. La Vieja, too, has brought food to her husband, though she resents not having a daughter to do it. With the untilled fields around them, the two women talk openly of themselves. La Vieja recalls her gay life, her two marriages which resulted in fourteen sons, her desire to live a long time. Yerma is more reserved in her comments at first. But inspired by the confidence aroused by the old woman, she asks:

> "I've wanted to talk with an old woman for a long time. Because I want to find out. . . . Why am I barren? . . . You can tell me what I must do, and I'll do whatever it is, even if you tell me to pierce the most sensitive part of my eyes with needles."

La Vieja hesitates in answering. She knows nothing, she says, having allowed Nature to awaken her instincts in the act of love:

> "I have lain face up and begun to sing. Children come like the rain."

Yerma detains her longer. Seeing the desperation in her face, La Vieja proceeds to interrogate her, more to satisfy Yerma than her own curiosity:

"Listen. Do you like your husband? . . . Well, do you love him? Do you want to be with him? . . . Don't you tremble when he comes near? Don't you feel something like a sleep when his lips come close? Tell me."

La Vieja senses that Yerma does not love her husband. Her answers confirm the doubt and bring out the true repository of her passions, Victor. He was the only man who ever aroused her emotionally and physically, but that had been before her marriage. In her confession there exists a parallel to the life of La Novia in *Bodas de sangre*, especially as to the dissatisfaction she exhibits towards her husband. This congruity of attitudes is traceable in most of Lorca's drama; similar circumstances are evident in La Zapatera, in Belisa, in La Novia in *Asi que pasen cinco años*, and even in the heroines of the puppet plays. They exhibit discontent with their married states or their approaching weddings and seek to satisfy their particular needs either through daydreams, as do La Zapatera and Yerma, or through sexual fulfillment outside marriage, as do Belisa and La Novia in *Bodas de sangre*. Similarly, Victor is associated with Leonardo and with El Jugador de Rugby insofar as he is the great sexual force forbidden to Yerma, just as Leonardo and El Jugador are that in their respective plays. Yet, Juan's attitude towards Yerma is very close to Leonardo's towards La Mujer; in his state as husband, Juan resembles El Novio. But to repeat what had already been stated elsewhere was not Lorca's intention and the similarities are valid primarily as integrating elements. Each play, and the characters within it, stand singularly within the whole of Lorca's theatrical union.

Yerma, continuing, had gone to her arranged marriage without love but with happiness in the thought of the children she would bear. She could be expected to love a man of her choosing but not one selected by her father. Yet, she had not cried or been afraid on the wedding night and gave herself gladly because of the child she desired so much:

". . . and I keep on giving myself to see if it comes,

never just for pleasure. . . . Is it necessary to seek in a
man only the man? . . . Should I just think of him or on
what could come gloriously from my breast?"

She implores La Vieja to guide her. La Vieja, however, pitying the miserable woman before her, decides not to meddle.
Yerma reproaches her and the code which dictates that such
things must not be discussed:

"Girls who are raised in the country, like I was, have
all the doors closed to them. Everything turns into half
words, gestures, because they say these things should
not be known. And you, too; you also keep quiet and
leave with the manner of a doctor, knowing everything,
but hiding it from one who is dying of thirst."

La Vieja tries only to awaken in Yerma a new outlook towards her marriage, one of dependence upon her husband
rather than on her own desires. As the old woman departs,
Yerma is in a worse state of agitation than previously. The
most significant part of the scene, however, is in the implication of Yerma in her tragedy. No longer is it all Juan's fault
as it had appeared earlier. Yerma, too, is to blame for her
aridity, having accepted Juan as less than a husband and
having given herself only to quench her own selfishness—the
desire for a child. Hence, the paradox.

Two young wives invade Yerma's short privacy. They
greet her warmly but only one stops to continue the conversation. The other has to return quickly to her home since
she had to leave the baby alone. Yerma warns her against
such carelessness:

"Children shouldn't be left alone. . . . you don't realize
what a small child is. What seems most harmless to us
can be dangerous to him."

Again, her words display a sincere concern. But they also
convey a silent reproach that children should be given to
those least aware of their worth. As the woman is made
more aware of her duty, she exits hastily. Yerma and the
other one continue on the subject. La Muchacha is also bar-

ren but the difference between the two women is simply
stated by her:

> "Anyway, you and I live more peacefully by not having
> any. Why does my husband have to be my husband?
> We did the same things as sweethearts that we do now.
> . . . Well, I'm going to give my husband his food. See
> what I mean? What a shame not to be able to say my
> sweetheart."

She is happy in her unfertile state because she never wanted
marriage, only the pleasures it condones. Yerma looks after
her, tortured by the thought that so many waste the opportunity for motherhood while she longs for it with her entire
being. Her suffering mounts with each ironic encounter with
life. It builds slowly, punishingly.

Victor's voice is heard approaching, singing a shepherd's
song. Yerma begins to sing also, and as she starts to return
to her house Victor enters. This second encounter, which her
eyes reveal to be poignant, is less formal than the first. Victor's gaiety is foiled by her sadness as they stand close to
each other and a struggle begins. But it is not an attraction of
passion like that evidenced in *Bodas de sangre;* instead, there
is an unmistakable recognition by Victor and Yerma that it
is they who should have been joined in marriage. That she
senses her fulfillment to be in him is seen in her words:

> "Do you hear that? . . . Don't you hear the crying? . . .
> I thought a child was crying. . . . Very near. And it cried
> as if drowning. . . . It's the voice of a small child."

The child's cry is coming from within Victor, as if it were
suffocating in his imprisoned love for her. Victor has become,
in Yerma's mind, the symbol integrating paternity and filia-
tion. And though Victor cannot hear the imagined cries, he
senses her need. Their glances are locked in understanding;
for a moment nothing matters to them but the rapport of
these seconds. Then, as if he feared the implication of her
eyes, Victor slowly lowers his own.

Juan's entrance interrupts the innocent scene, but his

suspicions make him react harshly towards Yerma as Victor exits. Juan, neither accusingly nor forgivingly, but dryly, sends Yerma back to the house. It will be another night with him away from their bed for Juan declares his intention of remaining in the fields. To Yerma it will be one night less in which her child could be given life. The first act ends.

This scene between Yerma and Victor, with its insinuations, serves to complete the preface to Yerma's inner conflict. All the principal characters have been observed and the possibilities open to Yerma uncovered. All but the one which will climax her torment, the tragic action which ends the drama. The complication of the situation, through Yerma's participation in her own barrenness, has added depth to the plot and made the heroine even more pitiable because her recognition of her fault is not forthcoming.

The first scene of the second act enshrines a group of women on various levels of an age-hewn mountainside, pounding clothing with stones to the rhythm of the river's fast-flowing waters. Yerma is not among them, but she is the subject of their gossip and laughter:

> "What is certain is that the husband has taken his two sisters to live with them. . . . They were in charge of the church and now they take care of their sister-in-law. . . . they're frightening. They're like those huge leaves that suddenly appear on sepulchres. They're covered with wax."

Juan's spinster sisters have become Yerma's jailers, insuring that she doesn't leave the house against Juan's wishes. Her only relief is sitting alone at night on the steps while Juan works in the fields. But the women do not blame the husband. Their acid comments jeer at Yerma's state:

> "The woman who wants children has them. But the pampered ones, the lazy and soft ones, are not fit to have a wrinkled womb."

Only one of the women defends Yerma but her lone voice is

not enough to dispel the gossip which joins Yerma and Victor:

> "There's something about certain glances. . . . A woman looking at roses is not the same as a woman looking at a man's thighs. She looks at him. . . . And when she isn't looking at him, because she's alone, because he's not in front of her, she carries his image in her eyes."

The argument which ensues is only quelled by the appearance of Juan's sisters, silent and somber in their black dresses. For a moment, as they take their places by the stream, there is silence. The looks of the washer-women are candid, revealing the scorn they bear for these desiccated figures. When the spinsters begin to launder, the others return to their places. Tauntingly, they begin to speak of the shepherds. One of them, the one who had voiced such strong indictments of Yerma, brings Victor's name into the conversation. The spinsters wince. The women begin a gay song of great sensuality whose topic is the barren wife. Each adds her own verse, one more erotic than the other:

> Lavandera 5a: "Tell me if your husband
> bears the seed
> to make the water sing
> through your chemise."
> Lavandera 2a: "My husband is coming
> from the mountain to eat.
> He brings me one rose
> and I give him three."

The song gives way to a litany accompanied by the pronounced rhythm of the women beating the clothing in unison. It is a slow tempo which makes everything deliberate—words, movements—and the atmosphere increases in sensuality:

> Lavandera 1a: "Flower to flower must be joined
> when summer dries the reaper's blood."
> Lavandera 4a: "And wombs must be opened to
> sleepless birds
> when trembling winter calls at the door."

The chant continues, always increasing in pace as the fertile women offer the absent Yerma a lesson in love. The beat of the pounding is hypnotic. And the song is taken up by all as the scene ends with an overpowering mixture of voice and rhythm, climaxing the slowly building progress of the chant.

Wrought in the tradition of Greek tragedy, this scene serves to accentuate Yerma's unsought separation from her neighbors, from tradition, hence from society itself. Through this choral chapter, the tragic sense of the drama is enhanced, emphasizing not only the spiritual separation of Yerma from her community but the reason why such a barrier exists. Also, the scene points out the physical apartness of Yerma and society. In the eyes of her neighbors, she is a freak who exists to be laughed at and sometimes given condescending pity. The scene, though not directly in the line of the plot's development, is important as a serious attack on society's refusal to accept what it will not understand because it lacks compassion. As such it is an apt comment and rightly included in the drama. Finally, the scene serves yet another purpose, minor, but nonetheless important:

> The scene of the washerwomen . . . has a coloring, a brightness and a light poetry which are relaxing.[5]

In the second scene, the action is returned to Yerma's house where Juan and his sisters await her return; Juan reprimands the spinsters for allowing Yerma to go out alone, even if only to the fountain. It is not jealousy that prompts his remarks, but fear of the gossip Yerma causes whenever she leaves the house alone:

> "One of you should go out with her, that's why you're here. . . . My life is in the fields, but my honor is here. And my honor is also yours."

But what he does not understand is that Honor is just as important in Yerma's life as it is in his; perhaps it is more so,

---

5. Arturo Aldunate-Phillips, *Federico Garcia Lorca a traves de Margarita Xirgu* (Santiago de Chile, Nascimento, 1937), p. 56.

as will be discovered later. Juan mistakes Yerma's intentions.
Her bitterness over being unfertile implies in his mind that
she seeks satisfaction elsewhere. But he cannot understand
that what she seeks most is that he turn his power for making the earth yield its wealth upon her, to make her fruitful.
Juan's overconcern for the land's productivity is another instance of the irony in the drama.

When Yerma returns, Juan's accusing eyes force her to
defend herself. She is less withdrawn than in previous scenes,
and her voice shows the increased hatred of her state; Juan's
insistence that she remain in the house elicits her spirited
defense:

> "Rightly. Women in their houses. When those houses are
> not sepulchres. When chairs break and the linen sheets
> wear out with use. But not here. . . . I don't offend you
> in anything. I'm submissive to you and what I suffer I
> keep close to my flesh."

Yerma's attitude is more desperate than before as it is enhanced by the passage of time. It is now five years since their
marriage. Juan, however, is still puzzled at the continued
agony over her childlessness. He thinks that time should have
taught her to be resigned. But Yerma's earlier hope has given
way to a growing frustration. However, she still looks at Juan
pleadingly, as if a spark still remained with her.

Yerma chooses the company of her thoughts to Juan's at
dinner and he enters to eat with his sisters. Alone, Yerma retreats into herself:

> "I ask to suffer with child, and the wind
> offers me dahlias from sleeping moon.
> These two springs of warm milk which I bear
> in the depths of my flesh are two horsebeats
> making the branch of my anguish throb.
> ....
> But you will come, my love, my child,
> because water yields salt, the earth fruit,
> and our wombs hold tender children,
> like a cloud bears sweet rain."

As in the first scene of the first act, Yerma's daydream is interrupted by Maria. She passes by quickly, a child in her arms. When Yerma calls to her, she enters hesitantly knowing that Yerma cries whenever she sees the child. In the presence of the young mother, Yerma feels her own poverty. Again, all her despair is expressed to Maria who listens understandingly. Maria's comforting words still have no effect on Yerma who declares narcisistically:

> "I'll end up believing that I am my own child. . . . when I walk through the darkness of the shed my footsteps sound to me like those of a man."

And then, as the conversation turns to the spinsters and Juan's suspicions, Yerma returns the child to Maria. At the door, she explains her captivity:

> "They think I may like another man and they don't realize that even if I did the first thought of my people is honor."

And thus the final element in Yerma's tragedy—the strict code of honor—is notably unveiled, joining with the theme of sterility to form an unbreachable wall against which Yerma's hopes are constantly dashed. The only outlet in her search for satisfaction—another man—is closed by her own hand. It is the governing code which prevents her from seeking the child she desires in Victor or in any other man.

As Maria exits, another visitor appears. La Muchacha, the one who had spoken with Yerma in the previous act, now speaks secretively; she reveals that her mother and two neighbors are expecting Yerma but the purpose of the visit is not discussed, though both know the reason. Yerma instructs the young woman that her mother must wait even if it becomes late. La Muchacha exists as yet a third visitor enters.

Victor is framed in the doorway, stating that he has come to say his farewells. After calling Juan, Yerma looks at Victor with a great sadness and speaks of their youth, noting how time elapses while:

"Some things never change. There are things locked behind walls that can't change because no one can hear
them. . . . But if they suddenly escaped and screamed,
they would fill the world. . . . How sad it is not to hear
the advice of the old!"

As Victor is leaving his lands to tend others in a new town,
so must these hidden things be forsaken. But as the lands cannot be forgotten, neither can these forbidden thoughts be
erased. One of the spinsters crosses to the door and stands
watching suspiciously. Shortly, Juan enters, offering to escort
Victor to the stream where his journey begins. As they leave,
Victor turns for a last look at Yerma. Their hands meet in
an innocent gesture. When they have left, Yerma looks at the
hand for a moment and then, in a sudden decision, puts on
her shawl. Yerma exits into the darkness led by La Muchacha. The two spinsters follow her into the darkness with
candles, calling her name, as the act ends.

Where the first scene presented the possibility that Yerma
might seek refuge from her torment in Victor, this last scene
abolishes even the insinuation of such a remedy. Yerma could
not conceive of such a union with anyone. As she has said:
"Honor comes first." This code imposes a blind obedience of
the marriage laws, hence of the husband, on the woman's part,
yet looks less strictly on the behavior of the man. It demands
and subjects; and, as here, it destroys.

Though Yerma cannot consider breaking the code of hon-
or, she tries to circumvent it by relying on the strange superstitions and rites which are available to such women as face
her problem. Thus, in the third act, Yerma places her hopes
on the powers which these superstitions attribute to some
women in her village. It is one of these women, Dolores, whom
Yerma has sought out. As the first scene of the final act begins, Yerma, along with the two old women, enters Dolores'
house. The dawn breaks as the quartet terminates the journey from the cemetery where Yerma had been taken for the
ritual prayers of fulfillment. Now, she receives words of en-

couragement from the conjurers who promise that she will soon be pregnant through supernatural aid if the recommended prayers are followed faithfully. As a sign of good faith, Dolores defers payment for her services until after the event. Yerma relies on their assurances because, as she says of Juan:

> "When he covers me he does his duty, but I feel his waist is cold, as if his body were dead; and I, who've always been disgusted by passionate women, want to be like a mountain of fire at that moment. . . . The trouble is that he doesn't want children. . . . I see it in his glance, and since he doesn't want them, he doesn't give them to me."

Afraid that the townspeople will see her leave the house in daylight, Dolores tries to hasten Yerma's exit. But it is too late. As Yerma opens the door, Juan and his sisters enter. Flushed with suspicions, Juan accuses her of dishonorable behavior, releasing the venom which has been disturbing him all the years of their marriage as he addresses first her and then the others:

> "You deceive me, you cheat me. . . . She's been doing it since the very day of our wedding. Looking at me with two needles, spending the nights beside me in vigil with her eyes open, and filling my pillows with evil signs. . . . And I can't take anymore."

Juan's troubled attitude is thus uncovered. Though it is less imposing than Yerma's suffering, it is, nonetheless, important because it shows that his behavior towards Yerma is not based on unfounded selfishness but rather on the demands of Honor. To him, disgrace is a terrible curse and Yerma's acts lead to such in the eyes of the neighbors. The silence of the crowds and their knowing looks whenever he passes nearby are enough to convince him that his name is on the verge of being tainted by scandal. Human respect is his ruling passion.

In spite of Dolores' assurance that Yerma has done nothing dishonorable, Juan persists in his accusations. Yerma's defense is gallant:

> "Come close and smell my clothing; come close! See where you can find a scent that isn't yours, that doesn't come from your body. . . . don't dare to set a man's name on my breasts. . . . I search for you. . . . it's you I seek day and night without finding shade where I can breathe. It's your blood and your protection I want."

But Juan's fixedness allows no deviation. He pushes her away and she falls. A look of hatred crosses her face as her screams pierce the small room. The approach of some neighbors adds tenseness to the scene. Afraid of the disgrace, Juan half-drags Yerma to her feet. She, yelling her curses and derisions for the town to hear, fights his every effort. Juan is helpless to stop the disgrace he so greatly feared. The curtain falls on the violent sequence.

The tragedy's final scene takes place in a mountain hermitage near the town. It is the annual pilgrimage to the shrine where barren women and those without husbands gather to seek their particular favors either from the saints or from the many willing men that follow them. The area is alive with barefoot women bearing offerings, with children, with old mothers escorting their unwed daughters, with sarcastic onlookers. Everywhere, in the tents and on the hillside there is much activity, but the preparations aren't all for the procession; as a brief song proclaims:

> "I couldn't see you
> when you were single
> but now that you're wed
> I will find your bed.
> I'll take off your clothes
> oh, pilgrim and wife,
> when in the darkness
> midnight brings raptness."

One of the cynical onlookers is La Vieja, the old woman of the first act, who adds more information as to what really occurs during these excursions. Slyly, she inquires of one of the women:

> "You come to beg the saint for children, but every year more single men come on this pilgrimage. What is going on?"

Her laughter emphasizes the sordidness into which the holy purpose is turned in the attempt by some to overcome their aridity. The sacred rites have become an excuse for promiscuity. La Vieja exits to entertain herself with the obvious hypocrisy of the women, and to look after her son who has joined the anxious men.

Maria, who has accompanied Yerma, and another woman speak further of the debauchery of past years and of the preparations for the present feast. Both the wine and the men are ready to make the "miracles" occur. Afraid of the solitude of the area, Maria and her companion retire, seeking the company of other people. For a moment the setting is vacant, but the sound of a chant introduces a small procession in which Yerma and six women appear. Their feet are bare and they carry twisted candles to guide them in the failing light of evening. As they walk, very slowly, their lips form the words of petition:

> "Lord, let my rose blossom,
> do not leave it in shadow."

First uttered by Yerma, the prayer is continued by all the women in turn. The chant is long and deliberate, as if the ponderance of cadence could add strength to the pleas. Finally, the group disappears into the church.

A very dissimilar aggregation populates the stage upon their exit. Women enter carrying garlands as a festive clamor of bells accompanies others who appear from all sides. Guitars are heard in diapasonal tones. The beginning of the feast signals the end of the religious rites. Two figures, prominent in their disguises, emerge from the crowd. The children recognize them as the representations of the devil and his wife.

The large masks emphasize the sensual mood which the scene is quickly adopting. The male mask, El Macho, symbol of virility, holds a bull's horn in one hand; La Hembra, his female counterpart and symbol of fertility, twirls a large necklace of bells. They dance with abandon. The whole atmosphere is of great physical beauty and earthiness. La Hembra begins to sing of the barren wife and the children and men add comments of their own. Then, El Macho approaches La Hembra in a very sensual dance; his words give the theme of the pagan ritual:

> "If you have come to this shrine
> to ask that your womb be unsealed,
> do not wear a veil of mourning,
> instead a fine dress of batiste.
> Go walking alone by the walls
> where fig trees stand so dense,
> and support my earthy body
> till the white whimper of dawn."

Each verse quickens the pulse of the spectators. When the dance ends, girls run happily into the night followed by the young men.

But Yerma is as preoccupied as before; Juan has accompanied her to prevent the unfaithfulness which he still believes she could commit. He sits elsewhere, drinking. La Vieja, trying to convince Yerma that her cause is hopeless with Juan, offers her son if she will leave her husband. Her son awaits Yerma behind the hermitage walls. La Vieja tries to convince her by revealing what she knows of Juan's family:

> "I wasn't able to say anything to you before, but now I can. . . . It's your husband's fault. . . . Neither his father, nor his grandfather, nor his great grandfather behaved like men of good breeding. For them to have a son it was necessary for heaven and earth to meet."

Yet, Yerma is beyond being offended by words. La Vieja's offer is rejected without emotion for Honor cannot be so easily defiled. Yerma's is no longer a mere desire of the flesh; it is her very soul that must be satisfied. And that satisfaction can come only from her husband. Bitterly resigned to the denial of motherhood, Yerma can no longer even hope that the means she has employed will bring fruition. Disgusted with Yerma's attitude, La Vieja goes off to seek another woman for her son.

Juan approaches Yerma when she is alone. Apparently, he has heard everything and is angered by her continuing expectance. His anger forces the disclosure of his true feelings about the child:

> "This is the last time I'll put up with this continuous lament for dark things, beyond life, for things that drift in the air. . . . For things that don't matter to me. Do you hear it? That don't matter to me. Now I must tell you. What matters is what I have between my hands. What I can see with my eyes. . . . Many women would be happy to live as you do. Life is sweeter without children. I'm happy without them. We're not to blame."

That which she had suspected, which La Vieja had told her, is now openly stated by Juan. He does not want children, he says, nor can she ever expect to have any. To Yerma it is obvious that the fault lies entirely with Juan, and that he could make her happy if he so chose. But the reality is not as evident. There is a curious state which remains mysterious: whether Juan is impotent or whether his selfishness commands his abstention.

Juan embraces Yerma in an attempt to conquer her conscience through the physical appeal of their union. But, as she detests a marriage without purpose, Yerma resists Juan's actions. Her last hope has been extinguished by his declaration. With it has gone the necessity of giving herself to him. She fights his grasping hands and with a scream torn from her deepest despair, Yerma strangles Juan. Over his body, as people gather around them, she pronounces on herself the double sentence of murder:

> "Don't come near me, because I've killed my son; I myself have killed my son!"

The crowd remains apart as the woman stands desolately. In
killing her husband, she has, in fact, killed her son. It is at
this moment that she fully realizes the consequence of her
action and that the climax of the tragedy is reached. To the
weight of the murders is added that of her moral death, or
suicide, because the child which she killed in Juan was the
reason for her existence. Her tragedy is now complete.

Yerma, therefore, though the tragedy of the individual,
finds its outlet through two main arteries which enrich the
drama with elements of tradition and psychology. First,
Yerma is the woman tortured by her own mind, whose obses-
sion with maternity drives out all other aspects of the real
world which surrounds her. This condition causes her rejection of Juan, her husband, as a lover; in her mind, his role
is limited to being the procreator of her child. Nothing more.
But Yerma is not entirely to blame for this view of marriage.
Her outlook is fashioned from the traditional and religious
consequences that have been characteristic of Spanish morality. These powers, and they are unmistakably that, force her
to accept life as it has been taught her. Free will is, then, no
more than an agency of this heritage. This is Yerma's internal
or moral tragedy. The death of her spirit makes it complete.

The second aspect of the tragedy is present in the attitude of Juan towards Yerma. Because the tragedy concen-
trates on his wife, Juan's mind is never as fully explored. Except for his apparent selfishness, disclosed in cameo scenes,
Juan is never allowed to speak as freely as Yerma. He cannot
bare his soul and show the reasons for his actions, or lack of
actions. Juan is the mute man and must remain, as most male
figures in Lorca's theatre, the physical cause of a woman's
anguish. As many of these other male characters, Juan exists
only on the physical level and seems totally unaware of
values based elsewhere. Thus the conflict.

Yerma with her clamoring need for motherhood is pitted
against Juan, the man of the earth, with his fanatical desire
to remain free of encumbrances. Each has a passionate attach-

ment to these physical goals and each must meet the demands on different levels. And the sense of tragedy arises because these two lines of existence are parallel, travelling
jointly into oblivion, never meeting. Yerma cannot accept
Juan in the fulness that love demands. He will always be
just the man who can give her a child. And Juan cannot accept Yerma as the mother image. To him she can only be a
companion in sexual satisfaction. Yet, each ardently believes
his view is correct and proper to their station in life. In order
for their life together to be whole and balanced, each must
strive to bend to the other's wishes. But since their paths are
so set by traditionalism, this is not possible. The result of the
double act of selfishness is, once again, death. Hers is a spiritual entombment; his, a physical death. And Honor is the
conveyor.

X. DOÑA ROSITA LA SOLTERA

CONCEIVED IN 1924 and not finished until June of 1935, *Doña Rosita la soltera* was premiered on December 13, 1935. Margarita Xirgu was cast in the title role under the direction of Ciprano Rivas Cherif at the "Teatro Principal Palace" in Barcelona. The decor was by Burmann.

IT IS TYPICAL of Garcia Lorca that at the height of his emergence as a tragic dramatist—*Bodas de sangre* and *Yerma*—he should turn away from the successful and resume work on projects which had first occupied him many years before. This deviation is best exemplified by the play which ingratiated itself after the completion of *Yerma, Doña Rosita la soltera.* The move was not unlike that which had followed the earlier success of his book of poems, *Romancero Gitano;* there, he had concentrated on the folk idiom, but the instant popularity of the work made him desert its path momentarily. In that instance he had become very depressed, doubting his artistic integrity. Now, however, having matured in outlook and feelings, Lorca approached his private problem of popularity with the "savoir faire" of a diplomat. His depression and anxiety were replaced with foresight and determination. Always wary of being categorized, Lorca turned his interest to a play which would be separated from his recent successes by technique and history, if not thematically. *Doña Rosita la soltera* is set in the Granada of 1890 and its action spans the twenty years thereafter. Superficially, the play is an evocation of the gaiety and elegance which marked those carefree years. In 1934, after the completion of *Yerma*, Lorca detailed the foundations of the new play in an interview:

> "I'm writing a comedy on which I place all my illusion: *Doña Rosita la soltera o el lenguaje de las flores.* 'Family reveille divided into four gardens.' It will be a work of sweet ironies, of pitiable bits of caricature; a bourgeois comedy of soft tones, and diluted in it, the grace and delicacy of times past and distant eras. I think the

241

evocation of those days, in which nightingales really sang and gardens and flowers had a romantic connotation, will surprise many. That marvellous age of our parents' youth. The era of the bustle; and later of pompous skirts and the 'cutrovi,' 1890, 1910."[1]

In this recalling of an era, *Doña Rosita la soltera* bears a close resemblance to Lorca's *Mariana Pineda*. Both plays are conceived in the spirit of an unchanging Granada, a spirit of many facets, intricate and often incomprehensible. Both plays share in the romantic and melancholic overtones which characterize the ancient spirit of Granada. Life in that city is complex and it is that atmosphere which is always at hand in *Doña Rosita la soltera*. Its cryptic past prevents stylization in the present. Therefore, though both plays are set in different eras, the atmosphere of the city is of similar stature, mystically present in spite of the changes of time.

But there are more than these general similarities between the plays. They also share the air of frustration which dominates most of Lorca's drama. In *Mariana Pineda* the heroine awaits the return of Don Pedro with faith in his love; even with the certainty of death before her, Mariana remains constant until her final moments bring disillusionment. Likewise, Doña Rosita awaits the return of her fiancee. She dreams of their reunion, of their marriage and of their life together. But as the years pass comes the finality of frustration. Thus, in the sharing of a common attitude and spiritual betrayal both women are very alike. However, in spite of a tragic set of circumstances, Doña Rosita is not the tragic heroine that Mariana becomes. Mariana, unlike Doña Rosita, remains true to her ideas; where the latter resigns herself to an empty life, Mariana cannot live without love. Within her heart she knows that only death for the cause of love has any meaning. It is this heroic sacrifice that really differentiates the two women.

In *Yerma*, also, can be found a kinship with *Doña Rosita*

---

1. Alardo Prats, "Los artistas en el ambiente de nuestro tiempo," *op. cit.*

la soltera, particularly in the theme of frustration, but a greater similarity is evident in *Asi que pasen cinco años*. This is shown best in the concern of Lorca in both plays with the idea of timelessness. Both plays place the burden of emphasis on this element, tinting it with subtle irony. In *Asi que pasen cinco años*, El Joven is made to wait five years for his intended bride, then another five years for La Mecanografa; but in the end, time mocks his monastic abstinence by showing that not even a second has elapsed. In *Doña Rosita la soltera*, Rosita has the expectation that her fiancee will return. But as the years pass into spinsterhood, her fidelity is mocked through the symbol of the withering rose whose life is only twenty-four hours long.

Conceived in the same year as *Mariana Pineda*, *Doña Rosita la soltera* was, no doubt, an outgrowth of that play. However, it was a more tangible source which gave impetus and shape to the embryonic thoughts scattered in Lorca's mind. Without this impetus, the play might never have been written since its theme had already been exposed in its predecessor. Lorca presents the causation of the play:

> "I conceived my latest comedy, *Doña Rosita la soltera*, in 1924. My friend Moreno Villa told me one day: 'I'm going to tell you the beautiful story of the life of a flower—the mutable rose—from an XVIII century book on roses.' Then, he began. 'Once there was a rose . . .' and when he had finished the marvellous story of the rose, I had my comedy already finished. It occurred to me completed, unique, impossible to change."[2]

Apparently, the play had remained in Lorca's mind for many years thereafter, for Moreno Villa, the poet who introduced him to the French botany book which contained the story of the rose,[3] declared many years later:

One afternoon while drinking coffee in the Palace Hotel

---

2. Felipe Morales, "Declaraciones de G. L. sobre teatro," *op. cit.*
3. Bouvet (ed.), *Lenguaje de las flores, su historia, cultivo y modo de escribir y hablar por medio de ellas* (Paris-Mexico, 1878).

with him (Lorca), Dali and Pepin Bello, I remember I told them of my find of the day: a book on the Rose. A French book of the beginning of the 19th century which was very suggestive, with all the known varieties and their latin or modern names. I soon forgot about it, but two years later he appeared with *Doña Rosita la soltera* and some of the names I mentioned were in it, among them that of the 'Rosa Mutabile,' which is all an evocation.[4]

The error on Lorca's part in citing the century of the book's publication is minor. What is important, however, is Moreno Villa's statement that two years after the incident Lorca had completed the play. Its seed, originated in 1924, had remained dormant until it was revived by the tale of the mutable rose. In all those years, the theme had matured to the extent that the simple story line of the rose crystallized it. This, according to Moreno Villa, was in 1933; it was not until 1935, however, that the play was fully realized:

This play haunted the poet's imagination for many years and was the longest in maturing among all that he wrote. Its conception was such a task to him that I know that when he saw it finished it was a load off his shoulders. . . . I believe that with *Doña Rosita*, written with great care, he overcame the private failure of *Mariana Pineda*.[5]

Lorca's interest in this play is evidenced not only by the many comments he made upon it, but also by the frequent promises he gave to read the manuscript to friends. The first of these readings took place in the quarters most favored by Lorca—the home of Carlos Morla Lynch and his family. Later, Lorca expressed further sentiments as to this most laborious of his plays:

"*Doña Rosita* is life tame on the outside and burning on the inside, of a Granadine maiden who, little by little, is converted into that grotesque and pitiable thing that is a

4. Jose Moreno Villa, *Vida en claro* (El Colegio de Mexico, 1944), p. 121.
5. Francisco Garcia Lorca, in *Three Tragedies, op. cit.,* p. 18.

spinster in Spain. Each act of the play takes place in a
different era. The first act is set in the starched and affected years of 1885. Bustle, complex hairdos, wools and
silks over the skin, colored parasols. . . . Doña Rosita is
twenty years old at this moment. All the hope of the
world is in her. The second act takes place in 1900.
Fitted waists, pompous skirts, the Paris Exposition,
modernism, the first automobiles. Doña Rosita reaches
the full maturity of her charms. Third act: 1911. Ruffled
skirts, airplanes. Another step, the war. Suffice it to say
that the principal upheaval in the world caused by the
conflagration can be felt very near in the spirit and ways
of the century. Flat bosoms, straight hips, eyes with a
distant gleam, ashes on the mouth and tresses knotted
unattractively."[6]

Within the framework of this reality, Lorca places his
characters. They are to live, love and suffer within the ridiculous, though attractive, Granada of those years. Their lives
are governed by a society in which some of the prime requis-
ites for love are strictly interpreted through "the language of
ffowers, "hand signals," "fan talk," and "umbrella conversations." These are the external trappings Lorca uses most effectively to satirize that society.

But beyond this mode of behavior, of social acceptance
and rejection, exist the secrets of women such as Doña Rosita who wait for love and never receive more than the glance
of a promise. That is the heart of the drama. It is the quiet
tragedy of many Spanish women who are defeated, not so
much by a frustrated love, as by a society which makes such
rejection a symbol of shame. The woman caught in that predicament becomes a pitiable creature, subject to the gossip of
her neighbors, and an outcast in all but outward appearances.
Such is the story of Doña Rosita, mirror of that seclusion:

"How many mature women will see themselves reflected
in Doña Rosita as in a mirror! I've wanted only the
purest line to lead my comedy from beginning to end.

6. Armando de M. y Campos, "Lope de Vega y Garcia Lorca en
    Mejico," *Presencias de teatro,* Mexico (1937), p. 271.

Rather than comedy, it would be best to call it drama, drama of Spanish distastefulnss, of the desire for fruition which women must forcefully repress in the deepest part of their fevered heart."[7]

But covering all these inner problems is a veil meant for those not directly concerned. The veil of human respect, imposed by the same artificial society which created the necessity for it, attempts discreetly to cover the sufferings of the individual and hypocritically to pass over the real attitude of society. This aspect of life is one of Lorca's principal concerns in this play.

The first act of *Doña Rosita la soltera o El lenguage de las flores*, with the further subtitle of "Poema granadino del novecientos, dividido en varios jardines, con escenas de canto y baile," is set in the home of Rosita's uncles—El Tio and La Tia. The large and comfortable livingroom has a very noticeable door leading into a greenhouse. El Tio is seen entering from there, followed by La Tia and their servant, El Ama. El Tio is upbraiding the servant-woman for her mistreatment of his flowers and she is returning his comments with the authority of one who is almost a part of the family. La Tia, seemingly proper in the attempt to discourage the argument, is unable to prevent El Ama's expression of disgust with the flowers which have invaded the house. El Tio returns to his greenhouse when El Ama's opposition becomes too strong. To illustrate her point that all things in life must be useful, El Ama sings a salacious refrain to La Tia:

> "The mouth serves well for eating,
> the legs serve well to dance,
> and there is something a woman has . . ."[8]

The last phrase is whispered to La Tia who then crosses herself in indignation at the sayings of the common people. It is clear that El Ama enjoys shocking her mistress.

---

7. *Ibid.*
8. All textual quotations, unless otherwise specified, are from *Obras Completas, op. cit.,* pp. 1261-1348.

Lorca has already, in these first moments, detailed these three characters so that they promise to be more than mere foils to the heroine, Rosita, who enters quickly and after a whirlwind search for her hat exits in like manner. Behind her she leaves two women who obviously love her very much and subsequently have spoilt her somewhat. El Ama praises the devotion of the uncles to the orphaned Rosita as El Tio re-enters. Still in a rage, he orders the servant to sweep the floor of his indoor garden. When she is gone, a twinkle replaces his seriousness. Approaching La Tia with the pride of a father, he declares:

> "It's a rose you've never seen; a surprise I've prepared. Because this 'declining rose' is incredible with its drooping petals, and its stem has no thorns. . . . Botanists have named it 'rosa mutabile' which means mutable, changing."

His own words seem inadequate to describe the beauty of the changing rose he has cultivated, and so he resorts to a small book which contains a poetic description of the rare flower:

> "When it blossoms in the morning,
> it has the redness of blood.
>
> Full blown at mid-day,
> it is as hard as the coral.
>
> And as afternoon faints
> in the violet of the sea,
> it turns to white, as white
> as a cheek of salt.
> And when the night is sounding
> its soft metallic horn
>
> its petals start to fall."

Rosita is to be the human counterpart of this mutable rose as her life follows the simple pattern of its existence throughout the three acts of the play. Each act will symbolize an aspect of the rose's life—morning, afternoon and night —through the life of Rosita. Thus, the many years which the drama covers are represented by the one day existence of the flower. The use of this symbolism unifies the play.

Rosita's re-entrance emphasizes the simile. The action continues, returning to the physical level which preceded the reading of the poem, as Rosita looks for her parasol. El Ama brings the object of the latest search. But to her horror, Rosita opens the parasol in the room. El Ama tries to contradict the evil spirits with a superstitious incantation that produces laughter. It is an incident which recalls the one in *La Zapatera Prodigiosa*. El Tio returns to his flower, looking at Rosita as he leaves. She, too, exits. Once more, La Tia and El Ama are alone in the room; the opportunity presents itself to speak of El Sobrino, Rosita's fiancee. In the background, as El Ama departs later, is heard the typical "pregon" of the wine seller.

El Sobrino's appearance is heralded by the "pregon." He enters with a face that betrays the agitation a letter from his father has caused. La Tia senses his unquietness. He gives her the fateful letter which calls him back to their home in South America. The dialogue which follows between aunt and nephew serves to reveal an important segment of the plot, until now undiscovered. La Tia had been opposed to the romantic interest of the cousins because she feared that such a separation would occur. Now her suspicions have been confirmed. El Sobrino, however, stands indecisive:

> "Do you think I want to leave? I want to stay here; that's why I've come. . . . What can you advise me to do?"

In her eyes, marriage cannot be the solution because El Sobrino has yet to make his own way. Her opposition is strong and, reinforced by El Sobrino's duty to his father, it becomes impregnable. His feeble attempts to find a solution result only in resignation to his father's command. All that he can do is make a faint promise to return and marry Rosita. He exits amid the cries of El Ama who has heard the conversation from the doorway. The two women watch his retreat with mixed feelings. La Tia, trusting in God's ways, sits pensively; but El Ama, emotionally upset by the declarations of El Sobrino, curses him loudly as she depicts the curse on the floor. Both retire as Rosita's laughter reaches them, an irony not to be ignored.

The next sequence is light, filled with the laughter of Las Manolas, three young women who have accompanied Rosita on her stroll. They are pretty things who tell each other secrets and sigh at the least provocation. Playfully, Rosita taunts them with rumors she has heard about their romances. They listen attentively to her ballad, taking each rumor as a jewel in their crowns:

> "Granada, the street of Elvira,
> where live all the Manolas,
> who go to the old Alhambra,
> they three alone at four.
> ....
> What lovers could await them?
> Under what trees are they lying?
> What hands caressing the perfumes
> stolen from their two round flowers?"

But the half-hearted denials of such affairs are not very convincing. The girls continue with their sighing and Rosita smiles knowingly. Her attitude changes quickly, however, when El Ama enters the room. It is obvious to Rosita that she has been crying and, afraid that something may have happened to La Tia, she runs out. Sensing the urgency of the moment, Las Manolas follow El Ama in their eagerness to know the cause of the trouble.

For a short time the scene is empty. A distant piano plays a study by Czerny. Then, El Sobrino enters and crosses to the center of the room where he halts as Rosita appears. As they embrace, Rosita expresses her sadness:

> "Why did your treacherous eyes
> fuse themselves to mine?

Why did your hands interweave
flowers upon my head?"

And, though his words cannot soothe, El Sobrino attempts to
ease her pain with promises that he will return to marry her.
But her depression grows constantly as the realization of their
separation dawns on her. In their final embrace, as if to reassure Rosita, El Sobrino affirms his intent to return for her
after his fortune is made. The piano accompanies his departure with its tune. Alone with her tears, Rosita picks up the
book of flowers as her uncle crosses to the greenhouse. She
recites the words previously read by El Tio and the first stage
in the life of Rosita, symbolized by the mutable rose, con-
cludes.

Already, the separation of this drama from Lorca's *Yerma* and *Bodas de sangre* is recognizable in technique. Particularly varied is the relationship between Rosita and El Sobrino. It is very far from the fiery liaison of La Novia and
Leonardo, or the tormented union of Yerma and Juan. There
is nothing improper or incorrect here to mar the relationship
of the lovers. These are normal people in a typical situation.
Everything is as it should be in their class. In short, they
are entirely different, not as human beings but as people in
a different environment, from the characters in the other
tragedies. Rosita and El Sobrino could never react to their
predicament as did the lovers in *Bodas de sangre* because the
very artificiality of the society in which they live is stronger
as a bond than the natural laws which governed Leonardo
and La Novia. The latter were able to break the bondage of
their society because that society was founded on basic
truths; the fact that these truths were twisted to work against
men made their escape even possible. In *Doña Rosita*, however, the very artificial foundations of that society make it
unthinkable that any but the prescribed manners should be
obeyed. Leonardo and La Novia, fashioned in the mold of
Nature, could discard their governing rules because instinct
became paramount; Rosita and El Sobrino do not even think

of fleeing together because there is no such power that makes
that action imperative. The superficiality of their society has
erased the strong connection with Nature that the other lovers possess.

In this light, Rosita's metaphorical connection with the
mutable rose becomes ironic. While the rose is part of Nature, living and dying according to its dictates, Rosita is
only physically so. The rest of her is dominated by a stifling
artificiality which is the hallmark of the society in which she
exists. While the rose's life is precarious because Nature so
ordains, Rosita has to face a double jeopardy—that imposed
by the actual rules of life and that superimposed by society.

The second act commences many years later, at the turn
of the century. The setting wherein El Tio and another gen-
tleman converse is unchanged from the first act. Señor X is not
as mysterious as his name implies, being a professor of "Political Economy." He is, however, a curious person greatly
given to "name-dropping" and the espousing of theories prevalent in the early 1900's. He is a man of his age in every
respect, advanced in thought and prolific in the bits of information he has gathered. To him everything new is of interest—automobile racing, science, philosophy, politics—and
progress its best recommendation:

> "I shall always belong to this century. . . . of greater ad-
> vancement than the one which ended. . . . Of course, the
> Earth is a mediocre planet, but civilization must be
> aided."

El Tio, on the other hand, is the antithesis of these sentiments as he resents the intrusions of progress into his ideal
world of the late 1800's. He prefers his flowers and their intricacies to all the advances of science:

> "The century we've just begun will be a century of ma-
> terialism. . . . where are they all going in such a hurry?
> . . . You cannot convince me."

The conversation continues along these argumentative lines

until Señor X calls a halt to it with an adopted "Voila" as
he inquires after Rosita. She is also of interest to him, but
romantically. He entrusts a replica of the Eiffel Tower to El
Tio as a gift to Rosita. His mission completed since Rosita
is not at home, Señor X begins his exit by performing, to extreme, the niceties required after such visits. The scene takes
on a comic pace as El Tio counters each compliment with a
corresponding "Thank you." When his visitor finally departs,
El Tio faces El Ama who had listened to the conversation
from her usual place outside the door. But he returns to his
flowers as if to seek reinforcement of his ideas after his mental bout.

La Tia, seeing that Señor X has left, enters, but she does
so not knowing that El Ama is warming up to the topic of
El Sobrino's desertion of Rosita:

> "Do you think it's right that a man should leave and
> keep this woman, who is the fairest of flowers, waiting
> for fifteen years? She should marry."

El Ama is upset by Rosita's patient waiting for El Sobrino.
La Tia receives El Ama's ire because she knows that she is
as responsible as El Sobrino for the abandonment. While he is
guilty of failing to fulfill his promise, La Tia is tainted by her
encouragement of his departure. The conversation becomes a
series of accusations and denials in which each accuses the
other of not loving Rosita. The result is a breakdown, both
women crying, and La Tia discharging the servant after forty
years of service. But the skirmish is brief and soon they are
reconciled. It is a charming reversal in which one compliments the other for their love of Rosita. However, as their
insistences mount, the argument is resumed. El Ama leaves
hotly, followed by La Tia; but the latter meets El Tio who
has apparently been eavesdropping, for he says:

> "Your laces turn to thorns from living together so long.
> . . . And yet, you can't do without her."

Rosita, still wearing a rose-colored dress but one of contemporary fashion, sweeps into the room and stops only to ask if the postman has arrived. The urgency of her question shows the importance of his daily tour. Each day brings the hope of a letter from El Sobrino. Her impatience at the postman's lateness creates some tension and a short argument between El Tio, Rosita, El Ama and La Tia ensues. The words of El Tio, uttered but a few moments before take added significance:

> "There comes a time when people who've lived together for many years make the smallest things a reason for quarreling and unrest to create intensity and anxiety over what is definitely dead."

Both El Tio and El Ama go their separate ways leaving Rosita and La Tia together. Their conversation discloses the preoccupation both women have with the passage of time. La Tia is concerned over the length of Rosita's engagement and tries to convince her that other men are still interested in her. Rosita, however, lives in hiding from time, afraid to recognize the many years which have elapsed since El Sobrino left the town. Her loneliness satisfies her delusion:

> "If I couldn't see people, I would think that he'd only left a week ago. I wait as I did that first day. After all, what is a year, or two, or five?"

The doorbell interrupts Rosita's attempted justification of her position. She becomes anxious at the thought that it is the mail, but El Ama announces instead the arrival of La Madre and her three spinster daughters, characterising them promptly with her ready wit.

The ostentatious foursome greet Rosita and La Tia. Their manner and bearing are stylized to the period; everything, from dress to speech, seems false and overdone. The artificiality of the age is well represented by their entire appearance. While the spinsters are perfect caricatures of the type, La Madre is an even better representation of the overbearing mother who passes herself off as a sacrificing woman. Although their pretense is distasteful to the entire household, La Tia treats them with courtesy as they have come to congratulate Rosita on her birthday. Their gift to Rosita, a card with a fancy barometer, is similar to El Ama's gift of a portable thermometer. Through this Lorca makes another subtle indication of Rosita's likeness to a rose which needs the right warmth and atmospheric conditions to live. The two gifts are symbolic.

The occasion also brings other visitors. Las Ayola, daughters of the local photographer, are well contrasted to the spinsters. Not only is their dress different—it is rich and tasteful—but their gaiety is at odds with the prudish attitude of the others. While the spinsters sit silently, Las Ayola giggle incessantly, finally recruiting Rosita. The older women continue their petty conversation over the girlish laughter. The approach of the postman, however, excites Rosita quite differently. She becomes serious at the thought of El Sobrino whose letter she awaits. Again the emphasis turns to the passage of time. Las Ayola recall their childhood when Rosita and El Sobrino taught them the alphabet and gave them candies. The spinsters remain quiet, disdainful of the younger women whose thoughts are only on marriage, until the conversation of Las Ayola turns to single women:

> "And if I'm Rosita's friend it's because she has a fiancee! Women without men are discolored, overcooked, and all of them . . ."

La Tia interrupts her thoughtless comments but an argument tinged with cynicism erupts between the spinsters and and Las Ayola. La Tia's intervention alone prevents its continuation. The scene resolves itself into quiet contempt as Rosita tries to overcome the hurt feelings by asking one of the spinsters to play the piano. All but the Ayola girls join in the "Language of the Flowers," a song resembling the poem of the mutable rose in theme. Rosita sings of the meanings of flowers:

"The willow herb is jealousy;
the dahlia's cold contempt;
the tuberose is the sighs of love
and France's gall is merriment.
The yellow flowers are for hate;
the crimson one for rage;
the white ones are for marriages
and blue ones for the dead."

El Ama appears with the long-awaited letter. Rosita exits
rapidly, anxious to read its contents. The visitors are almost
as impatient, but with Rosita's departure the quarrel resumes.
The letter has caused consternation on both sides; Las Ayola
hoping it contains a marriage proposal and the spinsters
afraid of an offer of marriage because they would lose the
comfort of another wasted woman. La Tia and El Ama, too,
have their expectations. La Tia sees an end to the reign of
doubt no matter what the answer, while El Ama hopes it
will bring Rosita the happiness she deserves. Her re-entrance
is met with the din of questions. Rosita answers in a shocked
voice:

"He wants to marry me . . . He wants to marry me because he can't bear it any longer. . . . But since it's impossible for him to come now, the wedding will be by
proxy and he'll come later."

But the celebrating voices do not count with El Ama's. She
does not share the instantaneous joy of La Tia and Las
Ayola, nor the pretended happiness of La Madre and the
spinsters. The marriage by proxy, proposed by El Sobrino,
is beyond El Ama's comprehension: "And at night, what?
. . . Let him come himself and get married!" Everyone laughs,
but El Ama's objections are founded on natural instincts
rather than on convention; she cannot understand a wedding
without a bridegroom or a bride alone on her wedding night.
But her disapproval is lost in the entrance of El Tio who has
accidentally cut the mutable rose upon hearing the news. He
presents it to Rosita:

". . . almost without realizing it I've cut the only mutable rose I had in my greenhouse. It was still red. . . . If I had cut it two hours later, it would have been white by now."

The cutting of the rose is emblematic of what is to follow. Its introduction in this sequence seems equivocal because it contradicts the fact of the marriage proposal. However, its presence indicates that all will not pass as might be expected in view of the letter. The symbolic identification of Rosita and the mutable rose having been established, its meaning here cannot be ignored. The feeling of uneasiness is accentuated by El Ama's look as everyone begins to dance a polka; she exits as everyone sings joyously. The act ends on this uncertain note. The second phase of the rose's existence, its afternoon, has concluded.

This last act develops primarily as a satire on the social scene and its prerogatives. The first indication of it is evident in the broad outlines with which the character of Señor X is endowed. He is the typical pseudo-intellectual of an era whose receptiveness to anything labelled "Progress" made the real thing sought that much more difficult to discover. His many interests make him a man without focus. Lorca presents him as an obvious caricature, just as La Madre and her spinster daughters are drawn satirically. With these characters as examples of a foolish and ridiculous society, Lorca then enlists the aid of Las Ayola, themselves a part of it, to cast stones at the pretense. It is a fine touch of the irony always prevalent in Lorca's drama. El Tio is more of a character than a caricature, but he also receives his share of satirical treatment in this act. His single purpose of caring for his garden in general and the mutable rose in particular makes him a social recluse. Thus, his discussion with Señor X cannot have any meaning.

Even El Ama, the one person in the play whose primary asset is common sense, is made the object of ridicule. She is laughed at for her superstitious antics on the one hand, and on the other for her well-meant opinions. The first can be excused in any society; the second, however, shows the bias of the era. As a servant she is not to be taken seriously. But to point out these faults, Lorca made El Ama a well-rounded character. Because common sense and natural instinct direct her actions, her mind is uncluttered, free from the artificialities of society. She possesses a directness and clear vision not possible for La Tia or El Tio, nor for Rosita or El Sobrino. Each of the principal characters, except El Ama, is so concerned with one aspect of life that they lose sight of the whole. El Tio exists only for his garden; his death after the cutting of the rose (not disclosed until the third act) verifies this attachment. Likewise, La Tia sees herself as the protector of Rosita; La Tia is to Rosita what El Tio is to the mutable rose. El Sobrino is concerned with his own welfare, his progress in a demanding society; it is this selfishness which makes him cling to Rosita even after fifteen years. Rosita, so much in love with a hope, cannot face the reality of her abandonment by El Sobrino.

Yet, in spite of El Ama's good intentions and common sense, she is the cause of Rosita's continued poverty of spirit. Along with La Tia, her over-protectiveness of Rosita has led to her disillusionment. Between La Tia's insistence on proper conduct of the courtship and El Ama's appeal against a proxy marriage, Rosita has been denied even a fictitious happiness.

The third act, which transpires in 1910, is set in the same room. It is conspicuously quiet as a clock strikes six o'clock in the afternoon. El Ama crosses silently and then exits with a cargo of large boxes and a suitcase. La Tia enters and sits on a chair. The clock again sounds, broaching the intense silence. The opening dialogue, as El Ama returns, discloses the events which have taken place in the years since the last act. El Tio is dead. His death has left the three women to struggle valiantly in the large house. But now they must leave it because they are poor. And so they prepare their belongings and look sadly at their ancient home. The dispossession is more than physical; with the house remain the hopes and aspirations of the women. This is particularly seen in La Tia. No longer does she argue with El Ama as her disillusionment with life becomes more pronounced. El Ama, however, tries to maintain an optimistic attitude in the presence of La Tia's despair. But even then she cannot hide the revengeful hatred she bears for El Sobrino. Together, they plot a cruel but deserved death for El Sobrino who had betrayed Rosita's hopes by marrying another eight years before. The selfishness of his action is declared by his having hidden the fact of the marriage for that time. But they have kept it a secret from Rosita. All that is left to her is a spark of hope kindled by his untruthful letters.

When Rosita appears, La Tia and El Ama adopt an innocent pose; but no sooner is she in the greenhouse than their thoughts return to her misfortune. Rosita—older, wasted— is no longer desirable to the previous suitors. Her fate will be in the lonely life of the spinster. The love which El Ama has for Rosita pushes aside the feigned optimism and makes her see only the dark colors of her existence. Her own sadness at the loss of her husband and daughter were not as tortuous:

> "But what's happening to my Rosita is the worst. It is waiting and not finding the object; it is crying and not knowing for whom; it is sighing for a person one knows does not deserve the sighs."

Rosita's is a death of the spirit rather than of the body, and to El Ama it is the worst punishment that can befall anyone. In this thought she establishes a kinship with La Madre in *Bodas de sangre;* Rosita, in turn, becomes associated with Yerma as a victim of the mental anguish caused by a man's selfishness.

The pathetic tenderness of the sequence in which La Tia nobly releases El Ama because she will no longer be able to pay her salary and El Ama turns a deaf ear in total devotion ends with a sincere embrace that declares their inseparability. While La Tia still protests El Ama's sacrifice, a new personage makes his appearance. Don Martin is a venerable old man of recognizable dignity which contradicts the physical disability that forces a crutch to support his weight. His presence is alleviative in that the retelling of his own problems, so comically effective, retards sentimentality or heaviness in the plot line.

The old school teacher is nervous and concerned over the pranks which the pupils play on other teachers. His physical impediment, alone, has separated him from the lot of his colleagues but he fears that his music class will one day be disrupted by a serious prank directed at him. As the pupils are the sons of rich parents who look down upon teachers, discipline is almost impossible. The occasion serves for an aside at the unfortunate commercialization of even such essentials as education. Yet, it goes beyond that. The sensitive Don Martin is a poet without recognition who has been forced into teaching to support himself. Because of his poor state, he had likewise been forced to abandon the hopes of a career as a pharmacist. Frustrated, he apprehensively looks at his present life. Only an old poetic drama and some few stories are the mainstays of his hopes as a writer. Yet, he continues to write because the only thing that pleases him is the idea of doing what he wants to do. But Don Martin cannot completely escape the preoccupation with his school. El Ama enters to announce that he must return there immediately because the children have flooded the classrooms. With difficulty, Don Martin prepares for the unpleasant duty of fixing the pipes:

"I dreamt of Parnassus and now I have to be mason and plumber. Well, as long as they don't push me and I don't slip."

Upon his departure, El Ama curses the wealthy classes which have brought such fine men as Don Martin to their deprived situations. Her ire turns to visionary sentencing of such despoilers to hell. Her daydream is completed by the picture of her loved ones and herself nestled in heaven accompanied by Rosita's spouse. But the vision is dispersed by the entrance of workmen who have come for the furniture. El Ama directs them.

Rosita returns with a packet of old letters in her hand. Recognizing them as El Sobrino's, La Tia reveals the real reason for the dispossession:

"Had I known, I would never have consented to your uncle mortgaging the house with furniture and all."

And Rosita, realizing that the mortgage was obtained to provide her with appropriate furnishings when El Sobrino proposed marriage, is hurt that their condition has been worsened because of her. La Tia, in an unsatisfactory pretense, tells her that she will use the wedding gifts yet. But Rosita, no longer able to bear La Tia's suffering, falls on her knees and makes a confession:

"I knew everything. I knew he had married; a kind soul told me, and I've been receiving his letters with an illusion full of sobs that even surprises me. . . . Now I am old."

The pretense is discarded as all the facts are known by Rosita. She is revealed in her own terms for the first time and she emerges as a woman of deep feelings and great dignity. Unlike Yerma and Mariana Pineda, she has kept her sorrows to herself. Her frustrations have been her burden and no one else's as they were in *Yerma* and *Mariana Pineda*. Only at this moment does she allow her heart to be viewed in its compassionate state. But, true to her character, Rosita retreats within herself again, refusing the pitying caresses of El Ama and La Tia.

Here, to accentuate further the passage of time, Lorca introduces another new character. El Muchacho is the son of Maria one of the three sisters in the first act, the girls who had accompanied Rosita on her walk. Now dead, she has left behind her an eighteen year old son. His youth and his resemblance to his mother recall for Rosita and La Tia those happy

years when hope was not necessary because there was no
sight of despair. Now, as La Tia escorts him to the greenhouse, El Muchacho formally takes his leave of Rosita, addressing her as her years demand. Twice she repeats what
must now be her new name: "Doña Rosita." The simile of
the mutable rose again comes to her lips.

Another throwback to the past, one of the spinsters, appears as Rosita prepares to leave. Rosita does not see her, but
El Ama convinces the woman to pay her respects at their
new house. As she exits, a storm's strong winds attack the
shutters and doors of the greenhouse. The decay of the garden
has started. La Tia notes sadly:

> "It's as if someone wanted to make the garden ugly so
> we wouldn't be sorry to leave it."

The last words are Rosita's, whose white dress announces
the decay visibly; while La Tia and El Ama hold her firmly to
prevent her from fainting, Rosita repeats:

> "And when the night arrives
> its petals start to fall."

The depetalling of the rose has begun. The drama ends with
this suggestive picture as the three women exit, accompanied
by the wind and rain.

As in *Asi que pasen cinco años*, the element of time is important in this drama. In both plays there occurs a substan-
tial time lapse—five years in one, twenty-four in the other.
But Lorca's technique in both plays, though emphasizing this
passage of time, brings about a "coup" which would make
everything seem to have taken place beyond the confines of
time. It is more obvious, perhaps, in *Asi que pasen cinco
años*, but the same spirit prevails here through the incorpora-
tion of the mutable rose symbol. The flower possesses life for
a scant twenty-four hours. It is first introduced in the origin-
ating act of the play, contemplated through its growth in the
second, and observed in its decay in the third. For the rose

the twenty-four years of the play are only twenty-four hours. This is the vegetable aspect of the symbol.

Rosita forms the human counterpart. The twenty-four hours of the flower's life are the twenty-four years of Rosita's hope. As the flower begins to decay when its life-span is completed, so Rosita deteriorates spiritually when her hope dies. The parallel is complete; it is this which is important and the actual passage of time is only a servant of the symbolism. It is for this reason that the ambience is well developed throughout the play. Lorca dedicates much attention in the early moments of the play to establishing the identity of the mutable rose and creating interest in its habitat—the greenhouse—importantly placed near the family's livingroom. This interest is maintained by integrating the life in the garden with that in the human household. In this complete identification between the flower and its human counterpart exists the core of the drama.

XI. LA CASA DE BERNARDA ALBA

COMPLETED ON June 19, 1936, shortly before Lorca's death, *La casa de Bernarda Alba* received its much-delayed premier performance on March 6, 1945. The production enacted by Margarita Xirgu and her company, was held at Buenos Aires' "Teatro Avenida."

THE LAST COMPLETE play in the repertory of Federico Garcia Lorca, and the one which added the final stanza to the ambitious trilogy on tragic love, is *La casa de Bernarda Alba*. As in its predecessors, *Bodas de sangre* and *Yerma*, Lorca's theme is tangent to frustration, honor and death. This play is the logical culmination of the trilogy, containing as it does both the passion of *Bodas de sangre* and the torment of *Yerma* in the intense struggle of a group of women held in check even from the thought of love by a tyrannical mother. Bernarda Alba is the mother, a statuesque dramatic personality, whose words carry the authority of the supreme ruler and whose life betrays little emotion. In this austerity she rules her household, never sparing from her wrath anyone who attempts to revoke the stifling atmosphere she has superimposed on herself and her daughters. As a result, all —Bernarda, the daughters, the servants—exist in Usher-like darkness and depression ultimately leading to mass sterility of emotions and to suicide:

> In *La casa de Bernarda Alba* the theme of spinsterhood is again introduced; now expressed with an almost melodramatic gesture. The solitude of the five daughters, their desire and sadness, inundate the three acts.[1]

As prisoner of her own virginity, each daughter has a spiritual cell which is of greater consequence than the mere white walls and shuttered windows which prevent her physical release. As in all of Lorca's plays, the moral and spiritual bonds that surround life overpower his characters irremedi-

---

1. Roberto Sanchez, *Garcia Lorca: estudio sobre su teatro* (Madrid, 1950), pp. 65-66.

ably; the physical boundaries within which they move restrictedly are no more than outward indications of the greater imprisonment. The harsh concept of honor, the frustration of sexual fulfillment, the impossibility of love, the importance of human respect, and Fate—these are the incarcerators. In *La casa de Bernarda Alba* they are brought together in a powerful and shocking story of domination and revolt.

The origins of this play, perhaps the least defined in Lorca's drama, are obscured somewhat by his note in the subtitle:

> "The poet points out that these three acts are intended
> as a photographic documentary."[2]

Obviously, then, the final tragedy is intended as a photographic documentation of Spanish life in the middle class society of Andalucia. As such it had a basis in reality. Where Lorca had assimilated a newspaper account as the seed for *Bodas de sangre*, *La casa de Bernarda Alba* resulted from a vicarious experience of the playwright. It is retold by Carlos Morla Lynch after Lorca's conversation with him in June of 1936:

> "There's a small village, not far from Granada, where my parents owned a small property—Valderrubio. In the house which was neighbor and adjacent to ours, lived 'doña Bernarda,' a very old widow who exerted an inexorable and tyrannical vigilance over her unmarried daughters. As they were prisoners deprived of all free will, I never spoke with them; but I could see them pass like shadows, always silent and dressed in black. . . . there was a joint dry well in the confines of their patio and I would descend into it to spy on that strange family whose enigmatic attitude intrigued me. And I was able to observe them. It was a mute and cold hell under that African sun, the sepulchre of live people under the inflexible rule of the gloomy incarcerator. And that is how *La casa de Bernarda Alba* was born."[3]

---

2. *Obras Completas, op. cit.,* p. 1349.
3. Morla Lynch, *op. cit.,* pp. 488-489.

Another reporter, Claude Couffon,[4] whose source for much
of his information was Lorca's cousin, Maria, adds that the
character Pepe el Romano is drawn directly from Pepe de
la Romilla, the real-life lover of one of the unfortunate
daughters. Like the newspaper story, again, this occurrence
served only as a point of departure for the playwright. In
that sense, then, the plot is of personal originality and the
characters more creations than copies.

Where characters are concerned, *La casa de Bernarda
Alba* is also the climactic point in Lorca's theatre because
it is populated solely by women. The tendency of his drama
towards female protagonists has already been noted (only
El amor de don Perlimplin and *Asi que pasen cinco años*
give the principal roles to male characters). The ascendency
of the female could only have culminated in a drama such as
La casa de Bernarda Alba. Within the austere realism of
Bernarda's domain live eight women of different ages and
attitudes. Bernarda herself is sixty years old; her mother,
Maria Josefa, is eighty and mad in Bernarda's eyes; La Poncia, her mistress' contemporary, is a person of the common-
est lineage; Bernarda's five daughters range in age from
Adela's twenty years to Angustia's thirty-nine and are as
unlike each other as their ages. Other women—La Criada,
Prudencia, La Mendiga—also enter, if only partly, into the
rarified atmosphere of the household.

Bernarda bears little resemblance to any of Lorca's earlier
conceptions except in her role as mother. Only La Madre in
Bodas de sangre approaches Bernarda in her concern with
honor and human respect. Both women place the strict code
of behavior as the governing factors in their lives: both im-
pose upon themselves and their offspring an extended period
of mourning, both insist on controlling what is theirs, both
demand that honor be maintained at any cost and exon-
erated in spite of the threat of death. But the comparison

---

4. *op. cit.*

cannot be extended further because Bernarda possesses entirely different reasoning, sentiments, and therefore, attitude from La Madre or any other Lorquian character. Bernarda is a selfish and tyrannical matron who eventually forces her daughters into the pit of despair. They lose every vestige of hope; this loss leads directly to the moral death of each daughter and to the physical death of the youngest. Slowly, but unequivocally, Bernarda drains the minds and hearts of her daughters until they become as white and barren as the walls of their physical prison.

La Poncia, alone, is beyond Bernarda's influence, if not her venom. She is the only character who opposes Bernarda with any strength, but eventually her wit and common sense, typical of her predecessors in other plays, become mere pinpricks against the determination of her mistress. Bernarda's domination, based on absolute power, brings absolute corruption of her family's life. And all that remains is La Poncia's passive resistance which must be so because her dependence on Bernarda is economic.

Having brought together in *La casa de Bernarda Alba* much of what had been included in previous plays, Lorca was able to extract from them the exact situations and themes allied to his latest endeavor. But it is never a mere repetition. Rather, it is an enlargement of particulars, making possible a heightened background against which to draw sensitively the many women who take part in the tragedy. Consequently, each is delineated with great insight. The play contains the implication of maternal frustration of *Yerma*, the quiet loneliness of *Doña Rosita la soltera*, the spirited sacrifice of *Mariana Pineda*, the love offering of *El amor de don Perlimplin*, the searing passion of *Bodas de sangre*, and the deathly despair of *El maleficio de la mariposa* and *Asi que pasen cinco años*. In a real sense, then, this play is the summation of Lorca's theatrical artistry.

The first act is set in the principal room of Bernarda's house. Its walls and columns are thick—a sign of the strength and durability of the prison inhabited by Bernarda's daughters. The starkness is enhanced by the archways which define the windows and doors, by the coarse unadorning curtains, and by the baroque paintings which are obsolete against the mass of white. Outside, somewhere in the village, church bells toll mournfully. They continue as La Criada and La Poncia, Bernarda's two servants, converse freely while their mistress and her daughters are at the burial services for the deceased master, Antonia Maria Benavides. La Criada is La Poncia's underling, but the two women share the same bitter feelings for the oppression which Bernarda practices. La Poncia, however, carries the greater hatred, having served Bernarda for thirty years; they were years of dedication repaid with crumbs from her table and insults of hierarchical indifference.

"Tyrant over all who surround her. She's capable of sitting on your heart for a year and watching how you die without losing that cold sneer from her cursed face."[5]

The two women continue their denunciation of Bernarda, revealing as they do, the first hints of the daughters' plight. But only La Poncia sees their situation clearly; La Criada, oppressed by her own misfortunes and mistreatment, sighs longingly at the thought of being one of the daughters. Her words will prove most ironic as the action goes forward in time. As they talk, La Criada gathers a few bits of precious food and La Poncia eats revengefully. It is a day when Bernarda will not notice the missing food. As the bells cease, the servants begin the final preparations for the mourners' return. It will be the first time since the death of Bernarda's father that outsiders will enter the house.

As the last session of bells commences La Poncia hurries to the church. Upon her exit, La Mendiga and her daughter, the town's beggars, enter the room. La Criada wastes

5. All textual quotations, unless otherwise specified, are from *Obras Completas, op. cit.,* pp. 1349-1442.

no time in expelling them, showing none of the kindness she expects for herself. This point is important for it directs attention to another irony. La Poncia and La Criada both decry the injustices of Bernarda, but they, in turn, assume similar attitudes towards others. La Poncia's conversation with La Criada discloses a commanding tone although both are servants. Obviously, La Poncia's higher status in the household gives her a privileged position. La Criada accepts her commands without question, just as La Poncia follows Bernarda's directives without evident hesitation. Going down the line, La Criada, sees herself as well above the beggar woman. Her tone, too, changes when she speaks with La Mendiga. Immediately, then, there is evident a descending scale of society which Lorca points to with poignant irony in this preliminary episode. And the very cruelty of which La Poncia and La Criada complain is reflected in their actions toward those placed below them by circumstance and further denied equality by an artificial code of society.

As La Mendiga departs, La Criada's thoughts return to her own problems and her soliloquizing turns to sharp denunciations of the wealthy. These first shouts of rebellion, however, becomes hysterical sobs which reveal her love for the deceased husband, Antonio Maria Benavides; apparently it was not a one-sided affair.

"You won't be able to lift my skirts behind the doors of your corral anymore! Oh, Antonio Maria Benavides, you'll no longer see these walls. . . . I'm the one who loved you most of all your servants."

Pulling her hair and screaming, La Criada behaves in a manner opposite to the image of the austere household presented a few moments before. Her words imply the irony that is always present in Lorca's theatre. But her actions are not out of place because Lorca is stating that besides the black and white facade of Bernarda's grotto exists this other life filled with feelings. As the play develops, these "outside" emotions enter into the hearts of the daughters, invading Bernarda's self-imposed privacy. Thus, the cause for the conflict.

La Criada's tantrum occurs during the entrance of the mourners. She continues until Bernarda and her daughters appear, her mistress ordering her departure as if she were the lowest animal:

> "Get out. This isn't your place. The poor are like animals; they seem to be made of another substance."

La Criada retreats from the room crowded solely by women. The men have been kept outside the house, in the yard, as if to preserve the virginity of the house. The dialogue which follows is forced and unnatural with embarrassed pauses. Magdalena, who as La Poncia commented is the only one who really loved her father, sits apart in tears. In contrast, Bernarda's face shows no trace of sorrow; her chair is like a throne from which she surveys everyone with suspicious eyes. In her hand, a cane—symbol of matriarchal supremacy. She condemns the women's conversation unhesitantly, ignores their muttered remarks and begins a litany which forces the women to participate. As the prayer ends, the mourners begin to file out with the proper words to the unappreciative Bernarda. When they are gone, her maledictions echo in the room. Then, unsparingly, Bernarda decrees the sentence which will be the physical cause of the play's complications:

> "During the eight years of mourning the wind from the street won't enter this house. We'll pretend that the windows and doors are walled up with bricks. That's what we did in the houses of my father and grandfather."

The daughters listen without emotion, but the weight of Bernarda's words is felt by them in the most secret recesses of their hearts. Magdalena, who is thirty years old, expresses what is in all their minds: "I know I won't get married. . . . Cursed be all women."

The scene is in flux as Adela exits, the daughters prepare for their imprisonment and La Criada re-enters as Bernarda's name is spoken beyond the room. The voice is that of Maria Josefa, Bernarda's eighty year old mother who, like the daughters, is a prisoner in the house. In this case, however, it is her madness which prevents her freedom. In Bernarda's orders to La Criada for the care of Maria Josefa, it becomes evident once more that the tyrannical woman is not concerned with her mother's welfare but with preventing the neighbors from seeing that a madwoman lives in their house. Principally, and this is observable throughout the drama, Bernarda is moved to action only by a fanatical dedication to human respect and its demands—the basis of honor. But ironically, it is this adherence which has made her the topic of the town's gossip and the object of its hatred. Though Bernarda realizes fully that she is attacked daily, she refuses to abdicate her role of moralist because she considers her family better than any other in the village. It is this false pride which clouds her understanding and makes her insist on an aristocratic withdrawal from the life of the community. Therefore, it is paradoxical that in adopting the code of life typical of the society in which she lives, Bernarda has in fact divorced herself and her family from that very group.

Adela, the youngest of the daughters, returning, answers Bernarda's query for Angustias, the eldest. She points to the courtyard, anxious to reveal that her sister has been watching the men there and listening to their conversation. When Angustias enters in answer to Bernarda's call, she receives a cruel slap. La Poncia holds Bernarda until all the daughters have retreated and tells her the details of the men's story:

> "They were talking of Paca la Roseta. Last night they tied her husband to a rack and rode off with her on the horse's rump. . . . She didn't care. They say that her breasts were exposed and that Maximiliano held her as if he were playing a guitar. . . . They returned at dawn."

Both Bernarda and La Poncia act outwardly shocked by the events and by the fact that Angustias heard the men discussing the affair, but neither hesitates in the re-telling of the story. Each has received some satisfaction from it—for Bernarda, the satisfaction of meandering into the indecent side of life and not being tainted; for La Poncia, the pleasure in adopting, if only temporarily and hypocritically, Bernarda's attitude.

Continuing the development of Bernarda's one-sided character, Lorca leads the dialogue into La Poncia's justification of Angustias' actions. This allows Bernarda's reply to her daughters' marriage possibilities:

> "There's no one for a hundred leagues around who's worthy of being close to them. The men here are not in their class. Is it that you want me to turn them over to any laborer?"

The death of her husband has no doubt changed Bernarda into a more suspicious woman than before; no longer trusting even La Poncia in whom she had often confided, she swiftly destroys their relationship with words which stab the servant. La Poncia is silenced by orders to put away all the clothing of the deceased man—nothing is to be given to anyone. Her selfishness extends even to that extreme. They leave to attend to the details.

Two of the daughters, Amelia and Martirio, come into the room upon Bernarda's departure. In these two can be observed the subtle approach which Lorca employed in underlining the drama's intent. Through their names he conveys the individual: Amelia's is derived from the Arabic word meaning "a district governed by a chieftain," Martirio's is the equivalent of "suffering." Similarly, Amelia is controlled by Bernarda while Martirio, though only twenty-four, is accursed by being the homeliest and only deformed offspring. Because of her condition she adopts an attitude like that of a martyr.

Tired and discontented, they discuss the opposite lot of

one of their friends whose marriage to an extremely jealous man has broken her spirit until she is now forced by him to remain at home. Were not her name Adelaida, Yerma would be a proper comparison. Amelia is confused by their friend's unhappiness:

"Nowadays one doesn't know if it's better to have a lover or not. . . . it's always the fault of this criticism which doesn't let us live."

Martirio concurs, but there is a notion in her words of submission rather than of conviction. Her hatred of men is not real, but a matter of hurt pride as her own hopes of marriage were shattered when her lover had deserted her for a wealthier, and less attractive, woman. The incident has marked her thoughts and twisted whatever hope there had been inwardly into the diffusion of a tormented mind. Now, she lives in her state of martyrdom, grasping at all its innuendos, in a posture of self-abasement.

A third sister, Magdalena, joins Martirio and Amelia. She, too, shows a disinterest in life because she has faced the futility of their lives for the next eight years. Her attitude is promptly spotted by her lack of concern over an untied shoelace. No one who matters, she says, will see it, and, if she happens to trip on it while on the stairs, there will be one less to suffer the silent agonies of their stunted existence. Though Martirio listens with comparative feelings, Amelia is less reconciled. Her hope is bolstered upon Angustias' entrance for, as Magdalena discloses, the oldest sister is to be wed to Pepe el Romano. Behind the declaration, however, lies the hidden irony which Lorca interjects so frequently. It is that neither Martirio nor Amelia knew of their sister's match while all the town's women gossiped freely about it. Magdalena, however, is affected by the ridiculousness of the affair because of the difference in ages: Pepe is twenty-five while Angustias has passed her thirty-ninth birthday. It is obvious that he will marry her for the large fortune which Bernarda's husband, her foster father, left to Angustias. Magdalena presses her point:

"The normal thing would be for him to court you, Amelia, or our Adela, who's twenty; not to come looking for the darkest thing in this house, for a woman who speaks through her nose like her father."

But Magdalena has gone over the name of Martirio in naming the other choices Pepe could have made. Martirio, silent and brooding, again becomes the uncomplaining martyr.

When Adela enters, brightly dressed in green, the sudden color contrasts effectively with the drabness of the stage. Her youth and vigor, aspects of her undaunted spirit, are well apart from the tired and haggard expressions on her sisters. With her enter laughter and warmth. But true to the pattern which demands the continuous destruction of high-spiritedness, Adela's smile is quickly dissolved in the opposition to her sister's marriage. In a fit of temper she lashes out at the unnatural turn which their lives have taken:

"I won't get used to it. I can't be locked in. . . . I don't want to lose my fairness in these rooms. . . . I want to get out!"

Magdalena, fearful that her rebellious shouts will bring Bernarda, silences Adela. La Criada enters instead to announce that Pepe is outside the house. All but Adela rush out of the room with the curiosity of children. La Criada approaches Adela, comforting her with the assurance that Pepe will best be seen from her own window. As La Criada exits, Adela hesitates in following her hint. But the temptation of seeing Pepe from the privacy of her room overcomes her and she, too, runs out. Her reactions to his name are leading but, as yet, undefined.

The room is empty for a moment until Bernarda and La Poncia return. Their conversation clarifies Angustias' inheritance from her foster father as being much greater than the amount left to the other daughters. Consequently, only she will have a dowry sufficient for their status. The irony that the foster daughter received the legacy points out the twisted bonds that exist in the family, bonds that made such an unnatural bequest possible. Bernarda is greatly discontented and her anger finds a target in Augustias when she enters wearing makeup, in defiance of her orders. Coldly, Augustias disclaims kinship with the dead man and therefore with the necessity of her mourning. His generosity to her cannot overcome her bitterness. The others enter, their spirits buoyed by the sight of Pepe. But Bernarda, now at the peak of indignation, crushes them again:

"Don't have any illusions that you can cope with me. Until I leave this house feet first, I'll be in charge of my own affairs and yours!"

As Bernarda's cane hits the floor in a rhythm of anger, shouts are heard in the courtyard. Maria Josefa runs into the room, demanding her mantilla and pearls, and prophecies that none of the daughters will ever marry. She, however, wants to marry:

" . . . I want to marry a handsome male from the seashore. . . . I don't want to see these unmarried women longing for their wedding as their hearts turn to dust."

Upon Bernarda's direction, the daughters reluctantly help La Criada in returning the madwoman to her room. As she is taken out, her screams of pleading are lost and the act ends.

Maria Josefa's brief appearance towards the end of the first act is significant in that it serves several purposes: first, it emphasizes Bernarda's iron rule and depicts the extent of this tyranny; second, it is symbolic of the decay to which the daughters will fall if Bernarda is allowed to continue her oppression. Maria Josefa is not of minor importance as her relatively few entrances might suggest; she is an impressive symbol of the future. As such she voices all the fears and desires which the younger women feel but are afraid to disclose in the presence of Bernarda. Her shouts are their innermost secrets. Further, her escape from the guarded room and her subsequent re-incarceration are previews of what will occur later in the drama.

Act two is set in the same white room. Only Adela is missing from the artificial picture of the daughters and La Poncia sewing for Angustias' wedding. La Poncia has noticed Adela's changed attitude; her laughter and gayety have turned to sadness:

> "Something's wrong with her. I find her restless, trembling, afraid, as if she had a lizard between her breasts."

The concern which had shown itself in Adela's face earlier has become a physical reaction to the proposed marriage. But the reason for her behavior, though it may be guessed, remains uncertain. However, Adela is not the only one affected. Jealousy conquers her sisters' conversation with Augustias. The latter continues to sew with the satisfaction of the promised release from the stiflng atmosphere of the household. The talk, always disguised with hatred, turns to Pepe's courtship of Augustias and when she acquiesces to the fact that he left her window at one-thirty that morning, La Poncia adds quickly: "But I heard him leave around four. . . . I'm certain." The moment of suspicion is marked by a pause. But La Poncia senses the tension and continues talking about the courtship, finally recalling her own days. The women laugh at the sensual story, and Amelia runs to the door to see if Bernarda can overhear these revelations of the mysteries of love. La Poncia continues, the women listening as if it were a forbidden story.

As Magdalena exits to look for Adela, the others diagnose the youngest sister's strange actions. Martirio, who sleeps in the room next to Adela's hints cruelly at the reason without saying what she is thinking. Angustias, too, has noticed the change but attributes it to jealousy over her marriage plans:

> "Envy is gnawing at her. . . . I can see it in her eyes. She's starting to look like a crazy woman."

Martirio prevents further evocation of the forbidden word—madness. Not that the word is to be excluded out of charity for Maria Josefa; it is a selfish fear that the word will soon describe them which prompts Martirio's objection. She is afraid, recalling that things repeat themselves, as in the story of Adelaida whose mother and grandmother married the same man. The madness which resulted from the union troubles Martirio. She fears the idea of repetition. In her own family she sees the demented state of Maria Josefa and the growing fanaticism of Bernarda. Her own deformity adds to her worries.

When Magdalena returns with Adela, Martirio's gaze falls coldly on her younger sister. And, after the others have left in answer to Bernarda's call, the two face each other. Nervous with an unrevealed guilt which it is obvious Martirio knows, Adela retreats from her. Until Martirio is out of the room, Adela does not speak to La Poncia. Only then, seeing in the servant a friendly person, Adela unburdens herself:

> "She follows me everywhere. Sometimes she looks into my room to see if I'm asleep. She won't let me breathe. And always: 'What a poor body, not meant for any man!' "

Martirio's torture of Adela masquerades as kindliness, but the recipient of her "false charity" knows better. To La Poncia, however, her actions remain sisterly. Yet, Martirio's words cut deeply into Adela whose youthful passion receives constant frustration everytime Martirio reminds her of their imprisonment. Noting Adela's independence and afraid that it will disrupt her life, La Poncia confronts her with the evidence hinted at by Martirio:

> "Why did you stand by your open window nearly naked with the light on as Pepe passed on the second day he came to speak with your sister?"

Adela's denial is not enough to hide her shame. Her tears soften La Poncia who tries to calm the despair with a calculating logic:

". . . who says you can't marry him? Your sister Angustias is a sick woman. She won't survive the first birth. Then, Pepe will do what all the widowers do around these parts: he'll marry the youngest, the most beautiful, and that's you."

But Adela is unwilling to wait in order to have Pepe. She shouts at La Poncia for meddling. No longer afraid of her, her last obstacle is Bernarda herself:

". . . I would leap over my mother to extinguish this fire that breaks out through my legs and mouth. . . . Looking into his eyes, I feel as if I'm slowly drinking his blood."

Her words give the feeling that even Bernarda will be eliminated from the path of her consuming passion for Pepe.

The re-entry of Angustias and the others halts the manifested emotions. Instantly, however, the conflict between Adela and Martirio is resumed in sarcastic comments. But it is not allowed to develop. Distant bells proclaim the return of the reapers from the fields and La Poncia explains that the previous day many young men arrived from the mountains for the harvest. In contrast with the somberness of the daughters' life, these men have the carefree manners of rovers, taking their pleasure wherever they find it:

"A woman dressed in sequins came last night. . . . and fifteen of them made arrangements to take her to the olive grove."

The women listen with outward disapproval, but their eyes mock their words. The freedom of the men, so foreign to their own condition, torments all of them. The emphasis is on this difference as a chorus of male voices sings while passing the house. Only Amelia and Martirio remain in the room. The others run to watch the men.

Martirio sits in the small chair with her head in her hands. Her excuse is vague and Amelia cannot fathom the trouble. Except by the inference in her speech, not understood by Amelia, Martirio's words seem natural. Her problem, she claims, arises from a lack of sleep as her nights have been interrupted by strange sounds in the barn. Innocently, Amelia suggests it might be an untamed mule. The suggestion is favored by Martirio whose twisted mind interprets it as the figure of her sister, Adela. But the double entendre escapes Amelia. The devious words have been impregnated with pauses; silences give added weight to Martirio's sly accusations. Now, with the frantic entrance of Angustias, a new occurrence again heightens the scene. The missing picture of Pepe, which Angustias kept under her pillow, creates new tenseness. Both Martirio and Amelia disclaim having taken the picture, and, when Adela appears, all eyes turn accusingly on her. Adela and Martirio stare at each other, the hatred now plainly seen. The clamor of excitement reaches Bernarda's ears; she orders La Poncia to search the rooms and, until her return a few moments later, only Angustias and Bernarda speak.

Upon La Poncia's return, however, the mystery is clarified. In her hand she carries the picture, discovered underneath the covers of Martirio's bed. And Martirio, discovered in her frustration, finally shows the side of her character which had been hidden by the aura of martyrdom. Her jealousy is directed at Angustias; her hatred towards Adela; her defiance against Bernarda's authority. The scene becomes a marketplace of insults until Bernarda orders all to leave. The suspicions which Martirio had aroused earlier by her remarks have been fulfilled, as has the promise of a rivalry between Adela and her over Angustias' fiancee.

Bernarda, however, has not grasped the full implications which the insults have disclosed. Her solution is that Angustias' marriage be hastened so that Pepe will be removed from the area of their thoughts. She fails to recognize the seriousness of Martirio's action, accepting the incident of the photograph as a joke. Likewise, she missed the hatred between Martirio and Adela and their sense of rivalry. Her misconception is pointed out by La Poncia:

"You've always been wise. You've seen the evil in people at a hundred leagues; I often thought you could read thoughts. But one's children are always that. Now you're blind."

But Bernarda, perhaps afraid to face the real implications which have been disclosed because they point to dishonor, refutes La Poncia's stand. Undaunted, La Poncia resorts to a direct attack on her mistress:

"Bernarda, something very grave is happening here. I don't want to blame you, but you haven't allowed your daughters freedom. Martirio is inclined to fall in love. . . . Why didn't you let her marry Enrique Humanas? Why did you send word to him not to come on the very day he was going to her window?"

Martirio is unaware that her lover had deserted her because of Bernarda's pride which could not allow the marriage of a laborer to her daughter. But by attacking Bernarda's pride and honor, La Poncia has left herself open to a countering move:

"I have them because I can afford them. And you don't because you know very well where you came from."

The base origins of La Poncia are always at Bernarda's control when the servant becomes too familiar. Foiled in her attempt to rectify the mismatch by suggesting Adela or Martirio as Pepe's logical mate, La Poncia slyly returns to the incident of Pepe's late visit to the house. Angustias denies the fact corroborated by Martirio; her entrance is punctual, as if she had overheard the entire conversation:

"For more than a week, Pepe has been leaving at one. May God kill me if I lie. . . . I speak to him through my bedroom window."

But Martirio insists that Pepe has been at another window. Bernarda begins to realize that one of her daughters is seeing Pepe dishonorably. La Poncia, without naming any of them, foments her thoughts. Adela, who entered during the conversation, attacks La Poncia as an agitator. Bernarda is already convinced that La Poncia has little loyalty and discharges her words as rumors:

> "I was born to have open eyes. Now I will keep guard without closing them until I die. . . . And you watch over your own affairs."

La Criada interrupts to announce a commotion in the street. As all the neighbors are at their doors, Bernarda sends La Poncia to report. The women rush to the windows, but Bernarda herds them into the courtyard. Only Martirio and Adela have remained inside, facing each other with disdain. Their brief meeting unmasks their true feelings. Martirio threatens to destroy Adela before she will allow her to continue with Pepe; at first indifferent, Adela then pleads with Martirio not to destroy the love which exists between them. But the jealousy within her has drowned all sisterly feelings, and Martirio remains the enemy.

La Poncia and Bernarda return. Speaking of the commotion, La Poncia tells of the adulterous woman who is being stoned by the populace for having murdered her illegitimate child. Bernarda, true to the stunted code of honor, rushes out of the room demanding the death of the impure woman. Her daughters follow. But Adela, horrified by their savagery, tries to prevent their participation. As they leave, Adela remains in the room holding her womb, terrified at her own fate if Bernarda should uncover her sin. In the accused woman Adela sees herself. The curtain on the second act descends as the roar in the street grows.

The final moments of the act are the climax of the increased tension which had been built on the accusations and suspicions of La Poncia, Martirio and Angustias. The logical end would have been to castigate Adela, but Bernarda's attitude towards honor did not allow the conclusion that her house was tainted. Yet the strong passions created by the conflict had to be expended. The incident of the adulterous woman allowed this release in an effective manner. By creating an identification of Adela with the woman, Lorca allows the entire aspect of her affair with Pepe to be crystallized. In the climactic moment of the act when Adela holds her womb, the reality of the accusations becomes certain. Bernarda and her daughters' participation in the unjust stoning serves as a temporary release; however, the most important moment lies in Adela's realization of what her fate will be when Bernarda is forced to face the truth as promised by Martirio. Confronted by that evidence which Adela carries within her womb, Bernarda's code will dictate, she fears, a sentence of death. But what Adela does not realize, and never will, is that Bernarda cannot react equally to a similar situation in her house. Though her code is unflinchingly applied to those outside her house, Bernarda detests the thought of scandal and would not allow the notice of her daughter's fornication to be known. Adela's failure to understand this aspect of Bernarda's character has its tragic conclusion in the final act.

The third stanza of the play has a changed setting—the patio of the house. The walls are again white, but with a slight shading of blue in the pigment. The light of the inner rooms favors the darkness of the patio with a subtle glow. In it are Bernarda, her daughters, and a visitor, Prudencia. The latter sits somewhat apart from the dinner table shared by the women. The silence is intermittently broken by the noise of silverware and plates. La Poncia serves them. As the dinner ends, Prudencia starts to leave but Bernarda detains her in her eagerness to converse with someone other than her family and servants. Their talk is directed elsewhere than they intended, however, when a breeding stallion corraled next to the house begins to pound the wall with his hooves. The horse, in heat, continues to be uneasy, and Bernarda commands an unseen groom to let it roll in the straw.

The introduction of the stallion into the drama is significant because it continues a tradition very evident in Lorca's poetry and drama. The horse is an outstanding symbol used by the playwright primarily to embody man's hurtling journey through life into death. It is thus used in *Bodas de sangre, Mariana Pineda, El amor de don Perlimplin,* and as the symbol of an ideal in *La Zapatera Prodigiosa.* However, in *La casa de Bernarda Alba* Lorca employs the horse as a more definite, if less somber, tool by making it embody the bridled passions which torment Bernarda's daughters. Because the horse is prevented from mating, he tries to break down the walls of his corral; similarly, the women, prevented from fulfilling their natural desires to be married, try to break out of their prison. The symbol is clear and obvious. But its second purpose, the ironic, is not as evident. The stallion will have satisfaction in the morning while its human counterparts, particularly Adela, cannot expect such consideration.

Angustia's marriage plans occupy Bernarda and Prudencia briefly, after which, at the sound of church bells, the visitor departs. The dinner completed, Adela's exit is followed by Martirio's. Amelia also leaves while Magdalena chooses to sit apart. Bernarda and Angustias speak softly, intimately, of Pepe; the daughter's words reveal an apprehension not without basis. But Bernarda, in her most motherly attitude to the moment, consoles and advises her. The words are unlike any she had spoken previously. They are free of venom or suspicion and dedicated solely to her daughter's benefit. Magdalena, who has fallen asleep during the conversation, can not hear these nor can any of the others because they are words meant only for a marriageable daughter.

Thus, the episode is marked by the exit of the daughters at its start and by their re-appearance at its conclusion. The pleasant mood is continued as Adela is involved with the beauty of the stars, but it begins to deteriorate as Martirio's still bitter offerings slowly bring back the reality of the previous act. Cynically, she begins to rebuff Adela's mood. Angustias retires since Pepe told her he would not come that evening; the others follow her example, but Martirio leaves less quickly, her eyes on the corral door and its surrounding shadows as if she expected to see something. Bernarda, sitting like a bastion, derides La Poncia's prediction of danger:

"Enjoying this silence and not finding that 'something very grave' that is supposed to be taking place. My watchfulness is too strong. . . . There's nothing wrong here. I'm alert against your suppositions. . . . Tonight I'm going to sleep well."

As La Criada enters, Bernarda retires in her smugness. But La Poncia senses that trouble will come of the affair between Adela and Pepe. Her words have a feeling of urgency:

"Adela has made up her mind to what is necessary and the rest watch continuously. . . . (Martirio) is the worst. She's a pool of poison. She sees that El Romano is not to be hers and she would sink the world if it were in her power. . . . In such affairs even blood ties are forgotten."

La Poncia, awake to every possible sound because of her premonition, rises from her chair and looks intently into the shadows when dogs begin to bark. At the same moment, Adela re-appears in the patio in her white petticoat. La Poncia looks at her suspiciously but the girl merely takes a drink of water and goes back to her room. As the dogs continue to bark, the servants also retire.

In the next moments the stage is empty; the setting is almost in complete darkness. After a while a figure appears in the doorway, but it is only Maria Josefa who enters the patio. In her arms she tenderly bears a small lamb which she treats as a child. To it she sings a lullaby whose verse ridicules Bernarda and her daughters:

"Bernarda,
face of a leopard.
Magdalena,
face of a hyena."

After her song, she fades into the shadows. Another figure, this time that of Adela, takes her place. She cautiously enters the courtyard and then runs into the barn. Her exodus is followed by Martirio who now pauses nervously. She, too, is dressed only in her petticoat. She waits, as if expecting something to happen whereby to discredit Adela, whom she knows has gone to meet Pepe. However, before Martirio can follow Adela, Maria Josefa emerges from the shadows. The lamb still in her arms, she asks Martirio to open the gate. Maria Josefa wants to go to the sea in search of her lover and, therefore, happiness. And this is an interesting symbol.

Though the sea seldom appears in Lorca's plays except as a casual mention, it has been an important aspect of nature to the man. In the reality of his life the sea had a great attraction and he held most precious his visits to such idyllic places as Cap de Creus in Gerona:

> "Ana Maria, I would like at this moment to hear the sounds of the chains of all the ships which weigh anchor on all the seas, but the roar of the sea makes it impossible. . . . How often I've recalled that real threat of shipwreck we had at Cap de Creus! . . . That is my sea, Ana Maria."[6]

He had "discovered" the northern Mediterranean waters in the company of Ana Maria Dali and her brother, Salvador. Later, in search of those happy memories, he returned to the sea. This time it was that of Malaga, the southern port, which renewed his vigor:

> "I've worked hard, but I had an enormous anxiety to be by the sea. Later, I went and was completely cured. I can say that Malaga has given me life. . . . Tell me of all that occurs in Cadaques and how the sea is."[7]

Thus, the sea is an important, if seldom reflected, influence on Lorca. The most generous evidence of this is in this occasion where Maria Josefa attempts to reach the sea. Both in the reality of Lorca's life, then, and in the kaleidoscopic world of *La casa de Bernarda Alba*, the sea becomes a source of life,

---

6. *Obras Completas, op. cit.*, p. 1580; letter to Ana Maria Dali (not dated).
7. *Ibid.*

of symbolic rebirth, and the passage-way to a freedom from
the encumbrances of society. Such are the implications in
the old woman's desire to journey to the sea. There, away
from the oppression of Bernarda's household she can find a
new youth in the spray of the waves. But her hope is frustrated by Martirio who succeeds in locking the grandmother
in the house.

Martirio pauses in the shadows, taking up her interrupted
watch over the door through which Adela had fled. Then, she
calls to her sister. Adela, her hair dishevelled and her petticoat colored by the yellow straw, faces her sister defiantly.
The two women argue vehemently over Pepe until Martirio's
confession of love for him. Adela tries to console her, but the
pitiful woman is beyond such sisterly acts. She is consumed
by a hatred engendered by the union of Pepe and Adela:

> "My blood is no longer yours. Although I would like to
> see you as my sister, I can only see you as a woman. My
> heart is so full of an evil force that, without desiring it,
> it chokes even me."

And Adela, unable to soften Martirio's hatred, becomes the
woman her sister has chosen to create, devoid of any blood-
ties, and willing to desert her family for an illicit union with
Pepe. Even his marriage to Angustias would not prevent her
chosen life. But Martirio bars her return to the tryst. In the
struggle that ensues, Bernarda answers Martirio's screams.
She faces Adela. Both women know the truth now and pre-
tence is put aside. Confronted by the reason which has driven
her to seek dishonor, Adela is transformed into a heroine
fighting boldly, if hopelessly, for her cause. The straw which
adorns her petticoat points to her disgrace, but nonetheless
she faces Bernarda resolutely. Flaunting her authority, Adela
breaks the cane which had been Bernarda's emblem. As the
others enter, Adela reveals her actions to them. Hearing the
confession, Bernarda rushes out to kill Pepe with a rifle. Martirio accompanies her. A few moments later, a shot is heard.

Bernarda and her daughter re-enter, triumphantly declaring that Pepe is dead. Adela rushes to her room madly, unable to hear Martirio's revelation that Pepe had really fled on his horse. The combined cruelty of Bernarda and Martirio led them to lie to Adela. A noise is heard inside the room into which Adela fled. Bernarda pauses and then begins to pound on the door. The noise awakens the neighbors, La Poncia explains, but Bernarda continues. Then, where Bernarda had failed to open the door, La Poncia pushes through into the room. Her horrified scream startles everyone. The sight of Adela's body, self-sacrificed to love by hanging, stuns Bernarda. But her state is momentary. Recovering, she orders the servants to take her down in a gesture to the decadent society that governs their lives:

"Take her down! My daughter has died a virgin! Take her to her room and dress her like a virgin. Let no one say anything! She has died a virgin. . . . The youngest daughter of Bernarda Alba has died a virgin!"

Martirio listens, but she thinks only of Adela's happiness in having had Pepe to fulfill her as a woman. The weeping continues as Bernarda orders a sincere mourning for Adela, a final bow to convention. The play ends with her order for silence.

As do most of Lorca's other plays, *La casa de Bernarda Alba* contains a plot built upon the evocation of Fate and the exploration of intricate human patterns. As elements, these are present in varying proportions making the characters proceed through the maze of life, tortuously into a complex of behavior, and finally to death. Fate has always at her disposal, as here, dependable allies such as jealousy, human respect, tyranny, hatred, and even love. These are the artifacts which Fate allows human hands to toy with, to use experimentally, to use toxically. With unswerving sureness, the result is death—be it spiritual, as it is for Martirio and her sisters, or physical, as it is for Adela. The momentum of Fate carries these characters along until they can no longer control their lives. Fate ordains that life continue along its traditional paths, says Lorca, and those who try to destroy or abandon the system achieve only their own extinction. Lorca's final comment in the theatre arrived on the eve of the Spanish Civil War and will always stand as an imposing prefix to a struggle which tried to remedy the social-political mores of a nation.

CONCLUSION

XII. A SUMMATION OF LORCA'S THEATRE

THEMATICALLY, Garcia Lorca's theatre revolves on a single axis: *the preservation of Honor leads to the frustration of love, hence, of life itself; this frustration, in turn, becomes a despair which leads to Death.* This is always the major theme, the premise which serves as a point of departure for many variations. Starting there, he develops richly colored situations and populates them with strong central characters, personages who live passionate lives whether their emotions find expression or are repressed. However they react, they are primarily pawns of Fate, for it is this dark force which governs the entire premise. The theme, with Fate as its primary cause, represents the nucleus of Lorca's drama.

The first definable element of the theme is Honor. As Lorca sees it, it is a traditional code based on law, superstition and religion which orders a strict interpretation of Spanish life. Though originally the code served the desires of society for betterment, its gradual twisting by taboos and pharasaical dominance has made it an instrument of oppression. Because Fate so decrees, however, it is an instrument of self-torture rather than a weapon in another's hand. Thus, Lorca's characters are their own enemies. Prevented by this gnarled idea of the preservation of Honor, his creations fail to live "normally." Bernarda Alba deprives herself of her daughters' love by her tyrannical hold over them, of the respect of her servants by her vicious pride, and of her own happiness by her unnatural attitude. Mariana Pineda sacrifices herself for Honor, choosing death rather than the mercy of Pedrosa to pass on an unsoiled name to her children. La Novia in *Bodas de sangre* tries to expurgate her social "sin" by confessing that she has remained virginal in observance of Honor, yet two men died upholding the honor of their names. Likewise, Adela, in *La casa de Bernarda Alba*, commits suicide after breaking the code and in rebellion from Bernarda's cruelty. Yerma prefers her mental torture to a dishonorable solution, while Don Perlimplin kills himself to teach Belisa the honorable meaning of love and to maintain the honor of his life. And El Joven in *Asi que pasen cinco años* wastes away and finally dies for having been honorable enough to wait upon the fickle wishes of his sweetheart. Even Cristobita, the wicked old man of the puppet plays, fits into this pattern of self-sacrifice for the sake of Honor as he dies in defense of his name and his wife's virtue. Therefore, the instigating force behind every one of Lorca's plays is Honor. His central characters all live, react and die in the shadow of the burdensome code.

But this is only an aspect of his drama to be balanced, if somewhat precariously, by those characters who live beyond the reach of the code. At least, their existence is not governed as strictly as is that of the principals. They are the common people, or the peasant and laboring classes, who are not held in check by the falseness of middle-class morality. In this fold are included the servant-women, the beggars, the townspeople and other assorted types who venture in and out of the plays with regularity. These are individuals who are close to the earth and who act according to the basic instincts of humanity rather than under the influence of artificial codes. Laughing is possible for them, in spite of their social disadvantages, because they are free of such encumbrances. As a result, these people survive while the principals become the victims of their own code. Honor, therefore, cannot survive in its misshapen form, nor can that society which adheres to a blind dedication to it. This is an important phase of the Lorquian theme.

Lorca connects the preservation of Honor with the frustration of love by making the latter result entirely from the former. Hence, Honor represses love. And this process is activated primarily through another important element in the dramas—Time. It is only through the lapse of time that the code of Honor becomes more and more excruciating. Time always has an undeniable role, one that serves to point out and emphasize the torment of frustration within the charac-

ters of respective plays. It, therefore, fits into the pattern of
plot development as a catalytic agent.

In *El maleficio de la mariposa*, Time heals the wounds
of the butterfly who flies into her realm beyond the tall grass;
Time is the agency for her lover's frustration because with
Time has gone his hope. Likewise, in *Doña Rosita la soltera*,
Rosita is forced by Time, which has destroyed her hopes, to
retire into a life without meaning. Time, also, will certainly
bring the physical counterpart of her spiritual death. Yerma,
particularly, suffers in the passing of the years because each
one that elapses certifies further the barrenness of her life
and the loss of hope. The echoes of Time are less obvious in
Mariana Pineda, but they are present throughout in the anxiety of waiting and in particular in the final scenes where
the heroine's hopes hang on the thread of her lover's attempt
to save her. But the short hours allotted her soon disappear
and she is led to her death. In *La casa de Bernarda Alba*,
Time is made an important aspect of the frustration of Bernarda's daughters by the mother's pronouncement that eight
years of strict mourning must be observed before they can
resume their normal lives. This bleak outlook actually forces
the complications that lead to open conflict and eventually
to death. One of the most poignant examples of Lorca's concern with the catalyst, of course, is seen in *Asi que pasen
cinco años*. There, Lorca treats Time as a theoretical and
mysterious value whose certainty cannot be impeached but
whose integrity can be questioned.

With the aid of Time, the element of frustration appears
in some aspect in all of Lorca's drama. From the simple and
direct statement in *El maleficio de la mariposa*, it follows a
line that rises climactically through the succeeding plays until the pinnacle is reached in the tragic trilogy—*Bodas de
sangre, Yerma*, and *La casa de Bernarda Alba*. It is Lorca's
consistency in the treatment of frustration that serves to
unite his theatre in spite of the diversification of situation. All

⌐the plays contain a connection with this umbilical cord: *Mariana Pineda* and *Doña Rosita la soltera* deal with abandonment and sacrifice; *El maleficio de la mariposa* is the original treatment on disillusionment; *Asi que pasen cinco años* is an exact study of despair; *Bodas de sangre* is the picture of remorse and defeat; *La casa de Bernarda Alba* is a view of hopelessness expressed through suicide; *Yerma* is the most striking presentation of maternal and sexual repression; *El amor de don Perlimplin* is the exploration of the love sacrifice. Even *La Zapatera Prodigiosa*, the play most apart from the central thematic control which Lorca created, possesses this one unifying factor. All have in common the element of frustration.

The last phase of the primary theme is the topic of Death. This frustration of love, of life itself, leads unequivocally to Death. The path is inevitable in the context of life as Lorca sees it. Death, through its infallible presence, adds the intrigue that permeates the plots. And yet, it is not always the horrible and bloody Death of *Bodas de sangre, Yerma* and *La casa de Bernarda Alba*. It is often otherwise: heroic, as in *Mariana Pineda;* poetic, as in *El maleficio de la mariposa* and *El amor de don Perlimplin;* ridiculous, as in the puppet plays; pathetic, as in *Doña Rosita la soltera;* or nihilistic, as in *Asi que pasen cinco años*. But there is always Death, be it of the principals or of minor characters, as in *La Zapatera Prodigiosa*.

The thematic content of Lorca's theatre, therefore, resolves itself into a pattern. Fate supersedes all action. Honor is a tool, the means through which Fate controls Man. Time provides the stimulus to plot, dissolving illusions that usually maintain human actions on a predictable level. Once Hope is eliminated by Time, the mind becomes frenzied with despair. The subsequent frustration leads directly to the separation of soul and body, by violence or through the spiritual death of the soul by seclusion from life.

HONOR

Name   Tradition   Law

TIME

FRUSTRATION

Love   Instinct   Sex

DEATH

The burden of carrying this thematic heirarchy falls mainly on the female characters. Lorca sees woman as the more tragic figure because of her role as bearer of children, prisoner of tradition, and servant of man. As he views her, Lorca observes the great sorrows which Fate has bestowed upon her existence. Man, however, appears as a passionate creature whose selfishness oppresses woman. He is free to act beyond the rules, ironically the same precepts which strictly govern her life. While she must remain at home obeying his commands, he experiences the freedom of the fields or expresses his natural instincts with another woman or may even choose not to satisfy his wife. These actions or inactions, depicting the unevenness of life under artificial rules, prompted the playwright to adopt the woman's cause and to portray her as the tragic figure reality had made her. Thus, the most memorable of his characters are women. And they can be as cruel as Bernarda Alba without losing this sense of having been betrayed by Fate.

Man's role in Lorca's theatre is, therefore, necessarily less imposing. His most notable participations occur in *El amor de don Perlimplin, Asi que pasen cinco años,* and in the puppet plays. Don Perlimplin is the hero of the tragicomedy as he kills himself in a poetic renunciation of life to teach Belisa the meaning of love. El Joven, in the second play, is the sole participant in his despairing death. While both characters are interesting and well-drawn, neither achieves the proportions which Lorca was able to give such female creations as Yerma, Doña Rosita or Bernarda Alba. Though these male characters, including Leonardo, Juan, El Tio and the others, are well-suited for their respective roles, none of them reach the firmness of purpose or the tragic values of Lorca's women. Leonardo and Juan, respectively, are boldly drawn types whose actions result in the tympanic climaxes of their separate plots. But they exist as subordinates when compared to their women. El Zapatero, too, is principally a foil to La Zapatera, whose actions create the most interest. El Novio in *Bodas de sangre*, El Sobrino in *Doña Rosita la soltera*, Victor in *Yerma* and Don Pedro in *Mariana Pineda* are cast in the same mold—mild, ineffective men whose actions are conditioned more by dictates than by convictions. Thus, El Novio duels with Leonardo after their women make it impossible for them to follow any other action; El Sobrino deserts Doña Rosita when a letter orders his return home and La Tia prevents his following another course; Victor lacks the strength to confront Juan with his love for Yerma; and, Don Pedro flees, leaving Mariana to die after she has obtained his safety.

The other male characters who appear at intervals in Lorca's plays are conceived, generally, as universal types; they are more caricatures than individuals, though El Tio in *Doña Rosita la soltera* and Pedrosa in *Mariana Pineda* fit less well into this category. It is not unusual, therefore, after observing the secondary role of the male in Lorca's theatre, to find that the final male figure, Pepe el Romano in *La casa de Bernarda Alba* never appears. Though there is frequent reference to him and he, like the males in other plays, has a direct influence on the plot, Pepe is never seen. Consistently, then, with Lorca's descending interest in the male of the species as a character, his final drama eliminates all but reference to him.

The attitude of the playwright towards the organization of his ideas in the creation of his drama make the usual concept of "poetry in the theatre" less applicable to Lorca than to any other modern playwright. It applies at all because of his earliest attempts to fuse his poetic talents to the dramatic form. *El maleficio de la mariposa* and *Mariana Pineda* are examples of how the poet learned the craft of the theatre. Both are written entirely in verse. Yet, as their study recognizes, they are dramatically valid pieces. The failure of the first was not due to its poetry, but to its unusual treatment of an even more unusual subject matter. *Mariana Pineda*, on the other hand, was instantly accepted. Yet, it was also in verse. Obviously, then, the plays were being judged, not on their form, but on their content. It is true, nonetheless, that these two plays are the least theatrical in Lorca's repertory. But this is due to the inexperience of the poet as playwright. As the knowledge of the man was amassed by his frequent excursions with "La Barraca," the playwright developed a particular style attuned to the subtleness of life, a poetic drama full of convictions, imagery and music. It became a complete theatre.

The transition period was achieved in his puppet plays. And it is in the two farces which followed, *La Zapatera Prodigiosa* and *El amor de don Perlimplin*, that an innovation in Lorca's dramatic style is most evident. These plays are written almost exclusively in prose. The exceptions are a few songs and recitatives sprinkled throughout with restraint but in sufficient amount to heighten the particular occasions. Lorca's dialogue takes on a new strength of purpose and an overall vigor not previously found in his first two works. The dialogue in these two farces is characterized by a lightness of pacing and an auditory appeal, a combination which has made the plays among the most popular of Lorca's collection. Part of this lies with the playwright's extension as a man of the theatre, part of the reason with his creation of a poetic prose—in imagery, function and general conception—which is based on the language of the people. Enriched by folk tradition, poetic insight and symbolistic content, Lorca's drama stemmed from the basic solution discovered in these farces.

Asi que pasen cinco años is one of the outstanding examples of the power and diversity Lorca's drama could achieve through the mastery of this poetic prose. Though the play's symbolism is complex because of its interdependence, it is never a matter of interfering with the dramatic movement of the drama. Part of its very function is to intensify this movement. The interesting aspects of the play are found in intermeshing values—the erotic tonality of the imagery, the opiumesque atmosphere of the plot, the unresolvable mystery of Time, and the rationalization of despair. All these phases are cleverly interpreted through a language which is vivid and poetic without divorcing itself from life.

The tragic trilogy—*Bodas de sangre, Yerma* and *La casa de Bernarda Alba*—comprises Lorca's greatest achievement in the theatre. The first two works are written mainly in prose, but poetry, in the form of songs, litanies and recitative, enter occasionally into the dialogue. In *Bodas de sangre*, for example, there are large portions of scenes presented in verse: the lullaby scene in the first act, the wedding sequence in the second, and the forest episode in the last. In these scenes, especially, Lorca's dialogue reaches its best level of theatricality through symbolic poetry. This drama marks the playwright's best claim to fame as it contains an excellent balance of the theatrical and the poetical elements that are required for poetic drama.

Yerma, also, makes use of many elements employed in its predecessor, but as it is a very different type of play its effectiveness lies in other directions. Here again are scenes composed primarily in poetry, but the greater portion of the tragedy is in prose. A further example of Lorca's timely use of poetry in his plays is evident in *Yerma*. Though prose sustains the action on a high plane by its veracity and force, it is poetry to which the author resorts when a situation invites more pronounced concentration on dialogue or a more intense expression. *Yerma* is the play most exemplary of Lorca's strategic technique in the use of poetry, song and dance—to reinforce the plot, to underline a conflict, or to contrast with a situation (alienation).

Although it is separate from the trilogy, *Doña Rosita la soltera* was written before *La casa de Bernarda Alba*. It is an important drama not only because of its individual merits, but also because it supplements Lorca's other historical drama, *Mariana Pineda*. Unlike that play, however, the playwright chose to conceive *Doña Rosita* in his well-tested poetic prose. In this way he overcame the private failure which *Mariana Pineda* had come to imply after his maturity. The several songs and the poem of the rose are so well integrated into the plot that the transfer is achieved without interruption or abruptness.

Finally, in *La casa de Bernarda Alba*, there are only two instances where poetry, as such, appears, and these are small interludes: the song of the reapers in the second act, and Maria Josefa's cradle song. Though songs rather than poetry, these ballads are the remains of a once generous sampling of pure poetic content in Lorca's drama. Notwithstanding this, the play remains one of his most poetic pieces. And this results from the mastery of his poetic prose which enabled the playwright to reach a goal he had long sought—a drama free of any pure poetry yet poetic in idea, expression and vision. In this final episode of his theatre, Lorca actually reached a stance opposed to that manifested in his first play. The drama conceived exclusively in poetry had been replaced by a drama created entirely in prose.

The final values of Garcia Lorca's theatre are found in the concept of totality of expression. As Lorca's life clearly shows, the playwright had an intensive background in many of the major art forms—music, painting, poetry, recitation. His early contact with Manuel de Falla had provided the inspiration for greater concentration on his piano studies and on the traditional music of Spain. Friendships with painters such as Salvador Dali, Rafael Barradas, and Miguel Prieto helped to formulate Lorca's outlook as a painter. His interests in poetry were abetted by poets of his and earlier generations: Rafael Alberti, Juan Ramon Jimenez, Gerardo Diego and Pedro Salinas among others. His childhood pastimes of recitation and puppetry were incited in his older life by Gregorio Martinez Sierra, Cipriano Rivas Cherif, Encarnacion Lopez ("La Argentinita") and Margarita Xirgu. Possessing such a diversified standing in the arts, Lorca was extremely aware of his opportunity to create a total theatre based on the marriage of these forms. Such awareness is manifested in the plays themselves: in the light and setting designs, in the direction, in the musical elements, in the effects and in the costuming. But awareness could not be immediate as his judgment was tempered with inexperience. As Lorca overcame this impediment, his theatre began to show his greater skill. Thus, his theatrical prowess can be seen developing as each play is studied in the approximate location within the whole.

The joint adventure, for Lorca's theatre is always that, of music, dance, art and poetry, contributes to a unified theatre of extensive range under the single purpose of his theme. His is a drama of dedication to humanity in which he longs for the freedom of the spirit from the artificial encumbrances of society. Lorca may laugh at the foibles and traditions of such a society, or he may show the human spirit naked at the whipping post of Fate, but his purpose is always the same. His theatre is a vivid interpretation of a codified existence and the evils it has engendered, and it remains as the undying hope his characters could never possess.

BIBLIOGRAPHY

BIBLIOGRAPHY

I. EDITIONS

A. PLAYS

TEN VERSES FROM A COMEDY written in a childhood collaboration with Ostos Gabella.
— **Malvarrosa,** Granada, Nos. 5-6, mimeographed.

EL AMOR DE DON PERLIMPLIN CON BELISA EN SU JARDIN
— García Lorca, Fed. **Obras Completas.** Buenos Aires: Losada, 1938, Vol. I; pp. 141-189.
— García Lorca, Fed. **(Tres Obras).** Buenos Aires: Losada, 1940.
— García Lorca, Fed. **Obras Completas.** Madrid: Aguilar, 1957; pp. 889-928.

ASI QUE PASEN CINCO AÑOS
— **Hora de España:** Valencia, 1937, No. 11; pp. 67-74; contains an excerpt from the play: "Romance del maniquí".
— **Repertorio Americano:** San José, Costa Rica, Dec. 18, 1937 contains excerpt from the play: "Romance del maniquí".
— García Lorca, Fed. **Obras Completas.** Buenos Aires: Losada, 1938, Vol. VI. op. 13-112.
— García Lorca, Fed. **Así que pasen cinco años.** Buenos Aires: Losada, 1948.
— García Lorca, Fed. **Cinco farsas breves, seguidas de Así que pasen cinco años.** Buenos Aires: Losada, 1953.
— García Lorca, Fed. **Obras Completas.** Madrid: Aguilar, 1957; pp. 955-1054.

BODAS DE SANGRE
— García Lorca, Fed. **Bodas de sangre.** Madrid: Cruz y Raya, 1935; 1936.
— García Lorca, Fed. **Bodas de sangre.** Buenos Aires: Teatro del Pueblo, 1936.
— **Revista de las Indias:** Bogotá, 1936, No. 3; pp. 69-79. Third Act only.
— García Lorca, Fed. **Bodas de sangre.** Santiago de Chile: Ed. Moderna, 1937.
— Moncayo, Hugo. **Federico García Lorca.** Quito: Grupo América, 1937. Selections.
— García Lorca, Fed. **Obras Completas.** Buenos Aires: Losada, 1938, Vol. I; pp. 25-140.
— **Grafos:** Havana, 1940, Vol. VII, No. 86.
— García Lorca, Fed. **Obras Completas.** Buenos Aires: Losada, 1944; with **El Amor de Don Perlimplín** and **Retablillo de Don Cristóbal.**
— García Lorca, Fed. **Obras Completas.** Madrid: Aguilar, 1957; pp. 1081-1182.
— García Lorca, Fed. **Bodas de sangre.** Buenos Aires: Losada, 1958.

LA CASA DE BERNARDA ALBA
— García Lorca, Fed. **La casa de Bernarda Alba.** Buenos Aires: Losada, 1945, 1953, 1958.
— García Lorca, Fed. **Obras Completas.** Buenos Aires: Losada, 1946, Vol. VIII.

303

— García Lorca, Fed. **Obras Completas**. Madrid: Aguilar, 1957; pp. 1349-1442.
— García Lorca, Fed. **Antología Poética**. Mexico: Univ. Nacional Autónoma, 1956.

LA DONCELLA, EL MARINERO Y EL ESTUDIANTE
— **Gallo:** Granada, April 1928, Vol. I, No. 2.
— Couffon, Claude. **Petit Theatre**. Paris: Les Lettres Mondiales, 1951.
— **Espiga:** Buenos Aires, 1952-53, Vol. I, No. 2.
— García Lorca, Fed. **Cinco Farsas Breves**. Buenos Aires: Losada, 1953.
— **Anales** — **Organo de la Universidad Central del Ecuador:** Quito, 1954, Vol. LXXXII, No. 337.
— García Lorca, Fed. **Obras Completas**. Madrid: Aguilar, 1957; pp. 806-13.
— García Lorca, Fed. **Tres Farsas**. Mexico: Ed. A. Arauz, 1959.

DOÑA ROSITA LA SOLTERA
— García Lorca, Fed. **Obras Completas**. Buenos Aires: Losada, 1938, Vo.l V; pp. 9-129.
— García Lorca, Fed. **Doña Rosita la soltera**. Buenos Aires: Losada, 1944; with **Mariana Pineda**.
— García Lorca, Fed. **Obras Completas**. Madrid: Aguilar, 1957; pp. 1261-1348.
— García Lorca, Fed. **Doña Rosita**. Buenos Aires: Losada, 1958.

EL MALEFICIO DE LA MARIPOSA
— García Lorca, Fed. **Obras Completas**. Madrid: Aguilar, 1957; pp. 579-631. Latest edition: 1960.

MARIANA PINEDA
— **La Farsa:** Madrid, Rivadeneyra, 1928, Vol. II, No. 52.
— García Lorca, Fed. **Mariana Pineda**. Santiago de Chile: Ed. Moderna, 1928; **Idem**, 1937.
— García Lorca, Fed. **Mariana Pineda**. Buenos Aires: Ed. Argentores, 1937.
— García Lorca, Fed. **Obras Completas**. Buenos Aires: Losada, 1938, Vol. V; pp. 131-252.
— García Lorca, Fed. **Mariana Pineda**. Buenos Aires: Losada, 1944; with **Doña Rosita la soltera**.
— García Lorca, Fed. **Mariana Pineda**. Mexico: Ed. Isla, 1945.
— García Lorca, Fed. **Obras Completas**. Madrid: Aguilar, 1954; pp. 691-801.
— Nadal, R.M. & Perry, Janet H. (ed.). **Mariana Pineda**. Boston: D.C. Heath, 1960; 1st ed. — London; Harrap. 1957.
— García Lorca, Fed. **Mariana Pineda**. Buenos Aires: Losada, 1958.

EL PASEO DE BUSTER KEATON
— **Gallo:** Granada, April 1928, Vol. I, No. 2.
— Couffon, Claude. **Petit Theatre**. Paris: Les Lettres Mondiales, 1951.
— **Espiga:** Buenos Aires, 1952-53, Vol. I, No. 16-17.
— García Lorca, Fed. **Cinco Farsas Breves**. Buenos Aires; Losada, 1953.
— **Anales** — **Organo de la Universidad Central del Ecuador:** Quito, 1954, Vol. LXXXII, No. 337.
— García Lorca, Fed. **Obras Completas**. Madrid: Aguilar, 1957; pp. 803-806.

— García Lorca, Fed. **Tres Farsas.** México: Ed. A. Arauz, 1959.

EL PUBLICO
— Only scenes from the five-act drama are known.
— **Los Cuatro Vientos:** Madrid, 1934, No. 3.
— García Lorca, Fed. **Obras Completas.** Buenos Aires: Losada, 1938. Vol. VI; pp. 113-39.
— García Lorca, Fed. **Obras Completas.** Madrid: Aguilar, 1957; pp. 1055-79.

QUIMERA
— García Lorca, Fed. **Obras Completas.** Buenos Aires: Losada, 1938.
— **Revista Hispánica Moderna:** N.Y., 1940, Vol. VI, Nos. 3-4; pp. 312-13.
— García Lorca, Fed. **Cinco Farsas Breves.** Buenos Aires: Losada, 1953.
— García Lorca, Fed. **Obras Completas.** Madrid: Aguilar, 1957; pp. 813-20.
— García Lorca, Fed. **Tres Farsas.** Mexico: Ed. A. Arauz, 1959.

RETABLILLO DE DON CRISTOBAL
— García Lorca, Fed. **Obras Completas,** Buenos Aires: Losada, 1938, Vol. I; pp. 191-218.
— García Lorca, Fed. **Retablillo de Don Cristóbal.** Buenos Aires: Losada, 1940.
— García Lorca, Fed. **Obras Completas.** Madrid: Aguilar, 1957; pp. 929-953.
— García Lorca, Fed. **Tres Farsas.** Mexico: Ed. A. Arauz, 1959.

LOS SUEÑOS DE MI PRIMA AURELIA
— Inedited work. Act One is in the possession of Lorca's estate.

TITERES DE CACHIPORRA: LA NIÑA QUE RIEGA LA ALBAHACA Y EL PRINCIPE PREGUNTON
— Inedited work, presumed lost, with dialogue adaptation from a traditional folk tale.

TITERES DE CACHIPORRA: TRAGICOMEDIA DE DON CRISTOBAL Y LA SEÑA ROSITA
— García Lorca, Fed. **Obras Completas.** Buenos Aires; Losada, 1940.
— **Raíz:** Madrid, Facultad de Filosofía y Letras, 1949, No. 3.
— García Lorca, Fed. **Cinco Farsas Breves.** Buenos Aires: Losada, 1953.
— García Lorca, Fed. **Tragicomedia de Don Cristóbal.** Buenos Aires: Losange, 1954.
— García Lorca, Fed. **Obras Completas.** Madrid: 1957; pp. 663-690.

YERMA
— García Lorca, Fed. **Yerma.** Buenos Aires: Ed. Anaconda, 1937.
— García Lorca, Fed. **Yerma.** Santiago de Chile: Ed. Moderna, 1937.
— García Lorca, Fed. **Yerma.** Lima: Ed. Latina, 1937; with **Llanto por Ignacio Sánchez Mejías.**
— García Lorca, Fed. **Obras Completas.** Buenos Aires: Losada, 1938, Vol. III; pp. 9-104.
— García Lorca, Fed. **Yerma.** Santiago de Chile: Ed. Iberia, 1939.
— García Lorca, Fed. **Yerma.** Buenos Aires: Losada, 1944, 1946, 1948, 1949.

— García Lorca, Fed. **Obras Completas.** Madrid: Aguilar, 1957; pp. 1183-1260.

LA ZAPATERA PRODIGIOSA
— García Lorca, Fed. **Obras Completas.** Buenos Aires: Losada, 1938, Vol. III; pp. 105-90.
— García Lorca, Fed. **La Zapatera Prodigiosa.** Buenos Aires: Losada, 1948.
— Helman, Edith. (ed.) **La Zapatera Prodigiosa.** N.Y.: W. W. Norton, 1952.
— García Lorca, Fed. **Obras Completas.** Madrid: Aguilar, 1957; pp. 821-888.

B. INTERVIEWS, LECTURES, PROSE

LOS ARTISTAS EN EL AMBIENTE DE NUESTRO TIEMPO
— **El Sol:** Madrid, Dec. 15, 1934. Interview with Alardo Prast.
— García Lorca, Fed. **Obras Completas.** Buenos Aires: Losada, 1938, Vol. VII.
— García Lorca, Fed. **Obras Completas.** Madrid: Aguilar, 1957; pp. 1626-31.

DECLARACIONES DE GARCIA LORCA SOBRE TEATRO
— **Heraldo de Madrid:** Madrid, April 8, 1936. Interview with Felipe Morales.
— García Lorca, Fed. **Obras Completas.** Buenos Aires: Losada, 1938, Vol. VII.
— García Lorca, Fed. **Obras Completas.** Madrid: Aguilar, 1957; pp. 1634-36.

DIALOGOS DE UN CARICATURISTA SALVAJE
— **El Sol:** Madrid, June 10, 1936. Interview with Luis Bagaria.
— García Lorca, Fed. **Obras Completas.** Buenos Aires: Losada, 1938, Vol. VII.
— García Lorca, Fed. **Obras Completas.** Madrid: Aguilar, 1957; pp. 1636-41.

ESTAMPA DE GARCIA LORCA
— **La Gaceta Literaria:** Madrid, Jan. 15, 1931. Interview with Gil Benumeya.
— García Lorca, Fed. **Obras Completas.** Buenos Aires: Losada, 1938, Vol. VII.
— García Lorca, Fed. **Obras Completas.** Madrid: Aguilar, 1957; pp. 1608-10.

FEDERICO GARCIA LORCA Y LA TRAGEDIA
— **Luz:** Madrid, July 3, 1934. Interview with J. Chabas.
— García Lorca, Fed. **Obras Completas.** Buenos Aires: Losada, 1938, Vol. VII.
— García Lorca, Fed. **Obras Completas.** Madrid: Aguilar, 1957; pp. 1622-24.

IMAGINACION, INSPIRACION, EVASION
— **El Defensor:** Granada, Oct. 12, 1928.
— **El Sol:** Madrid, Feb. 14, 1929.
— García Lorca, Fed. **Obras Completas.** Buenos Aires: Losada, 1938, Vol. VII.

— García Lorca, Fed. **Obras Completas.** Madrid: Aguilar, 1957; pp. 1543-1548.

UNA INTERESANTE INICIATIVA
— **El Sol:** Madrid, April 5, 1933.
— García Lorca, Fed. **Obras Completas.** Buenos Aires: Losada, 1938, Vol. VII.
— García Lorca, Fed. **Obras Completas.** Madrid: Aguilar, 1957; pp. 1619-22.

IRE A SANTIAGO
— **Blanco y Negro:** Madrid, March 5, 1933. Interview with L. Méndez Domínguez.
— García Lorca, Fed. **Obras Completas.** Buenos Aires: Losada, 1938, Vol. VII.
— García Lorca, Fed. **Obras Completas.** Madrid: Aguilar, 1957; pp. 1614-18.

MARIANA PINEDA
— **El Defensor:** Granada, May 7, 1929.
— García Lorca, Fed. **Obras Completas.** Buenos Aires: Losada, 1938, Vol. VII.
— García Lorca, Fed. **Obras Completas.** Madrid: Aguilar, 1957; pp. 1553-55.
— **La Nación:** Buenos Aires, Dec. 29, 1933.

EL POETA EN NUEVA YORK
— **El Sol:** Madrid, March 17, 1932.
— García Lorca, Fed. **Obras Completas.** Buenos Aires: Losada, 1938, Vol. VII.
— García Lorca, Fed. **Obras Completas.** Madrid: Aguilar, 1957; pp. 1611-13.

VACACIONES DE "LA BARRACA"
— **Luz:** Madrid, Sept. 3, 1934. Interview with Juan Chabas.
— García Lorca, Fed. **Obras Completas.** Buenos Aires: Losada, 1938, Vol. VII.
— García Lorca, Fed. **Obras Completas.** Madrid: Aguilar, 1957; pp. 1624-26.

LA ZAPATERA PRODIGIOSA
— **La Nación:** Buenos Aires, Nov. 30, 1933.

C. COMPLETE WORKS

FEDERICO GARCIA LORCA: OBRAS COMPLETAS
Prologue and compilation by Guillermo de Torre. (Buenos Aires: Ed. Losada, 1938-1942) 7 vols; Vol. VIII issued separately in 1946.
— Vol. I: "Bodas de Sangre," "El amor de Don Perlimplín," "Retablillo de Don Cristóbal."
— Vol. II: "Libro de Poemas," "Primeras Canciones," "Canciones," "Seis Poemas Galegos."
— Vol. III:: "Yerma," "La Zapatera Prodigiosa."
— Vol. IV: "Romancero Gitano," "Poema del Cante Jondo," "Llanto por Ignacio Sánchez Mejías."
— Vol. V: "Doña Rosita la Soltera," "Mariana Pineda."
— Vol. VI: "Así que pasen cinco años," "Poemas Póstumos."

— Vol. VII: "Poeta en Nueva York," "Conferencias," "Prosas póstumas."
— Vol. VIII: "La Casa de Bernarda Alba."
FEDERICO GARCIA LORCA: OBRAS COMPLETAS
Compilation and notes by Arturo del Hoyo. Prologue by Jorge Guillén. Epilogue by Vicente Aleixandre. (Madrid: Aguilar, 1957) 1971 pp.; 4th Ed.
— This single volume collection contains all the available material written by Lorca. It is the most complete edition of his works and includes: Bibliography, Chronology, Drawings, Music and Biographical materials.

II. ADAPTATIONS

EL AMOR DE DON PERLIMPLIN CON BELISA EN SU JARDIN.
— Don Perlimplín. Opera by Vittorio Rieti. Concert premiere in Chicago, 1952; staged in Paris, 1952.
— Don Perlimplín. Opera by Wolfgang Fortner presented at Schwetzingen Festival, Spring, 1962.
— Roter Mantel. Ballet by Luigi Nono presented in West Berlín, Autum, 1954. Choreography: Tatjana Gsovsky.

ASI QUE PASEN CINCO ANOS
— The Wind Remains. Zarzuela by Paul Bowles based on "Manikin Scene". Premiered in 1943 at New York's Museum of Modern Art. Conducted by Leonard Bernstein. Choreographed by Merce Cunningham. Recorded by MGM in 1957.

BODAS DE SANGRE
— Blood Wedding. Ballet by Denis ApIvor and Alfred Rodríguez. Presented by Sadler's Wells Ballet in London in 1953.
— Bluchozeit. Opera by Wolfgang Fortner. Premiered on June 8, 1957.
— Bodas de sangre. A 1938 Argentinian film with Margarita Xirgú.
— Bodas de sangre. Opera by Juan José Castro. Premiered in Buenos Aires.
— Bodas de sangre. Ballet by Esteban Cerda. Premiered in Buenos Aires.
— Der Wald. Operatic scene by Wolfgang Fortner; presented on radio on June 25, 1953 in Frankfort am Main. Concert premiere: Essen, Dec. 18, 1954.

LA CASA DE BERNARDA ALBA
— The House of Bernarda Alba. Ballet realized by Dale Edward Fern and performed by Florita Raup in a dance concert at Hunter College on February 1, 1953.

YERMA
— Yerma. Ballet by Leo Smit. Choreographed by Valerie Bettis.
— Yerma. Opera by Denis ApIvor with libretto by Montague Slater.
— Yerma. Opera by Paul Bowles. Presented at the University of Denver in July, 1958 with Libby Holman and Rose Bampton.
— Yerma. Ballet by Alan Hovhaness, choreographed by J. Marks. Presented by the San Francisco Contemporary Dancers, Sept., 1959.

LA ZAPATERA PRODIGIOSA
— **La Zapatera Prodigiosa.** Opera by Juan José Castro. Premiered in Buenos Aires.

III. TRANSLATIONS

A. PLAYS

EL AMOR DE DON PERLIMPLIN CON BELISA EN SU JARDIN
— Beck, Enrique. **Don Perlimplin.** In **Die Dramatischen Dichtungen.** Wiesbaden: Insel-Verlag, 1954.
— Belamich, Andre (trans.) **Les Amours de Don Perlimplin.** In **F.G.L. — Oeuvres Completes, Vol. III.** Paris: Gallimard, 1955.
— Camp, Jean (trans.). **Amour de Don Perlimplin avec Belise en son Jardin.** Paris: Librairie Theatrale, 1954.
— Chirone, Dimma (trans.). **Amore di Don Perlimplin con Belisa nel suo Giardin.** In **Il Dramma:** Turin: May 15, 1946.
— O'Connell, R.L.; Graham-Lujan, J. (trans.). **The Love of Don Perlimplin.** In **From Lorca's Theatre.** New York: Scribner's, 1941; In Bentley, Eric. **From the Modern Repertory — Series One.** Denver: Univ. of Denver Press, 1949.
— Soutou, Jean-Marie (trans.). **Amour de Don Perlimplin et de Belise dans leur Jardin.** Lyon: Barkzat, 1945.

ASI QUE PASEN CINCO AÑOS
— Auclair, Marcelle (ed.). **Lorsque Cinq Ans Auront Passe.** In **F.G.L. —Oeuvres Completes, Vol. V.** Paris: Gallimard, 1956.
— Beck, Enrique, (trans.). **Asi Que Pasen Cinco Años.** In **Die Dramatischen Dichtungen.** Wiesbaden: Insel-Verlag, 1954.
— O'Connell, R.L.; Graham-Lujan, J. (trans.) **When Five Years Pass.** In **From Lorca's Theatre.** New York: Scribner's, 1941.

BODAS DE SANGRE
— Alin, Karin; Gullberg, Hjalmar (trans.). **Blodsbrollop.** Stockholm: Norsted & Soners, 1947.
— Auclair, Marcelle; Prevost, Jean (trans.). **La Noce Meurtriere.** In **La Nouvelle Revue Francaise:** Paris, 1938, No. 295-296-297.
— Auclair, M.; Prevost, Jean (trans.). **Noces de Sang.** Paris: Gallimard, 1946.
— Auclair, Marcelle (trans.). **Noces de Sang.** In **F.G.L. — Oeuvres Completes, Vol. IV.** Paris: Gallimard, 1956.
— Beck, Enrique (trans.). **Bluthochzeit.** In **Mass und Wert:** Zurich. Jan. 2, 1939; pp. 642-57 in **Bluthochzeit.** Wiesbaden: Insel-Verlag, 1952. In **Die Dramatischen Dichtungen.** Wiesbaden: Insel-Verlag, 1954.
— Fink, V. **(Bodas de Sangre).** Moscow.
— Hughes, Langston (trans.). **Fate at the Wedding.** New York: Unpublished typescript in N.Y. Public Library Theatre Collection.
— Kelin, F.V.; Fevralski, A. (trans.). **Krovia Svad'ba.** Moscow-Leningrad: Iskusstvo, 1939.
— Namia, Robert (trans.) **Noces de Sang.** Algier: Ed. Edmond Charlot, 1945.
— Neiman, Gilbert (trans.). **Blood Wedding.** In **New Directions No. 5.** Norfolk, Conn.: New Directions, 1939.

— Nkatsos, Nikos (trans.). **Ho Matomenos Gamos.** Athens: Ikaros, 1945.
— O'Connell, R.L.; Graham-Lujan, J. (trans.). **Blood Wedding.** In **Three Tragedies of Fed.** García Lorca. N.Y.: New Directions, 1955. In Gassner, John. **A Treasury of the Theatre.** N.Y.: Dryden Press, 1957; In Watson, E.B. and Pressey, B. (Eds.). **Contemporary Drama-Fifteen Plays.** N.Y.: Scribners, 1959; in Flores, Angel (Ed.) **Spanish Drama.** N.Y.: Bantam Books, 1962.
— Oliver, William I. (trans.). **Blood Wedding.** New York: Columbia Univ. Microfilm No. F 1379, 1957.
— Tentori, Francesco (trans.). **Muerto con Amor.** Rome: Fiera Litteraria, 1946.
— Valentini, Giuseppe (trans.). **Nozze di Sangue.** In **Il Dramma:** Turin, 1943, No. 410-11.
— Vittorini, Elio (trans.). **Nozze di Sangue.** Milan: Bompiani, 1942.
— Weissberger, Jose A. (trans.). **Bitter Oleander.** N.Y.: Unpublished typescript in N.Y. Public Library Theatre Collection, 1940.

LA CASA DE BERNARDA ALBA
— Alin, Karin; Gullberg, Hjalmar (trans.). **Bernadas Hus.** Stockholm: Norsted & Soners, 1947.
— Auclair, Marcelle (ed.). **La Maison de Bernarda Alba.** In **F.G.L.** —**Oeuvres Completes, Vol. V.** Paris: Gallimard, 1946.
— Beck, Enrique (trans.). **La Casa de Bernarda Alba.** In **Die Dramatischen Dichtungen.** Wiesbaden: Insel-Verlag, 1954.
— Creach, Jean-Marie (trans.). **La Maison de Bernarda Alba.** Paris: Le Club Francais du Livre, 1947. In **France-Illustration Supplément:** Paris, Dec. 8, 1951, No. 96; pp. 1-20.
— O'Connell, R.L.; Graham-Lujan, J. (trans.). **The House of Bernarda Alba.** In **Three Tragedies of F.G.L.** N.Y.: New Directions, 1955.

LA DONCELLA, EL MARINO Y EL ESTUDIANTE
— Couffon, Claude (trans.). **La Doncella . . .** In **Petit Theatre.** Paris: Les Lettres Mondiales, 1951.
— Oliver, William I. (trans.). **The Lass, The Sailor and The Student.** New York: Columbia Univ. Microfilm No. F 1403, 1957.
— Reynolds, Tim (trans.). **The Virgin, The Sailor and The Student.** In **Accent:** Illinois, Summer 1957, Vol. XVII, No. 3, 134-36.
— Auclair, M. (ed.). In **F.G.L. — Oeuvres Completes, Vol. V.** Paris: Gallimard, 1956.

DONA ROSITA LA SOLTERA O EL LENGUAJE DE LAS FLORES
— Auclair, Marcelle (trans.). **Doña Rosita . . .** In **F.G.L. — Oeuvres Completes, Vol. IV.** Paris: Gallimard, 1956.
— Beck, Enrique (trans.). **Doña Rosita . . .** In **Die Dramatischen Dichtungen.** Wiesbaden: Insel-Verlag, 1954.
— O'Connell, R.L.; Graham-Lujan, J. (trans.) **Doña Rosita . . .** In **From Lorca's Theatre.** N.Y.: Scribner's, 1941.
— Sleyen, Sofia (trans.). **Doña Rosita . . .** Warsaw: 1953.

EL MALEFICIO DE LA MARIPOSA
— Belamich, Andre (trans.). **Le Malefice de la Phalene.** In **F.G.L. — Oeuvres Completes, Vol. III.** Paris: Gallimard, 1955.
— Oliver, William I. (trans.). **The Spell of the Butterfly.** New York: Columbia Univ. Microfilm No. F 1403, 1957.

MARIANA PINEDA
— Baldo, A. (trans.). **Mariana Pineda.** Modena: Guanda, 1946.
— Beck, Enrique (trans.). **Mariana Pineda.** In **Die Dramatischen Dichtungen.** Wiesbaden: Insel-Verlag, 1954.
— Belamich, Andre (trans.). **Mariana Pineda.** In **F.G.L.** — **Oeuvres Completes, Vol. III.** Paris: Gallimard, 1955.
— Graham, James R. (trans.). **Mariana Pineda.** In **Federico García Lorca: A critical essay on his plays.** N.Y.: Columbia Univ. Manuscript, 1950.
— Languasco, Nardo (trans.) **Mariana Pineda.** In **Il Dramma:** Turin, May 15, 1946.
— Massis, Andre (trans.). **Mariana Pineda,** Inedited version presented at Paris' Theatre Charles-de-Rochefort in 1946.

EL PASEO DE BUSTER KEATON
— Couffon, Claude (trans.). **El Paseo** ... In **Petit Theatre.** Paris: Les Lettres Mondiales, 1951.
— Reynolds, Tim (trans.). **Buster Keaton's Promenade.** In **Accent:** Illinois, Summer 1957, Vol. XVII, No. 3; pp. 131-33.
— Auclair, M. (ed.) In **F.G.L.** — **Oeuvres Completes, Vol. V.** Paris: Gallimard, 1956.

EL PUBLICO
— Auclair, Marcelle (ed.). **Le Public.** In **F.G.L.** — **Oeuvres Completes, Vol. V.** Paris: Gallimard, 1956.
— Belitt, Ben (trans.). **The Audience.** In **Evergreen Review,** Vol. II, No. 6. New York: 1958; pp. 93-107.
— **Le Public.** In **La Nouvelle Revue Francaise:** Paris, 1955.
— Viaud, P. (trans.). **Le Public.** In **Mercure de France:** Paris, July 1949; pp. 417-25.

QUIMERA
— Couffon, Claude (trans.). **Quimera.** In **Petit Theatre.** Paris: Les Lettres Mondiales, 1951.
— Oliver, William I. (trans.). **Chimera.** New York: Columbia Univ. Microfilm No. F 1403, 1957.
— Reynolds, Tim (trans.). **Chimera.** In **Accent:** Illinois, Summer 1957, Vol. XVII, No. 3; pp. 137-39.
— Auclair, M. (ed.). In **F.G.L.** — **Oeuvres Completes, Vol. V.** Paris: Gallimard, 1956.

EL RETABLILLO DE DON CRISTOBAL
— Belamich, Andre (trans.). **Le Guinol Au Gordin.** In **F.G.L.** — **Oeuvres Completes, Vol. III.** Paris: Gallimard, 1955.
— Bodini, Vittorio (trans.). **El Retablillo de Don Cristobal.** Rome: Aretusa, 1946.
— Camp, Jean (trans.). **Le Petit Retable de Don Cristobal.** Paris: L'Espagne Libre, 1946; Paris: Librairie Theatrale, 1954.
— Chirone, Dimma (trans.). **Quadretto di Don Cristobal. Farsa per Marionette.** In **Il Dramma:** Turin, May 15, 1946.
— Honig, Edwin (trans.). **The Frame of Don Cristobal.** In **New Directions No 8:** Norfolk, Conn., 1944.
— Namia, Robert (trans.). **Le Petit Retable de Don Cristobal.** Algier: Ed. Edmond Charlot, 1945.
— Oliver, William I. (trans.). **The Puppet Play of Don Cristobal.** N.Y.: Columbia Univ. Microfilm No. F 1403, 1957.

LA TRAGICOMEDIA DE DON CRISTOBAL Y LA
SEÑA ROSITA
— Belamich, Andre (trans.). Le Tragicomedie. In La Nouvelle Nou-
velle Revue Francaise: Paris, 1955, No. 26.
— Oliver, William I. The Tragicomedy of Don Cristobita and Doña
Rosita. In New World Writing No. 8. New York: Mentor Books,
1955.

YERMA
— Alin, Karin; Gullberg, Hjalmar (trans.). Yerma. Stockholm: Nor-
sted & Soners, 1947.
— Auclair, Marcelle. Yerma. In F.G.L. — Oeuvres Completes, Vol.
IV. Paris: Gallimard, 1956.
— Beck, Enrique. (trans.). Yerma. In Die Dramatischen Dichtungen.
Wiesbaden: Insel-Verlag, 1954.
— Camp, Jean. (trans.). Yerma. In L'Avant Scene: Paris, 1954, No.
98; pp. 11-30.
— Jaccobi Ruggero (trans.). Yerma. Rome: Edizioni del Secolo, 1944.
— O'Connell, R.L.; Graham-Lujan, J. (trans.). Yerma. In From
Lorca's Theatre. N.Y.: Scribner's, 1941; In Three Tragedies of
F.G.L. N.Y.: New Directions, 1955; In Ulanov, Barry. Makers of
the Modern Theatre. N.Y.: McGraw-Hill, 1961.
— Sleyen, Sofia (trans.). Yerma. Warsaw: 1953.
— Vauthier, Etienne (trans.). Yerma. Brussels: Imprimerie van Door-
slaer, 1939.
— Viet, Joan (trans.). Yerma, Poeme Tragique. Paris: Seghers, 1947.

LA ZAPATERA PRODIGIOSA
— Beck, Enrique (trans.). La Zapatera ... In Die Dramatischen Dich-
tungen. Wiesbaden: Insel-Verlag, 1954.
— Belamich, Andre (trans.). La Savatiere Prodigieuse. in F.G.L. —
Oeuvre Completes, Vol. III. Paris: Gallimard, 1955.
— Campbell, Roy (trans.). The Marvellous Shoemaker's Wife. New
York: Columbia Univ. Microfilm No. F 1404, 1957.
— Kagarlitski, A.; Kelin, Fedor (trans.). La Zapatera ... Moscow:
1941.
— Languasco, Nardo (trans.). La Zapatera ... In Il Dramma: Turin,
May 15, 1946.
— O'Connell, R.L.; Graham-Lujan, J. (trans.). The Shoemaker's Pro-
digious Wife. In From Lorca's Theatre. New York: Scribner's,
1941.
— Pomes, Mathilde. La Savatiere Prodigieuse. In Magasin du Spec-
tacle: Paris, 1946; Paris: R. Laffont, 1946.

B. INTERVIEWS, LECTURES

— Quattre Interviews Sur le Theatre. In Theatre Populaire: Paris,
1955, No. 13; pp. 3-14.
— Laffranque, Marie (ed.). F.G.L. — Declarations et Interviews Re-
trauves. In Bulletin Hispanique: Paris, July — Sept. 1956; pp. 325-
26, 328-31.
— Block, Haskell M. (trans.). A Talk About the Theatre In The
Creative Vision. N.Y.: Grove Press, 1960.
— Sloman, A.E. (trans.). The Authority of the Theatre. In Playwrights on Playwriting. N.Y.: Hill & Wang, 1960.

BIBLIOGRAPHY 313

MARIANA PINEDA
— Bernstein, Joseph (trans.). **Mariana Pineda.** In **Playwrights on Playwriting.** N.Y.: Hill & Wang, 1960.
LA ZAPATERA PRODIGIOSA
— Bernstein, Joseph (trans.). **The Shoemaker's Prodigious Wife.** In **Playwrights on Playwriting.** N.Y.: Hill & Wang, 1960.

C. COMPLETE WORKS

FEDERICO GARCIA LORCA — OEUVRES COMPLETES
— Translations into the French by Marcelle Auclair, André Belamich, Claude Couffon, Pierre Darmangeat, Bernard Sésé, and Paul Verdevoye. (Paris, Gallimard, 1954) 6 vols.

FEDERICO GARCIA LORCA — (COMPLETE WORKS)
— Translations into the Russian by Fedor V. Kelin, A. Fevralski and others. (Moscow, 1938) several volumes.

IV. STUDIES

A. BOOKS

Aldunate Phillips, Arturo: **Federico García Lorca a través de Margarita Xirgú.** Santiago de Chile: Nascimento, 1937; 74 pp.

Alonso, Dámaso: **Poetas españoles contemporáneos.** Madrid: Gredos, 1952; 446 pp.

Andrade, Raúl: **Gobelinos de niebla. Tres ensayos literarios.** Quito: Talleres Gráficos de Educación, 1943; 131 pp.

Arai Espinosa, Ma. del Rosario Sachi: **El teatro poético de Federico García Lorca.** Univ. of México: M. A. Thesis, 1942; 88 pp.

Assaf, José E.: **El teatro argentino como problema nacional.** Buenos Aires: Ed. Criterio, 1937; 196 pp.

Babín, María Teresa: **Federico García Lorca y su obra.** Univ. of Puerto Rico: M. A. Thesis, 1939.
———**El mundo poético de Federico García Lorca.** Columbia University: Ph.D. Dissertation, 1951; 315 pp.
———**El mundo poético de Federico García Lorca.** San Juan: Biblioteca de Autores Puertorriqueños, 1954; 316 pp.
———**García Lorca — Vida y Obra.** New York: Las Américas, 1955; 122 pp.

Barea, Arturo: **Lorca — The Poet and His People.** Trans. by Ilsa Barea. London: Faber & Faber, 1944; 103 pp.
———**Idem.** New York: Harcourt, Brace & Co., 1949; 176 pp.
———**Lorca — El poeta y su pueblo.** Buenos Aires: Ed. Losada, 1957; 137 pp.

Beck, Enrique: **Die Dramatischen Dichtungen.** Translations into German of **Mariana Pineda, Don Perlimplín, La Zapatera Prodigiosa, Bodas de sangre, Así que pasen cinco años, Yerma, Doña Rosita** and **La casa de Bernarda Alba.** With notes. Wiesbaden: Insel-Verlag, 1954; 441 pp.

Bedriñana, Francisco C.: **Papel de China. Tres ensayos.** Havana: Ed. Antena, 1941; 86 pp.

Benet, William Rose (Ed.): **The Reader's Encyclopedia.** New York: T.Y. Crowell Co., 1948; 1242 pp.

Benítez Claros, Rafael: Figuras representativas en el drama del siglo **XX.** Univ. de Oviedo: Lecture, 1959.

Bentley, Eric: **From the Modern Repertory — Series One.** Contains a translation of **Don Perlimplín.** With notes. Denver: Univ. of Denver Press, 1949; 406 pp.
———**In Search of Theatre.** New York: Knopf, 1953; Vintage Books, 1957; 385 pp.

Berenguer Carisomo, Arturo: **Las máscaras de Federico García Lorca.** Buenos Aires: Talleres Ruiz Hnos., 1941; 211 pp.

Bianchi, Sarah: **El guiñol en García Lorca.** Buenos Aires: Cuadernos del Unicornio, 1953; 14 pp.

Bo, Carlos: **Carte Spagnole.** Florence: Marzocco, 1948; 155 pp.

Bodini, Vittorio (Ed.): **Federico García Lorca — Teatro.** Turin-Milan: Einaudi, 1952; 519 pp.

Bowra, Sir Cecil M.: **The Creative Experiment.** London: Macmillan & Co., 1949; 255 pp.

Brenan, Gerald: **The Face of Spain.** New York: Grove Press, 1951; 310 pp.
———**The Literature of the Spanish People.** Cambridge: Univ. Pres, 1953; 495 pp.
———**Historia de la Literatura Española.** Translated by M. de Amibilia. Buenos Aires: Losada, 1958; 480 pp.

Campbell, Roy: **Lorca. An Appreciation of His Poetry.** London- New Haven: Yale Univ. Press, 1952; 79 pp.
———**Lorca.** New Haven: Yale Univ. Pres, 1959; 102 pp.

Cardoza y Aragón, Luis: **Apolo y coatlicue — ensayos.** México: Ed. "La Serpiente Emplumada", 1944; 202 pp.

Carrillo, José: **Ensayos literarios y didácticos.** México: Tipografía Mercantil, 1949; 303 pp.

Cavalheiro, Edgard: **García Lorca.** Sao Paolo: Livraria Martins, 1946; 165 pp.
———**Idem.** Rio de Janeiro: Ed. Civilizaçao Brasileira, 1956; 241 pp.

Chandler, Richard E., and Schwartz, K. **A New History of Spanish Literature.** Baton Rouge: Louisiana State Univ. Press, 1961; 696 pp.

Cirre, José Francisco: **Forma y espíritu de una lírica española.** México: Gráfica Panamericana, 1950; 180 pp.

Clark, Barret H. and Freedley, George: **A History of the Modern Drama.** New York: Appleton-Century, 1947; 832 pp.

Cole, Toby: **Playwrights on Playwriting.** Contains translations of two interviews and an article by Lorca. New York: Hill and Wang, 1960; 299 pp.

Contín Aybar, Pedro René: **Federico García Lorca, poeta popular.** Ciudad Trujillo: 1939.

Correa, Gustavo: **La poesía mítica de Lorca.** Eugene: Univ. of Oregon Press, 1957; 174 pp.

Couffon, Claude (Ed.): **Petit theatre — Federico García Lorca.** Contains French translations of **Quimera, El paseo de Buster Keaton** and **La doncella, el marinero y el estudiante.** Paris: Les lettres mondiales, 1951; 63 pp.

Crow, J. A.: **Federico García Lorca.** Los Angeles: U.C.L.A. Press, 1945; 116 pp.

Cuchí Coll, Isabel: **Del Madrid literario — 1933-1934.** San Juan: Imp. Venezuela, 1935; 88 pp.

Dalí, Salvador: **The Secret Life of Salvador Dalí.** Trans. by Haakon M. Chevalier. New York: Dial Press, 1942; 400 pp.

De Hoyo, Arturo: **Teatro mundial.** Contains plot outlines of **Bodas de sangre, Doña Rosita, La casa de Bernarda Alba** and **Yerma,** Madrid: Aguilar, 1955; 1,270 pp.

De Hoyos Ruiz, Antonio: **Las mujeres de García Lorca.** Genoa: Lecture at "Associación Cultural Femenina", 1959.
————**Las obras dramáticas de García Lorca.** Rome: Lecture at "Asociación Amici della Spagna", 1959.

De la Guardia, Alfredo: **García Lorca — Persona y creación.** Buenos Aires: Sur, 1941; 330 pp.; B.A.: Schapire, 1944; 440 pp.

De María y Campos, Armando: **Presencias de teatro (Crónicas 1934-1936).** México: Ed. Notas, 1937; 316 pp.

De Torre, Guillermo: **La aventura y el orden.** Buenos Aires: Losada, 1948; 190 pp.
————**Tríptico del sacrificio — Unamuno, García Lorca, Machado.** Buenos Aires: Losada, 1948; 148 pp.

Del Río, Angel: **Federico García Lorca (1899-1936). Vida y obra.** Bibliography by Sidonia Rosenbaum. New York: Hispanic Institute, 1941; 149 pp.
————**Vida y obras de Federico García Lorca.** Zaragoza: Heraldo de Aragón, 1952; 168 pp.

Díaz-Plaja, Guillermo: **L'Evolucio del teatre.** Barcelona: Ed. Barcino, 1934; 62 pp.
————**La poesía lírica española.** Barcelona: Ed. Labor, 1937.
————**Esquema de la historia del teatro.** Barcelona: Instituto del Teatro, 1944; 79 pp.
————**Historia de la poesía lírica española.** Barcelona: Ed. Labor, 1948; 456 pp.
————**Federico García Lorca. Estudio crítico.** Buenos Aires: Kraft, 1948; 284 pp.
————**Historia general de las literaturas hispánicas.** Vol. V — Romanticismo y Modernismo. Barcelona: Ed. Barna, 1956.
————**Modernismo frente a noventa y ocho.** Madrid: Espasa-Calpe, 1951; 366 pp.
————**Federico García Lorca, su obra e influencia en la poesía española.** Buenos Aires: Espasa-Calpe, 1954; 210 pp.
————**El teatro.** Barcelona: Noguer. 1958; 645 pp.

Diez-Echarri, Emiliano: **Historia de la Literatura Española e Hispanoamericana.** Madrid: Aguilar, 1960.

Eich, Christoph: **Federico García Lorca, poeta de la intensidad.** Madrid: Gredos, 1958; 200 pp.

Espina, Antonio: **Las mejores escenas del teatro español e hispanoamericano.** Madrid: Aguilar, 1959; 680 pp.

Esslyn, Martin: The Theatre of the Absurd. New York: Doubleday Anchor, 1961; 364 pp.

Federico García Lorca — Tutto il teatro. Milan: Mondadori, 1959; 448 pp.

Fergusson, Francis: The Human Image in Dramatic Literature. New York: Doubleday, 1957; 217 pp.

Fiskin, A.M.I. (Ed.): Writers of Our Years. Contains — Federico García Lorca by Fed. de Onis. Denver: Univ. of Denver Press, 1950; 117 pp.

Flecniakoska, Jean Louis: L'univers poetique de Federico García Lorca. Bordeaux: Biere, 1952; 144 pp.

Flys, Jaroslaw M.: El lenguaje poético de Federico García Lorca. Madrid: Gredos, 1955; 243 pp.

García López, José: Historia de la literatura española. Barcelona: Teide, 1959; 593 pp.

García-Luengo, Eusebio: Revisión del teatro de Federico García Lorca. Madrid: Política y Literatura, Aga, 1951; 34 pp.

Gassner, John: Masters of the Drama. New York: Random House, 1940; N.Y.: Dover, 1945; 804 pp.
———Form and Idea in Modern Theatre. New York: Dryden Press, 1956; 290 pp.
———A Treasury of the Theatre. New York: Dryden Press, 1957; 1,120 pp.
———The Theatre in Our Times. New York: Crown, 1960; 588 pp.

Gili, J. L.: Lorca. Baltimore: Penguin Books, 1960; 144 pp.

González Carbalho, José: Vida, obra y muerte de Federico García Lorca. Santiago de Chile: Ercilla, 1938; 81 pp.

González Muela, Joaquín: El lenguaje poético de la generación Lorca-Guillén. Madrid: Insula, 1955; 186 pp.

Gonzalo Sobejano: García Lorca y el surrealismo. Amsterdam: Lecture at the "Spain-Spanish American Assoc."

Granell, Eugenio F.: Ideas de escritores y pintores españoles. Columbia Univ.: Lecture on July 20, 1960 at the Hispanic Institute.

Gregersen, Halfdan: Ibsen and Spain — A Study in Comparative Drama. Cambridge: Harvard Univ. Press, 1936; 209 pp.

Guerrero Zamara, Juan: El teatro de Federico García Lorca. Madrid: Colección Raíz, 1948; 19 pp.

Guillén, Jorge: Language and Poetry. Cambridge: Harvard Univ. Press, 1961; 293 pp.

Hartnoll, Phyllis (Ed.): The Oxford Companion to the Theatre. New York-London: Oxford Univ. Press, 1957, 888 pp.

Haycraft, Howard and Kunitz, Stanley: Twentieth Century Authors. New York: H. W. Wilson Co., 1942; 1,577 pp.

Heiney, Donald: Contemporary Literature. New York: Barron's Educ. Series, 1954; 553 pp.

Hespelt, E. Herman: An Outline History of Spanish-American Literature. New York: Crofts & Co., 1941; 170 pp.

Hispanic Institute in the United States. New York: Columbia University's Casa Hispánica. Contains a wealth of material — clippings, magazines, books, theatre programs — related to Lorca.

Honig, Edwin: **García Lorca.** Norfolk, Conn.: New Directions, 1944; 242 pp.; 1947; New York: New Directions, 1951; 242 pp.; 1963.

Hornstein, Lillian: **The Readers Companion to World Literature.** New York: Mentor Books, 1956; 493 pp.

Hurtado, J. and Palencia, A. G.: **Historia de la literatura española,** Madrid: Tip. de Archivos, 1932.

Iglesias Ramírez, Manuel: **Federico García Lorca, el poeta universal.** Barcelona: Ed. Dux, 1955; 265 pp.

Infiesta, Roberto: **Itinerario lírico de Federico García Lorca.** Havana: Lecture on Oct. 30, 1951 at the "Club Femenino de Cuba".

Kelin, Fedor and Fevralski, A.: **Izbrannoe.** Moscow: 1944; 333 pp.

Kostetzky, Eaghor G.: **Vybranyi García Lorca — Poezija, Proza, Drama.** Neu Ulm: Na Hori, 1958; 132 pp.

Kunitz, Stanley: **Twentieth Century Authors.** New York: H. W. Wilson Co., 1955; 1,123 pp.

Lamm, Martin: **Modern Drama.** Trans. by Karin Elliott. Oxford: Blackwell, 1952; New York: Philosophical Library, 1953; 359 pp.

Lázaro Carreter, F.: **Las obras de Federico García Lorca.** Lecture: Univ. of Salamanca, 1959.
———**Veinte años de teatro español.** Tangiers, Casablanca, Rabat and Tetuan: Lecture, 1959.

Lima, Robert: **The Complete Theatre of Federico García Lorca — A Critical Analysis.** Villanova Univ.: M. A. Thesis, 1961; 308 pp.
———**The Theatre of García Lorca.** N.Y.: Las Americas, 1963.

Lumley, Frederick: **Trends in Twentieth Century Drama.** London: Rockliff, 1956; 273 pp.
———**Theatre in Review.** Edinburgh: R. Patterson, Ltd., 1956; 201 pp.

McCollom, William G.: **Tragedy.** New York: Macmillan Co., 1957; 254 pp.

MacGowan, Kenneth and Melnitz, William: **The Living Stage.** New Jersey: Prentice-Hall, 1956; 543 pp.

Machado Bonet, Ofelia: **Federico García Lorca — Su producción dramática.** Montevideo: Imp. Rosgal, 1951; 229 pp.

McVan, Alice Jane: **Antonio Machado.** New York: Hispanic Society, 1959; 256 pp.

Magill, Frank N.: **Cyclopedia of World Authors.** New York: Harper, 1958; 1,198 pp.

Mancini, Guido: **Storia della letteratura spagnola.** Milan: Feltrinelli, 1961; 698 pp.

Mantle, Burns (Ed.): **The Best Plays Series.** Vols. 18, 28, 32, 34, 41. New York: Dodd, Mead & Co.

Moncayo, Hugo: **Conferencias — Federico García Lorca.** Quito: Imp. Univ. Central, 1937; 79 pp.

Monner Sans, José María: **Panorama del nuevo teatro.** La Plata: Biblioteca de Humanidades, 1939; 273 pp.; Buenos Aires: Ed. Losada, 1942; 255 pp.

Mora Guarnido, José: **Federico García Lorca y su mundo.** Buenos Aires: Losada, 1958; 238 pp.

Moreno Villa, José: **Vida en claro.** Autobiografía. México, 1944; 278 pp.

———**Ensayos.** México: El Colegio de México, 1946; 155 pp.

Morla Lynch, Carlos: **En España con Federico García Lorca.** Madrid: Aguilar, 1957; 498 pp.

Muñoz, Matilde: **Historia del teatro dramático español.** Madrid; 338 pp.

Nalé Roxlo, Conrado: **Antología apócrifa.** Buenos Aires: Hachette, 1943; 186 pp.

Namorado, Joaquín: **Vida e obras de Federico García Lorca.** Coimbra: Saber, 1943.

Nathan, George Jean: **Theatre Book of the Year 1948-1949.** New York: Knopf, 1949; 363 pp.

———**Theatre Book of the Year 1950-1951.** New York: Knopf, 1951; 294 pp.

Newmark, Maxim: **Dictionary of Spanish Literature.** New York: Philosophical Library, 1956; 352 pp.

Northup, George Tyler: **An Introduction to Spanish Literature.** Chicago: Univ. of Chicago Press, 1947; 479 pp.

Nourissier, Francois: **Federico García Lorca, dramaturge.** Paris: L'Arche, 1955; 158 pp.

Novo, Salvador: **Continente vacío.** Madrid: Espasa-Calpe, 1935.

Núñez Arca, P.: **Presencia de García Lorca.** São Paolo: Letras Editora Continental, 1944; 269 pp.

O'Connell, Richard L. and Graham-Lujan, James: **From Lorca's Theatre.** New York: Scribner's 1941; 251 pp.

———**Three Tragedies of Federico García Lorca.** New York: New Directions, 1955; 212 pp.

Orcajo Acuña, Federico: **Teatro de hoy.** Buenos Aires-Montevideo: Sociedad Amigos del Libro Rioplatense, 1936; vol. XXVI.

Pandolfi, Vito: **Spettacolo del secolo — Il teatro dramatico.** Pisa: Nistri Lischi, 1953; 414 pp.

Parker, Jack Horace: **Breve Historia del Teatro Español.** México: Ediciones de Andrea, 1957; 214 pp.

Parrot, Louis: **Federico García Lorca — Une etude.** Paris: Seghers, 1947; 216 pp.

Peacock, Ronald: **The Art of the Drama.** London: Routledge & Kegan Paul Ltd., 1957; 263 pp.

Peers, Edgar Allison: **A History of the Romantic Movement in Spain.** London: Cambridge Univ. Press, 1940; 2 vols.

Perez-Minik, Domingo: **Debates sobre el teatro español contemporáneo.** Santa Cruz de Tenerife: Ed. Goya, 1953; 286 pp.

Poveda, J.: **Ensayos.** Ciudad Trujillo: Ed. Rincon, 1941; 94 pp.

Prapolini, (Ed.): **Historia universal de la literatura.** Buenos Aires: Utheu, 1941; vol. VI.

Robles, Emmanuel: **García Lorca.** Algiers: Editios du Cactus, 1949; 96 pp.

Romera-Navarro, M.: **Historia de la literatura española.** Boston: Health & Co., 1949; 704 pp.

Sagorski, B. (Ed.): **Federico García Lorca.** Moscow: The State Literary Press, 1943.

Sainz de Robles, Fed. Carlos: **Diccionario de la literatura.** Madrid: Aguilar, 1954; vol. II.

Salinas, Pedro: **Reality and the Poet in Spanish Poetry.** Trans. by Edith Helman. Baltimore: Johns Hopkins Press, 1940; 165 pp.

———**Literatura española del siglo XX.** Mexico: Ed. Séneca, 1941; 352 pp.

———**Ensayos de literatura hispánica.** Madrid: Aguilar, 1958.

Samachson, Dorothy and Joseph: **The Dramatic Story of the Theatre.** New York-London: Abelard-Schuman, 1955; 168 pp.

Sánchez, Robert G.: **García Lorca — Estudio sobre su teatro.** Madrid: Ed. Jura, 1950; 166 pp.

Santos Torroella, Rafael: **Salvador Dalí.** Madrid: Afrodisio Aguado, 1952.

Scarpa, Roque Esteban: **Poetas españoles contemporáneos.** Santiago de Chile: Zig-Zag, 1953; 320 pp.

Schonberg, Jean Louis: **Federico García Lorca — L'homme, l'ouvre.** Paris: Plon, 1956; 360 pp.

Schveitzer, Marcelle: **Souvenir sur Federico García Lorca, musicien.** Paris: Seghers, 1949.

Seghers, Pierre (Ed.): **Poetes d'Aujourd' hui.** Paris: Seghers, 1949.

Sharpe, Robert Boies: **Irony in the Drama.** Chapel Hill: Univ. of N. Carolina Press, 1959; 22 pp.

Shipley, Joseph T.: **Guide to Great Plays.** Washington, DC.: Public Affairs Press, 1956; 867 pp.

Smith, Horatio: **Columbia Dictionary of Modern European Literature.** New York: Columbia Univ. Press, 1947; 899 pp.

Sobel, Bernard: **The New Theatre Handbook and Digest of Plays.** New York: Crown, 1959; 749 pp.

Souvirón, José María: **La nueva poesía española.** Santiago de Chile: Nascimento, 1932; 53 pp.

Spicer, Jack: **After Lorca.** San Francisco: White Rabbit Press, 1959.

Stage Design Throughout the World Since 1935. Contains designs and photographs of actual productions of **Bodas de sangre, La casa de Bernarda Alba, Amor de Don Perlimplín, Yerma** and **Doña Rosita.** London-Toronto: Harrap & Co.

Starkie, Walter Fitzwilliam: **Federico García Lorca.** British Institute of Madrid: Lecture.

———**In Sara's Tents.** London-New York: Dutton & Co., 1954; 339 pp.

Stephens, Frances: **Theatre World Annual (1953-1954).** New York-London: Macmillan Co., 1954; 176 pp.

Theatre Collection — New York Public Library. Central Building, Room 315-T. Contains its own card catalogue of plays, programs, criticism, scripts, photographs and clippings. Lorca material is cross-indexed under play titles and author's name.

Torrente Ballester, Gonzalo: Literatura española contemporánea (1898-1936). Madrid: A. Aguado, 1947; 464 pp.
———Teatro español contemporáneo. Madrid: Ed. Guadarrama, 1958; 348 pp.
———Panorama de la literatura española contemporánea. Madrid: Ed. Guadarrama, 1961; 882 pp.
Torres Rioseco, Arturo: New World Literature. Los Angeles: Univ. of Calif. Press, 1949; 250 pp.
Trend, John Brande: Alfonso the Sage. London: Constable & Co., 1926; Boston-New York: Houghton Mifflin, 1926; 216 pp.
———Lorca and the Spanish Poetic Tradition. New York-Oxford: Macmillan, 1956; 178 pp.
Turnbull, Eleanor L. and Salinas, Pedro: Contemporary Spanish Poetry. Baltimore: Johns Hopkins Press, 1945: 401 pp.
Tynan, Kenneth: Curtains. N.Y.: Atheneum, 1961; 496 pp.
Ulanov, Barry: The Makers of the Modern Theatre. N.Y.: McGraw-Hill, 1961; 743 pp.
Usigli, Rodolfo: Itinerario del autor dramático. México: La Casa de España, 1940; 172 pp.
Valbuena Prat, Angel: Historia del teatro español. Barcelona: Noguer, 1960; 708 pp.
———Historia de la literatura española. Barcelona: Gili, 1960: 3 vols.
Vázquez Ocaña, Fernando: García Lorca. México: Ed. Grijalbo, 1957; 387 pp.
Vian, Cesco: Federico García Lorca, poeta e dramaturgo. Milan: Universita Cattolica, 1951.
Vittorini, Elio: Teatro spagnolo. Milan: Bompiani.
Vivanco, Luis Felipe: Introducción a la poesía española contemporánea. Madrid: Ed. Guadarrama. 1957: 662 pp.
Williamson, Audrey: Contemporary Theatre. London: Rockliff, 1956; 195 pp.
Young, Stark: Immortal Shadows. New York: Hill & Wang, 1948; 270 pp.

IV. STUDIES

B. ARTICLES (General)

———Un rato de charla con Federico García Lorca. In Correo de Galicia: Buenos Aires, Oct. 22, 1933.
———Federico García Lorca en Buenos Aires. In Revista de la Asoc. Patriótica Española: Buenos Aires, Nov., 1933.
———El teatro de Federico García Lorca. In Archivos de la Literatura Contemporánea — Indice Literario: Madrid, Feb., 1936; vol. V, No. 37, pp. 25-31.
———García Lorca en la Unión Soviética. In Cervantes: Havana, 1944; vol; vol. XIX, No. 4, pp. 11, 86.
———Lorca Cycle Set For Bow. In The N.Y. Journal-American: New York, Nov. 15, 1960; p. 17.

Aldunate, R.: **El teatro de Federico García Lorca.** In **Mercurio:** Santiago de Chile, April 11, 1937.

Altolaguirre, M.: **Nuestro teatro.** In **Hora de España:** Valencia, 1937; No. 9, pp. 32-37.

Aparicio, Antonio: **Federico García Lorca y su época.** In **Atenea:** Concepción (Chile), 1949; vol. XCIII, No. 286, pp. 41-61.

Aratari, Anthony: **The Tragedies of García Lorca.** In **Commonweal:** New York, Aug. 12, 1955; Vol. 62, pp. 472-476.

Babín, María Teresa: **García Lorca, poeta del teatro.** In **Asomante:** San Juan, 1948; vol. IV, No. 2, pp. 48-57.

———**La metáfora y la imagen en García Lorca.** In **Isla:** San Juan, 1939; vol. I, No. 3, pp. 11-12.

———**Narciso y la esterilidad en la obra de García Lorca.** In **Revista Hispánica Moderna:** New York, 1945; vol. XI, No. 1-2, pp. 48-51.

Barea, Arturo: **Las raíces del lenguage poético de Lorca.** In **Bulletin of Spanish Studies:** Liverpool, 1945; vol. XXII, pp. 3-15.

———**Federico García Lorca — el poeta y el pueblo.** In **Número:** Montevideo, 1951; vol. III, No. 15-17, pp. 229-245.

Barella, Carlos: **Federico García Lorca.** In **Toma y Lee:** Santiago de Chile, 1937; No. 10, pp. 45-58.

Barga, Corpus: **Amor místico y amor pagano.** In **La Nación:** Buenos Aires, April, 1933.

Bentley, Eric: **El poeta en Dublin.** In **Asomante:** San Juan, 1935; vol. VIII, No. 2, pp. 44-58.

Berenguer Carisomo, Arturo: **Las máscaras de Federico García Lorca.** In **Revista de la Asociación Patriótica Española:** Buenos Aires, 1941; vol. XIII, No. 154-158, 161, 162, 165, 168.

Blanco Aguinaga, Carlos: **Emilio Prados — Vida y Obra.** In **Revista Hispánica Moderna:** N.Y., vol. XXVI, July-Oct. 1960; pp. 8-9.

Bly, Robert: **Some Thoughts on Lorca and Rene Char.** In **The Fifties:** Minn., 1959; No. 3, pp. 7-9.

Cahn, Alfredo: **García Lorca en alemán.** In **La Nación:** Buenos Aires, March 3, 1957.

Camp, Jean: **Federico, mon ami.** In **L'Avant Scene, Journal Du Theatre:** Paris, 1954; No. 98, p. 13.

Campuzano, J. R.: **La sensibilidad infantil de García Lorca** In **Letras de México:** México, 1941; vol. III, No. 2, p. 4.

Cano, José Luis: **Recuerdos de Federico Garía Lorca.** In **Temas:** New York, June, 1959; vol. XVIII, No. 104, p. 10.

———**Federico en persona.** In **El Nacional:** Caracas, Dec. 13, 1959.

Carrier, Warren: **Meaning in the Poetry of Lorca.** In **Accent:** Urbana (Ill.), Spring, 1950; vol. X, No. 3, pp. 159-170.

Carrillo Urdanivia, Graciela: **El teatro de Federico García Lorca.** In **Inquietud:** Lima, 1939-1940; vol. I, No. 2 and 3, pp. 43-50, 79-81.

Cassou, Jean: **Coup d'oeil sur le theatre.** In **Les Nouvelles Litteraires:** Paris, Jan. 7, 1939; p. 6.

Chica-Salas, Susan: **Synge y García Lorca — Aproximación de dos mundos poéticos.** In **Revista Hispánica Moderna:** New York, April, 1961; vol. XXVII, No. 2, pp. 128-137.

Chirre Danos, Ricardo: Federico García Lorca. In Sustancia: Tucuman, 1939; vol. I, No. 2, pp. 213-234.

Cirre, José Francisco: El caballo y el toro en la poesía de Federico García Lorca. In Cuadernos Americanos: México, Nov. Dec., 1952.

Couffón, Claude: Federico García Lorca. In Le Figaro Litteraire: Paris, August 16, 1951.

——A Fuentevaqueros, sur le pas de Lorca. In Le Figaro Litteraire: Paris, Dec. 25, 1951.

——Federico García Lorca. In España Libre: New York, June 6 No. 13, 1952.

——Idem. In Nueva Democracia: New York, 1953; vol. XXXIII, No. 3, pp. 64-81.

——Idem. In Anales: Quito, 1953; vol. LXXXI, pp. 297-323.

Crow, J. A.: Bibliografía Hispano-Americana de Federico García Lorca. In Revista Iberoamericana: México, 1939; vol. I, pp. 307-319.

Cuartas Arboleda, Conrado: Símbolo en la poesía de Federico García Lorca. In Universidad de Antioquia: Medellin, 1950; vol. XXIV, pp. 541-547.

Cueva Tamariz, Agustín: Contenido del teatro de García Lorca. In Letras del Ecuador: Quito, 1951; No. 68.

D'Amico, Silvia; Teatro sulla sabbia. In Tribuna: Rome, 1935; vol. IX, No. 18.

Del Río, Angel: Federico García Lorca (1899-1936). In Revista Hispánica Moderna: New York, July-October, 1940; vol. VI, No. 3 and 4, pp. 193-260.

Devoto, Daniel: Notas sobre el elemento tradicional en la obra de García Lorca. In Filología: Buenos Aires, 1950; vol. II, pp. 293-341.

Diego, Gerardo: El teatro musical de Federico García Lorca. In El Imparcial: Madrid, April 16, 1933.

——Idem. In La Prensa: New York, July 3, 1933.

Diez-Canedo, Enrique: El teatro universitario "La Barraca." In El Sol: Madrid, August 22, 1932.

——Panorama del teatro español desde 1914 a 1936. In Hora de España: Valencia, 1938; No. 16, pp. 44-48.

Dionisio, Mario: Lorka em Lisboa. In Itinerario: Mozambique, 1948; vol. VIII, pp. 75-76.

Dudgeon, P.O.: Lo universal en la poesía popular europea: J. M. Synge y Federico García Lorca. In Cursos y conferencias: Buenos Aires, 1939; vol. XV, pp. 765-791.

——J. M. Synge and Federico Garcia Lorca. In Fantasy: London, 1942; No. 26.

Eichelman, Samuel: Lola Membrives repondra obras de Lorca. In Argentina libre: Buenos Aires, Jan. 30, 1941.

Emie, Louis: Federico García Lorca. In Cahiers Du Sud: Marseilles, Jan 1941; pp. 3-16.

Etchepare, Alberto: Margarita Xirgú, esencia y presencia de la España eterna. In Mundo Uruguayo: Montevideo, Jan 11, 1945.

Fallon, Gabriel: **Drama in Action.** In **The Standard Dublin:** Dublin.

Federico García Lorca Exhibit. New York: Columbia University Dramatic Museum. Feb.-March. 1958. Reproduced on Microfilm- N. Y. Public Library *ZC-20.

Fernández Almagro, M.: **El mundo lírico de García Lorca.** In **España:** Madrid, Oct. 13, 1923.

Ferreiro, A.M.: **García Lorca en Montevideo.** In **Poema del Cante Jondo.** Madrid: Ed. Ulises, 1937; pp. 135-147.

———Idem. In **Poema del Cante Jondo.** Santiago de Chile: Ed. Veloz, 1937; pp. 135-147.

Fletcher, John Gould: **Lorca in English.** In **Poetry:** Chicago, Sept. 1940; vol. LVI, pp. 343-347.

García, Romano: (Review) **García Lorca, poeta de la intensidad** by C. Eich. In **Indice de Artes y Letras:** Madrid, 1960; vol. XII, No. 140, p. 23.

García Lorca, Francisco: **El mundo de Federico García Lorca.** In **Meridiano:** Madrid, July, 1947.

———**Federico García Lorca.** In **Columbia Dictionary of Modern Literature.** New York: Columbia Univ. Press, 1947; p. 303.

———**El mundo de Federico García Lorca.** In **El Diario de Hoy:** El Salvador, August 26, 1951.

García Luengo, Eusebio: **Carta sobre revisión del teatro de Federico García Lorca.** In **Indice:** Madrid, March 15, 1952; vol. VII, No. 49.

Gassner, John: **Spanish Drama in the World Theatre.** In Flores, Angel: **Spanish Drama.** N.Y.: Bantam Books, 1962; pp. 1-12.

González Mena, J.: **El teatro de Federico García Lorca.** In **Todo:** México, March 12, 1936.

Honig, Edwin: **Dimensions of Imagery and Action in the Work of García Lorca.** In **Poetry:** Chicago, Oct. 1943; vol. LXIII, No. 1, pp. 32-44.

———**Toward a Lorca Theatre.** In **New Mexico Quarterly:** Alburquerque, 1950; vol. XX, No. 1, pp. 94-98.

Indice Cultural Español: Madrid. Monthly publication of Dirección General de Relaciones Culturales" which contains a record of lectures, exhibits, conferences and literary and artistic events related to Spanish life and culture.

Jarnes, Benjamín: **Letras españolas — García Lorca y su obra.** In **La Nación:** Buenos Aires, May 9, 1937 — Aug. 21, 1938.

Kelin, Fedor: **Federico García Lorca in Russia.** In **La Literatura Internacional:** Moscow, 1943; vol. II, No. 9, pp. 50-55.

Latcham, Ricardo A.: **Notas sobre García Lorca.** In **Atenea:** Concepción (Chile), 1936; vol. XXXVI, No. 136, pp. 13-22.

Lázaro Carreter, Fernando: **Apuntes sobre el teatro de García Lorca.** In **Papeles de Son Armadans:** Madrid-Palma de Mallorca, July, 1960; vol. XVIII, No. 52, pp. 9-33.

Levi, Ezio: **"La Barraca" di García Lorca.** In **Scenario:** Rome, 1934; vol. X.

Lima, Robert: **Federico García Lorca — A Bibliography of his Theatre.** In **La Voz:** New York, October-March issues, 1961-1962.

324 THE THEATRE OF GARCIA LORCA

Little, Stuart W.: **Lorca Cycle Due.** In **New York Herald Tribune:** N.Y., Nov. 8, 1960; p. 14.

Lo Presti, Liliana: **García Lorca en Italia.** In **Alcalá:** Madrid, Nov., 1954.

López Aranguren, Dolores: **Federico García Lorca, su paisaje y sus tipos.** In **América Española:** Cartagena (Colombia), 1941; vol. XI, No. 37, pp. 13-26.

Luisi, Luisa: **El teatro de García Lorca.** In **Ensayos:** Montevideo, 1937; vol. II, No. 16.

Macri, Oreste: **Teatro di Federico García Lorca.** In **La Rassegna d'Italia:** Milan, May, 1946.

McCarthy, Francis B.: **From the Vulgate to Lyric Grandeur.** In **Saturday Review:** New York, April, 1948; p. 23.

Martínez Nadal, R.: **Introduction.** In **Poems.** New York: Oxford Univ. Press, 1939; pp. VII-XXVIII.

Massa, P.: **Federico García Lorca, el romancillo popular y "La Argentinita."** In **Crónica:** Madrid, March 20, 1932.

Mora Guarnido, José: **El juglar.** In **Entregas de la Licorne:** Montevideo, 1957; Vol. IV, "9-10, pp. 147-154.

Nieto Arteta, Luis E.: **Universidad y sexualismo en el teatro — Casona y García Lorca.** In **Revista de las Indias:** Bogotá, Dec. 1941; No. 36.

O'Brien, Robert: **Modern Drama Bibliography.** In **La Voz:** New York, April 1961; pp. 8-9.

Ortiz Saralagui, Juvenal: **Federico García Lorca y Rafael Barradas.** In **Romance:** México, 1940; vol. I, No. 19.

Ostos Gabella, M.: **De mis memorias de la infancia de García Lorca.** In **Alne:** Madrid, Dec. 1954; vol. I, No. 5.

Pandolfi, V.: **García Lorca dalla poesia al dramma.** In **La Rassegna d'Italia:** Milan, Sept.-Oct., 1947.

Papparatti, Giovanni: **Federico García Lorca.** In **Giornale d'Italia:** Rome, Nov. 11, 1952.

Peers, E. Allison: **Aspects of the Art of Lorca.** In **Bulletin of Spanish Studies:** Liverpool, 1944; vol. XXI, No. 81, p. 19.

Perez Marchand, Monelisa Lina: **Apuntes sobre el concepto de la tragedia en la obra dramática de García Lorca.** In **Asomante:** San Juan, 1948; vol. IV, No. 1, pp. 86-96.

Pla y Beltrán: **García Lorca y yo.** In **Crucial:** México, 1952; Vol. III, No. 33.

Proel-Galeria: **Federico García Lorca, el poeta que no se quiere encadenar.** In **La Voz:** Madrid, Feb. 18, 1935.

Ramírez de Arellano: **García Lorca y su positiva influencia sobre nuestro teatro.** In **Ateneo:** Madrid, Aug. 30, 1952.

Rivas Cherif, C.: **Poesía y drama del gran Federico.** In **Excelsior:** Jan. 6, 1957.

Rivas Sainz, Arturo: **García Lorca y la metáfora.** In **Prisma-Revista de Cultura:** Guadalajara, April 1, 1940.

Rosenbaum, Sidonia C.: Federico García Lorca — Bibliografía. In Revista Hispánica Moderna: New York, July-Oct., 1940; vol. VI, No. 3-4, pp. 263-279.

Rubia Barcia, J.: Cómo murió Federico García Lorca. In Nuestra España: Havana, 1939; No. 2.

Rukeyser, Muriel: Lorca in English. In Kenyon Review: Gambier (Ohio), Winter, 1941; pp. 123-127.

Saenz de la Calzada: El teatro universitario español de "La Barraca." In América: México, 1940; pp. 35-37.

Salinas, Pedro: Lorca and the Poetry of Death. In Hopkins Review: Baltimore, 1952; vol. V, pp. 5-12.

Solana, Rafael: Mapa de afluentes en la obra poética de Federico García Lorca. In Letras de México: México, 1938; No. 29, pp. 5-8.

Spitzer, Leo: Nota sobre la poesía y el teatro de Federico García Lorca. In Atenea: Stgo. de Chile, May, 1937.

Starkie, Walter M.: The Demons of García Lorca. In Saturday Review: New York, Nov. 26, 1960; p. 49.

Surchi, Sergio: Sulla natura popolare del teatro di García Lorca. In Sipario: Milan, Jan. 1953; No. 81.

Tiempo, César: Conversaciones con García Lorca en Buenos Aires. In El Nacional: Caracas, July 11, 1957; pp. 8-9.

De Torre, Guillermo: Federico García Lorca (Boceto de un estudio). In Verso y Prosa: Madrid, 1927; vol. I, No. 3.

————F. G. L. — Síntesis de su vida y de su obra. In España Peregrina: México, 1938; vol. XXI, No. 431.

Trias Monje, José: La mujer en el teatro de García Lorca. In Asomante: San Juan, 1945; vol. I, No. 1, pp. 66-68.

Ugo Pane, Remigio: Bibliography of Lorca's Works in English Translation. In Bulletin of Bibliography: Boston, Sept.-Dec., 1950; pp. 71-75.

Uribe-Echevarria, Juan: Notas sobre la poesía y el teatro de Federico García Lorca. In Atenea: Concepción, 1937; vol. XXXVIII, No. 143, pp. 162-177.

————Poesía y teatro de Federico García Lorca. In Universidad: México, 1937; vol. IV, No. 19, 12-15.

Velázquez, Alberto: Poesía y sino trágico de Federico García Lorca. In Revista de Guatemala: Guatemala, 1947; Vol. II, No. 3, pp. 11-44.

Villarejo, José S.: García Lorca, su vida y su obra. In Revista del Ateneo Paraguayo: Asunción, 1940; vol. XIX, No. 19.

Von Kuehnelt-Leddihn, Erick: Letter. In Commonweal: New York, Sept. 23, 1955; vol. LXII, p. 615.

Wilson, Edmund: Federico García Lorca. In Twentieth Century Authors. New York: Wilson Co., 1942.

Williams, William Carlos: Federico García Lorca. In Kenyon Review: Gambier (Ohio), 1939; vol. I, pp. 148-158.

Young, Stark: Prologue. In From Lorca's Theatre. New York: Scribner's, 1941.

Zañartu, S.: Teatro de García Lorca. In El Sur: Concepción, Aug. 22, 1937.

Zardoya, Concha: **La técnica metafórica de Federico García Lorca.**
In **Revista Hispánica Moderna:** New York, 1954; vol. XX, No. 4,
pp. 295-326.
Zdenek, Joseph W.: **La mujer y la frustración en las comedias de
García Lorca.** In **Hispania:** Washington, 1955; vol. XXXVIII, pp.
67-69.

IV. STUDIES

C. ARTICLES (Specific)

EL AMOR DE DON PERLIMPLIN CON BELISA EN SU
JARDIN
— Fergusson, Francis: **"Don Perlimplín" — Lorca's Theatre Poetry.**
In **Kenyon Review:** Gambier, Ohio, Summer 1955; pp. 337-348; In
Ferguson, F.: **The Human Image in Dramatic Literature.** N.Y.,
Doubleday Anchor, 1957; pp. 85-97.
— Fernández Almagro, M.: "El amor de don Perlimplín..." In **El
Sol:** Madrid, April 6, 1933.
— Santana, Emilio: "El amor de don Perlimplín..." In **El Universal:**
Caracas, Sept. 17, 1957.

ASI QUE PASEN CINCO AÑOS
— Arce, Margot: **Palabras de introducción.** In **La Torre:** San Juan,
1955; Vol. III, No. 9, pp. 175-178.
— Aub, Max: **Nota sobre "Así que pasen cinco años."** In **Hora de
España:** Valencia, 1937; No. 11, pp. 67-74.
— Davila, Carlos: **García Lorca en Nueva York.** In **Revista Americana:** N. Y., 1945; Vol. II, pp. 158-159.
— Granell, Eugene F.: **Esquema interpretativo.** In **La Torre:** San
Juan, 1955; Vol. III, No. 9, pp. 178-188.
— **"If Five Years Pass."** In **La Prensa:** N.Y., April 9, 1954.
— Xiráu, Ramón: **"Así que pasen cinco años."** In **Prometeus:** Mexico,
March 1952; Vol. II, No. 2.

BODAS DE SANGRE
— A. C.: **"Bodas de sangre."** In **A.B.C.:** Madrid, March 9, 1933.
— Atkinson, Brooks: **"Bitter Oleander."** In **The New York Times:**
N.Y., Feb. 12, 1935.
— Atkinson, Brooks: **Theatre-García Lorca.** In **The New York Times:**
N.Y., April 1, 1958.
— Barnes, Robert: **The Fusion of Poetry and Drama in "Blood Wedding."** In **Modern Drama:** Univ. of Kansas, Spring 1960; Vol. II,
No. 4, pp. 395-402.
— Baus, F.: **Apreciación sobre "Bodas de sangre."** In **El Universal:**
Caracas, April 30, 1939; pp. 9, 14.
— **"Bodas de sangre."** In **Indice Literario:** Madrid, 1933; Vol. II, pp.
105-108.
— **"Bodas de sangre."** In **Indice Literario:** Madrid, 1936; Vol. V, No.
37, pp. 25-31.
— **"Bodas de sangre."** In **Suma Bibliográfica:** Mexico, 1948; Vol. III,
III, p. 449.
— **"Bodas de sangre"** bajo el título **"Bitter Oleander."** In **La Prensa:**
N.Y., Feb. 8 and 13, 1935.
— **"Bodas de sangre"** gana admiradores. In **La Prensa:** N.Y., Feb. 22,
1935.

— Brion, M.: ("Noces de sang"). In Les Nouvelles Litteraires: Paris, July 4, 1936.
— Brown, J. M.: "Bitter Oleander." In The New York Evening Post: N.Y., Feb. 12, 1935.
— D.F.: "Blood Wedding." In Saturday Review of Literature: N.Y., 1940; Vol. XXI, p. 21.
— Du Gard, M. M.: "Noces de sang." In Les Nouvelles Litteraires: Paris, June 11, 1938.
— E. A.: "Bodas de sangre." In Hoja Literaria: Madrid, March 1933; p. 9.
— E.F.R.: Margarita Xirgú. In Capitulo: Buenos Aires, 1937; Vol. I, No. 1, pp. 47-49.
— Fernández Almagro, M.: ("Bodas de Sangre"). In El Sol: Madrid, March 6, 1933.
— Fletcher, J. G. ("Blood Wedding"). In Poetry: Chicago, 1940; Vol. LXIV, p. 343.
— García Lorca, Francisco: From Granada to Bleeker Street. In The New York Times: N.Y., January 30, 1949; pp. 1, 3.
— Hammond, P.: "Bitter Oleander." In The New York Herald Tribune: N.Y., Feb. 12, 1935.
— Isaacs, Edith J. R.: "Bitter Oleander." In Theatre Arts Monthly: N.Y., 1935; Vol. XIX, pp. 248, 253
— J.E.A.: "Bodas de sangre" en francés In Criterio: Buenos Aires, 1938; Vol. XXXV, pp. 354-355, 401-402.
— J.E.A.: Del elogio inmoderado — ("Bodas de sangre" como film). In Criterio: Buenos Aires, 1938; Vol. XXXIV.
— Kreymborg, A.: "Blood Wedding". In The Living Age: Boston, 1940; Vol. CCCLXIII, p. 95.
— Lewis, Allan: The Folklore Theatre — Garcia Lorca. In Contemporary Theatre, N.Y.: Crown, 1962.
— Lockridge, R.: "Bitter Oleander." In The New York Sun: N.Y., Feb. 12, 1935.
— Mantle, Burns: "Bitter Oleander." In The New York Daily News: N.Y., Feb. 13, 1935.
— "Marriage of Blood." In The New Statesman: London, 1939; Vol. XVII, p. 458.
— Massa, P.: El poeta García Lorca y su tragedia "Bodas de sangre." In Crónica: Madrid, April 9, 1933.
— Merac, R.: "Noces de sang." In Gringoire: Paris, Jan. 26, 1939.
— Morby, Edwin.: García Lorca in Sweden. In Hispanic Review: Philadelphia, 1946; Vol. XIV, pp. 38-46.
— "Noces de sang" de F.G.L. au Studio des Champs Elysees. In Theatre de France: Paris, 1953; Vol. II.
— Pacheco, C.: "Bodas de sangre." In Criterio: Buenos Aires, 1934.
— Pego, A.: Crónica de norteamérica — Ni Benavente ni García Lorca. In La Vanguardia: Barcelona, March 13, 1935.
— Queiroz, Rafael: "Bodas de sangre." In Leitura: Rio de Janeiro, 1944; Vol. II, No. 15.
— Riley, E. C.: ("Bodas de sangre"). In Clavileño: Madrid, Jan.-Feb. 1951; Vol. II, No. 7, pp. 8-12.
— Ruiz Vilaplana: Recuerdos de F.G.L. — "Bodas de sangre" en París. In Mi Revista: Barcelona, 1938; Vol. III, No. 43.
— Salinas, Pedro: El teatro de Federico García Lorca. In Indice Literario: Madrid, 1936; Vol. V, No. 43, pp. 25-31.

— Scherder, Juan German: "Bodas de sangre" en Paris. In Indice de Artes y Letras: Madrid, 1952; Vol. VII, No. 50.
— Schmidt, Augusto Fed.: Mauriac, Lorca e a eternidade do theatro. In Revista do Brasil: Rio de Janeiro, 1938; Vol. I, No. 3, pp. 225-230.
— Taubman, Howard: Struggle to Survive. In The New York Times: N.Y., May 21, 1961.
— Young, Stark: ("Bitter Oleander"). In The New Republic: N.Y., 1935; Vol. LXXXII, p. 78.

LA CASA DE BERNARDA ALBA
— Altazor: "La casa de Bernarda Alba" de F.G.L. por "La Caratula." In Indice de Artes y Letras: Madrid, 1950; Vol. VI, No. 28.
— Bentley, Eric: El poeta en Dublin. In Asomante: San Juan, April-June, 1953; Vol. VIII, No. 2.
— Blanco Amor, José: Dice Margarita Xirgú: "La casa de Bernarda Alba" es la mejor obra de García Lorca. In España Republicana: La Plata, Arg., March 10, 1945.
— "La casa de Bernarda Alba." In Insula: Buenos Aires, 1945; vol. III.
— "La casa de Bernarda Alba." In Negro Sobre Blanco: Buenos Aires, 1945; Vol. III, No. 10.
— Casey, Calvert: Notes on "La casa de Bernarda Alba." Unpublished typescript accompanying the program of the 1957 production in N.Y. by Nuevo Círculo Dramático.
— Chica Salas, Francisca: Margarita Xirgú en "La casa de Bernarda Alba." In Saitabi: Valencia, 1944; Vol. V, No. 52, pp. 48-49.
— De la Guardia, Alfredo: "La casa de Bernarda Alba." In Latitud: Buenos Aires, 1945; Vol. I, No. 3.
— Dughera, Eduardo A.: Un aspecto de "La casa de Bernarda Alba." In Institute of Social Publications No. 66: Santa Fe, 1953.
— Eichelbaum, S.: Margarita Xirgú reaparecerá con la última obra de Lorca. In Argentina Libre: Buenos Aires, Sept. 26, 1940.
— Falangistas y frailes españoles prohiben representación teatral de García Lorca. In España Libre: N.Y., April 22, 1949.
— García Lorca en la escena soviética. In Boletín de Información URSS: Moscow, March 15, 1960; Vol. XVII, No. 6, pp. 32-33.
— Gardella, Kay: End of the Line. In The New York Daily News: N. Y., June 8, 1960; p. 75.
— "The House of Bernarda Alba." In TV Guide Magazine: Radnor, Pa., June 4-10, 1960; Vol. VIII, No. 23, p. A-35.
— Salazar, Adolfo: Un drama inédito de García Lorca. In Carteles: Havana, April 10, 1938; In El Universal: Caracas, Sept. 11, 1938.
— Shanley, John P.: García Lorca Work on "Play of the Week." In The New York Times: June 7, 1960.

DOÑA ROSITA LA SOLTERA O EL LENGUAJE DE LAS FLORES
— Bianco, José: García Lorca en El Odeon. In Sur: Buenos Aires, 1937; Vol. VII, No. 32, pp. 75-80.
— Blanco Amor, Eduardo: Nueva obra teatral de García Lorca. In Revista de las Indias: Bogota, 1937; Vol. I, No. 5, pp. 46-49.
— "Doña Rosita la soltera." In El Sol: Madrid, May 23, 1935.
— "Doña Rosita ou le lenguage des fleurs" au theatre des noctambules. In Theatre de France: Paris, 1953; Vol. III, pp. 120-122.

— Espina, A.: **Estreno de la última obra de García Lorca en El Principal Palace de Barcelona.** In El Sol: Madrid, Dec. 15, 1935.
— J. E. A.: **La verdad sobre García Lorca a propósito de "Doña Rosita la soltera."** In Criterio: Buenos Aires, 1937; Vol. XXXII, No. 480, 481, pp. 43-45, 63-65.
— Iduarte, Andrés: **F.G.L. en New York.** In El Mundo: N.Y., April 19, 1949.
— Linares, J.: ("**Doña Rosita la soltera**"). In El Hogar: Buenos Aires, May 14, 1937.
— Massa, Pedro: **Estreno de "Doña Rosita la soltera"—nueva obra de García Lorca interpretada por M. Xirgú.** In Crónica: Madrid, 1935.
— Vagabond Jim: **"Doña Rosita la soltera."** In Criterio: Buenos Aires, 1945; Vol. XVIII, pp. 440-441.

EL MALEFICIO DE LA MARIPOSA
— De la Guardia, Alfredo: **La primera obra dramática de Federico García Lorca.** In La Nación: Buenos Aires, Nov. 17, 1940.
— Fernández Almagro, Melchor: **El primer estreno de Federico García Lorca.** In A.B.C.: Madrid, June 12-13, 1952.

MARIANA PINEDA
— Ayala, F.: **Un drama de García Lorca — "Mariana Pineda."** In La Gaceta Litteraria: Madrid, July 1, 1927; No. 13.
— Ayala, F.: **"Mariana Pineda."** In La Gaceta Literaria: Madrid, Oct. 15, 1927; No. 20.
— Diez-Canedo, E.: **"Mariana Pineda," de García Lorca, en el Fontalba.** In El Sol: Madrid, Oct. 13, 1927.
— Fernández Almagro, M.: **"Mariana Pineda."** In La Voz: Madrid, Oct. 13, 1927.
— Floridor.: **"Mariana Pineda."** In A.B.C.: Madrid, Oct. 13, 1927.
— García Lorca y su obra **"Mariana Pineda."** In España Libre: N.Y., 1942; Vol. IV, No. 14.
— Lavandero, R.: **La heroína y su poeta.** In Verdades: San Juan, Jan. 1937; pp. 20-21.
— M.R.C.: **"Mariana Pineda."** In La Vanguardia: Barcelona, June 26, 1927.
— Machado, A.: **"Mariana Pineda."** In La Libertad: Madrid, Oct. 13, 1927.
— **"Mariana Pineda."** In The Times Literary Supplement: London, August 9, 1938.
— Matas Graupera, Julio: **"Mariana Pineda" en la Universidad de la Habana.** In Vida Universitaria: Havana, Sept. 1950.
— R. G.: **Representación de "Mariana Pineda."** In Hora de España: Valencia, 1937; No. 8, pp. 75-76.

EL RETABLILLO DE DON CRISTOBAL
— A.S.: **Vitrina del libro — Cinco farsas breves.** In España Libre: N.Y., Aug. 20, 1954.
— Guibourg, A.: **(El retablillo de don Cristóbal).** In Criterio: Buenos Aires, March 26, 1934.

TITERES RE CACHIPORRA: TRAGICOMEDIA DE DON CRISTOBAL Y LA SEÑA ROSITA
— De Torre, Guillermo: **Federico García Lorca y sus orígenes dramáticos.** In Cinco Farsas Breves. Buenos Aires: Losada, 1953; In Clavileño: Madrid.

330   THE THEATRE OF GARCIA LORCA

— Guerrero Zamora, Juan: **Una obra idédita de Federico García Lorca.**
In **Raíz:** Madrid, 1948-1949; No. 3-4.
— Mane, Bernardo: **Retablillo titiritero bajo el cielo español.** In **La
Prensa:** Buenos Aires, Nov. 14, 1954.
— Mora Guarnido, J.: **Crónicas granadinas. El teatro cachiporra de
Andalucía.** In **El Sol:** Madrid, Jan. 18, 1923.

YERMA
— A. C.: **"Yerma."** In **A.B.C.:** Madrid, Dec. 30, 1954.
— Avecilla, C. R.: **"Yerma."** In **El Pueblo:** Madrid, Jan. 1, 1935.
— Bárcenas, Angel: **García Lorca, su obra "Yerma" y una edición de
homenaje.** In **La Nación:** Buenos Aires, Oct. 5, 1952.
— Barga, Corpus: **Tragicomedia. "Yerma" y la política.** In **Diario de
Madrid:** Madrid, Jan. 7, 1935; In **Repertorio Americano:** Costa
Rica, Feb. 23, 1935.
— Carrillo Urdanivia, Graciela: **"Yerma" y su obsesión de inmorta-
lidad.** In **Inquietud:** Lima, 1940; Vol. I, No. 3, pp. 79-81.
— Colecchia, Frances: **El teatro de García Lorca visto a través de su
drama poético "Yerma."** In **Estudios, Revista de Cultura Hispánica:**
Duquesne Univ., 1952; Vol. I, No. 3, pp. 9-17.
— Correa, Gustavo: **"Yerma." Estudios estilísticos.** In **Revista de las
Indias:** Bogotá, 1949; Vol. XXXV, No. 109, pp. 11-63.
— Diez-Canedo, E.: **Un poeta dramático.** In **La Voz:** Madrid, Dec. 31,
1934.
— Espina, Antonio: **"Yerma" triunfa en París.** In **España Republi-
cana:** La Plata, Arg., July 10, 1948.
— Fernández Almagro, M.: **"Yerma."** In **El Sol:** Madrid, Dec. 30,
1934.
— García Lorca, Francisco: **"Yerma" dans l'oeuvre de Federico García
Lorca.** In **L'Avant-Scene:** Paris, 1954; No. 98.
— García Luengo, Eusebio: **"Yerma" y el teatro de Lorca.** In **Letra:**
Madrid, 1935; No. 1.
— Guibert, F.: **Margarita Xirgú en "Yerma."** In **Capitulo:** Buenos
Aires, 1937; Vol. I, No. 1, p. 46.
— Haro, E.: **("Yerma").** In **La Libertad:** Madrid, Dec. 30, 1934.
— J.E.A.: **"Yerma," un drama que da náuseas.** In **Criterio:** Buenos
Aires, 1937; Vol. XXXIII, pp. 259-261.
— Jarnes, Benjamín: **"Yerma."** In **La Vanguardia:** Barcelona, Dec.
20, 1936.
— Kemp, Robert: **El teatro en París — "Yerma" de Federico García
Lorca.** In **El Reproductor Campechano:** Campeche, Mexico, 1948;
Vol. V, No. 4, pp. 15-17.
— Marín Alcalde, A.: **("Yerma").** In **Ahora:** Madrid, Dec. 21, 1934.
— Mori, A.: **Una jornada gloriosa en El Español.** In **El Liberal:** Ma-
drid, Dec. 30, 1934.
— Novas Calvo, L.: **"Yerma."** In **Revista Cubana:** Havana, 1935;
Vol. I, pp. 266-269.
— Obregon, A.: **"Yerma".** In **Diario de Madrid:** Madrid, Dec. 31,
1934.
— Pedro, Valentín: **"Yerma."** In **El Hogar:** Buenos Aires, March 15,
1935.
— Perez de la Ossa, H.: **El teatro.** In **Revista de Estudios Hispánicos:**
Madrid, 1935; Vol. I, pp. 66-68.

— Rosell, A.: **Shakespeare y García Lorca, víctimas de los taquígrafos.** In **Pan:** Buenos Aires, 1937; Vol. III, No. 140, pp. 17, 52.
— Scheiner, Rosa: **Acotaciones al margen de "Yerma,"** de García Lorca. In **Claridad:** Buenos Aires, 1937; Vol. XVI, No. 315.
— Sender, R. J.: **El poeta en la escena.** In **La Libertad:** Madrid, Jan. 5, 1935.
— ("Yerma"). In **El Sol:** Madrid, Jan. 31, 1935.
— ("Yerma."). In **El Sol:** Madrid, March 12, and 13, 1935.
— "Yerma" et la critique. In **L'Avant-Scene:** Paris, 1954; No. 98.

LA ZAPATERA PRODIGIOSA
— Andrenio.: ("La Zapatera Prodigiosa"). In **La Voz:** Madrid, Dec. 25, 1930.
— Baralt, Luis A.: ("La Zapatera Prodigiosa"). In **Dirección de Cultura FEU:** Havana, May 20, 1954; pp. 25-26.
— Diez-Canedo, E.: ("La Zapatera Prodigiosa"). In **El Sol:** Madrid, Dec. 25, 1930. In **La Voz:** Madrid, March 19, 1935.
— Espinosa, Agustín: ("La Zapatera Prodigiosa"). In **El Sol:** Madrid, March 19, 1935.
— F.: **"La Zapatera Prodigiosa."** In **A.B.C.:** Madrid, March 19, 1935.
— Fernández Almagro, M.: ("La Zapatera Prodigiosa"). In **La Voz:** Madrid, Dec. 25, 1930. In **Ya:** Madrid, March 19, 1935.
— Gómez, Pedro: **"La Zapatera Prodigiosa."** In **Galería:** Santiago de Cuba, 1957; Vol. I, No. 3, pp. 12-13.
— González Ruano, C.: **Bajo la sonrisa de "La Zapatera Prodigiosa."** In **Crónica:** Buenos Aires, Jan. 11, 1930.
— Guibourg, E.: **"La Zapatera,"** fórmula teatral. In **Noticias Gráficas:** Buenos Aires, Dec. 4, 1933.
— Hale, L.: ("La Zapatera Prodigiosa" — **Transmission by the B. B.C.).** In **The Observer:** London, July 27, 1954.
— Helman, Edith F.: **Introduction.** In **La Zapatera Prodigiosa.** N.Y.: W. W. Norton, 1952.
— Mazzara, Richard A.: **Dramatic Variations On Themes of "El sombrero de tres picos"** — **"La Zapatera Prodigiosa" and "Una viuda difícil."** In **Hispania:** Washington, D.C., May 1958; Vol. XLI, No. 2, pp. 186-189.
— Obregón, A.: **"La Zapatera Prodigiosa"** de García Lorca. In **Diario de Madrid:** Madrid, March 19, 1935.
— Tezanos Pinto, Fausto: **"La Zapatera Prodigiosa"** de F.G.L. In **Criterio:** Buenos Aires, Dec. 1933.
— ("La Zapatera Prodigiosa"). In **Revista Hispánica Moderna:** N.Y., 1954; Vol. XX, No. 1-2.

INDEX

INDEX

Adams, Mildred 18
Aesop 56
Albeniz, Isaac 44, 67
Alberti, Rafael 10, 26, 27, 37, 300
Aldunate-Phillips, Arturo 230
Alfonso XIII 27
All Quiet on the Western Front 20
Alonso, Damaso 10, 18, 47
Altolaguirre, Manuel 46
Amalia 108
Amor brujo, El 34
Amor de don Perlimplin con Belisa
  16, 21, 33, 95, 141-156, 173, 199,
  265, 266, 282, 291-300.
Amorin 35
Apollinaire, G. vii
"Argentinita, La" 19, 34, 37, 55, 69,
  300
Aristophanes 56
Arquitectura del cante jondo 29, 31
Artesani-Lyons, R. 195
Asi que pasen cinco años 21, 22, 29,
  48, 125, 157-187, 189, 218, 225,
  243, 261, 265, 266, 291-300.
Auclair, Marcelle 32, 37
Auden, W. H. vii
Azaña, Manuel 29, 38, 46
Azcoaga 41
Aznar, Admiral 27
Azorin 8

Babin, Maria Teresa 169, 194
Bagaria, Luis 48
Balada de la placeta 10
Baldres, Alfredo 68
Ballagas, Emilio 24
Barcena, Catalina 55
Barea, Arturo 1, 191
Barnes, Robert 192
Baroja, Pio 8
"Barraca, La" 30, 31, 32, 33, 35, 69,
  95, 189
Barradas, Rafael 55, 299
Barrie, J. M. 12
Baty, Gaston 32
Beckett, Samuel 186
Bedard, B. J. ix
Belitt, Ben 18, 20, 44
Bello, Pepin 244
Benavente, Jacinto 55
Benitez Inglott, M. 44
Benumeya, Gil 28
Berenguer 27
Bestia hermosa, La 39

Bibliography 301
Bizet, Georges 216
Blanco Amor 35
Blood of the Poet 185
Bodas de sangre 32, 33, 34, 35, 36,
  39, 41, 42, 45, 119, 124, 161, 188-
  216, 217, 218, 219, 220, 221, 225,
  227, 241, 250, 258, 263, 264, 265,
  266, 282, 291-300.
Bola negra, La 39
Bouvet 243
Brenan, Gerald 49, 51
Brewster, Townsend viii
Brickell, Hershell 18
Browning, Robert vii
Buñuel, Luis 8, 21
Burgos Lecea 41
Burlador de Sevilla, El 32
Burmann 217, 241

Caballero de Olmedo, El 32
Calderon de la Barca, Pedro 30, 31,
  32, 55, 86, 219
Calvo Sotelo, Jose 48
Campbell, Roy 1, 37
Campins, General 49
Cancion de cuna 65, 112
Canciones 14
"Cante jondo" 29
Canto primitivo andaluz, El 35
Capek, Karel 56
Carmen 216
Carrier, Warren 213
Casa de Bernarda Alba, La 39, 48,
  68, 119, 161, 218, 263-287, 291-300.
Casona, Alejandro 30, 42
Cernuda, Luis 46
Cervantes, Miguel de 4, 30, 32, 36,
  56, 68, 86, 122
Cetina 56
Chabas, Juan 36, 218
Chabrol, Jean Pierre 50, 51
Christina of Hapsburg-Lorraine 141
Claudel, Paul vii
Clorinda 76
"Clubs teatrales" 33, 41, 141, 142
Cocteau, Jacques 160, 185
Cole, Toby 121
Columbia University 17, 18, 19
Couffon, Claude 50, 265
Count of Yebes 48
Crucifixion 44
Cueva de Salamanca, La 30, 32
cummings, e.e. vii

335

Cyrano de Bergerac 154
Czerny 249
Da Cal, Ernesto 30
Dali, Ana Maria 284
Dali, Salvador 8, 9, 10, 15, 16, 21, 96, 159, 244, 299
Dama boba, La 34
Dario, Ruben 10, 35
Debussy, Claude 67
De Falla, Manuel 6, 34, 67, 68, 299
Degollacion del Bautista, La 24
De la Guardia, Alfredo 56, 190
De los Rios, Fernando 7, 8, 17, 29, 30
De los Rios, Giner 8
De los Rios Giner, Laura 30, 69
Del Rio, Angel 18, 19, 21, 22, 141
De M. y Campos, Armando 245
De Onis, Federico 17, 18
Destruccion de Sodoma 39
De Torre, Guillermo 45, 48, 67, 68
De Ucelay, Pura 33, 41, 48
Diaz, Carmen 39
Diaz de Artigas, Josefina 32, 188
Diego, Gerardo 10, 32, 300
Diez Canedo, Enrique 41, 98
Divan del Tamarit, El 29, 45
Dolores 3, 4
Dominquez Berrueta, M. 6
Don Quixote 4, 5, 65
Doña Rosita la soltera 39, 40, 41, 43, 44, 161, 218, 241-262, 266, 291-300
Donato, Magda 16
Doncella, el marinero y el estudiante, La 16, 21, 160, 187
Dos habladores, Los 68
Dos Passos, John 20
Drama de las hijas de Loth, El 39
Dreams of My Cousin Aurelia, The 40
Dudgeon, Patrick O. 189
Duende 24-26, 70
Duprey, Richard A. ix
Elegia 218
Eliot, T.S. vii, 20
Epitafio a Isaac Albeniz 45
Escalera, Jose 97

Ferdinand VII 97
Fergusson, Francis 149
Fernandez Montesinos, Manuel 49
Ferrant, Angel 69, 70
Ferreiro, A. M. 31
Figaro 70

Flores, Angel 20
Florit, Eugenio ix
Franco, Francisco 38, 48
Fry, Christopher vii
Fuenteovejuna 32
Gacela de la huida 45
Gallo 15
Garcia, Enrique 4
Garcia, Federico 2
Garcia Lorca, Francisco ix, 1, 2, 3, 40, 189, 244
Garcia Lorca, Isabel 2, 30, 38, 68
Garcia Luengo, E. 161
Garcia Maroto, Gabriel 47, 56
Garcia Morejon, Julio ix
Gasch, Sebastian 16
Gassner, John 143
Genet, Jean 186
Gimenez Caballero, Ernesto 16, 69
Goethe 26
Goldoni, Carlo 12
Gomez de la Serna 160
Gomez, Jose 68
Gongora, Luis de 15
Gonzalez Carbalho 35
Graham-Lujan, James 40
Guarda cuidadosa, La 30, 32
Guillen, Jorge 48
Guillen, Nicholas 24
Hermosa, La 41
Hoffsmanthal, Hugo von vii
Hojas de hierba 20
Honig, Edwin 1, 11, 35, 124, 172, 199, 219
Hugo, Victor 4, 110
Huida de Nueva York 23
Ibsen, Henryk 12
Iguera Brothers 30
Imagen poetica de don Luis de Gongora 15, 31, 35
Imaginacion, inspiracion y evasion en la poesia 17, 20
Impresiones y paisajes 6
"Institucion libre de enseñanza" 8
Ionesco, Eugene 186
Jardin de las morenas, El 12
Jarnes, Benjamin 41
Javert, Inspector 110
Jerusalem Liberated 76
Jimenez, Alberto 8
Jimenez, Juan Ramon 8, 9, 12, 34, 41, 42, 300
Junco, Alfonso 51

Keaton, Buster 123
Kipling, Rudyard 56
L'Amic de les Arts 16
La Fontaine 56
La luna pudo detenerse al fin 24
Lanz, Hermenegildo 67
Lenormand 160
Lerroux, Alejandro 38
Les Miserables 110
Levi, Ezio 31
Lewisohn, Irene 32
Libro de poemas 12
Liliom 205
Linares Rivas 56
Llanto por Ignacio Sanchez Mejias 37, 42, 43
Lloyd, A. L. 2
Lluch Garin, Felipe 69
Lope de Vega 30, 32, 34, 41, 55, 56, 71, 86, 139, 140, 219
Lo que canta una ciudad de noviembre a noviembre 24, 35
Lorca, Doña Vicenta 2

Machado, Antonio 9
MacGregor, Robert ix
MacLeish, Archibald vii
Madariaga, Salvador 213
Maeterlinck, Maurice 56
Maleficio de la mariposa, El 11, 12, 55-66, 67, 82, 98, 100, 104, 123, 140, 141, 142, 161, 266, 291-300
Manhattan Transfer 20
Mariana Pineda 15, 16, 34, 45, 96-119, 120, 123, 140, 161, 218, 242, 243, 244, 260, 266, 282, 291-300
Marmol, Jose 108
Martinez Anido, Severiano 141
Martinez Nadal, R. 3, 17
Martinez Sierra, Gregorio 8, 11, 12, 55, 57, 98, 112, 300
Medina, Lola 5
Membrives, Lola 31, 34, 35, 42, 120
Mendez, Concha 46
Menendez Pidal, Ramon 122
Menor de las comedias, La 11
Merce, Antonia (see "La Argentinita")
Midsummer Night's Dream 189
Mignoni 55
Misterio de los Reyes Magos 68
Moliere 12, 71, 140
Molina, Jose 68
Molnar, Ferenc 204

Mora Guarnido, Jose 40, 56, 57, 96, 98, 186
Morales, Felipe 47, 90, 161, 243
Moreno Villa, Jose 243, 244
Morla Lynch, Carlos 25, 37, 45, 48, 69, 159, 177, 206, 244, 264
Mussolini 27

Nanas infantiles, Las 20, 24, 35
Neruda Pablo 35, 44, 45
Nieto Pena 41
Niña que riega el albahaca y el principe pregunton, La 67, 69
Nocturno del Generalife 25
Nocturno del hueco 45
Novo, Salvador 47, 157

Ocampo, Victoria 35
O'Connell, Richard L. 40
Oda a Salvador Dali 14
Oda a Walt Whitman 20, 33
Oda al Rey de Harlem 33
Oliver, Eusebio 48
Ontañon, Santiago 30, 141
Ortega 34
Ortega y Gasset 8
Ortiz, Manuel Angeles 30
Ortiz Saralegui, Juvenal 68, 69

Paganini 26
Palencia, Benjamin 30
Paseo de Buster Keaton, El 14, 15, 21, 160, 187
Pedrell 67
Pedrosa, Ramon 97
Pequeño poema infinito 24
Pequeño vals vienes 23
Peralta, Manuel 97
Perez de Ayala, Ramon 8, 9
Pi y Margall, Francisco 97
Piccaso, Pablo 120
Pineda, Mariana 96, 98
Pinter, Harold 186
Poema del cante jondo 20, 28
Poeta en Nueva York, El 19, 21
Poetica 32
Ponce de Leon 30
Pound, Ezra vii
Prats, Alardo 39, 43, 90, 242
Prevost, Jean 31, 32
Prieto, Miguel 30, 299
Primeras canciones 46
Primo de Rivera 27, 142
Publico, El 21, 23, 29, 187, 189
Puck 70

Quevedo 56
Quimera 16, 21, 160, 187
Quintero Brothers 55
Ravel, Maurice 67
Realidad y el deseo, La 46
Reinhardt, Max 33
Remarque, Eric Maria 20
"Residencia de estudiantes" 8, 9, 10, 11, 12, 17, 28, 34, 43
Residencia en la tierra 44
Retablillo de don Cristobal, El 29, 43, 87-95, 156, 291-300
Revista de Occidente 14, 16, 28
Reyerta de gitanos 14
Reyes, Alfonso 34, 47
Ricasens Siches 41
Riders of the Sea 189
Rivas Cherif, Cipriano 16, 39, 50, 120, 141, 217, 241, 300
Robles, Gil 38, 46
Rodriguez Espinosa, A. 3
Rodriguez Rapun, Rafael 30
Rolan, Feliciano 41
Romancero gitano 14, 16, 17, 37, 44, 241
Romeo and Juliet 23
Rosales Brothers 49, 52
Rostand, Edmond 56, 154
Ruiz Alonso, Ramon 51
Sacrificio de Ifigenia, El 29
Saint John of the Cross 65
Saint Teresa of Avila 40, 65
Salazar, Adolfo 24, 42
Salinas, Pedro 10, 300
Sanchez, Alberto 30
Sanchez, Roberto 263
Sanchez Mejias, Ignacio 18, 36
Sanchez Vocisa, Joaquin 30
Sangre no tiene voz, La 39
Schonberg, Jean Luis 51
School for Scandal, The 83
Segovia, Andres 18
Seis poemas gallegos 43
Semana santa en Granada 47
Shakespeare, William 7, 12, 70, 189
Shaw, G. B. 12
Sheridan, Richard 83
Sobejano, Gonzalo ix
Solana, Rafael 21
Soldiers Who Do Not Want To Go To War, The 40
Son de negros en Cuba 24
Soto de Rojas 24

Starkie, Walter ix
Strauss, Joann 157
Suite de los espejos 12
Suñer, Serrano 51
Swan, Michael 5, 25
Synge, J. M. 189
Tancredo 76
Tasso, Torquato 76
"Teatro de la Anfistora" 41, 48, 157, 161
"Teatro del Pueblo" 30
"Teatro Universitario" 30
Teoria y juego del duende 24, 35
Tierra baldia 20
Tierra y luna 43
Tirso de Molina 30
Titeres de Cachiporra, Los 16, 67-95
Torres, Manuel 25
Torres Martinez, Cesar 48
Torrijos, General 108
Tragedia de ensueño 190
Tragicomedia de don Cristobal y la seña Rosita 69-87, 88, 93, 94, 156
Trend, J. B. 19

Ugarte, Eduardo 30, 31
Unamuno, Miguel de 9
Valle-Inclan, Ramon 42, 190
Valdes 52
Vals de las ramas 23
Vazquez Ocaña, F. 1, 18, 29, 39, 157
Vicente, Gil vii
Vida es sueño, La 32

Wasteland, The 20
Weissberger, Jose 32, 42
Whitman, Walt 20, 23
Williams, William Carlos vii
Xirgu, Margarita 15, 28, 31, 37, 45, 47, 69, 96, 120, 217, 230, 241, 263, 300
Yeats, W. B. vii
Yerma 36, 37, 39, 41, 42, 43, 119, 122, 125, 161, 217-240, 241, 242, 258, 260, 263, 266, 291-300

Zapatera Prodigiosa, La 14, 20, 21, 28, 33, 34, 42, 66, 95, 120-140, 142, 143, 145, 155, 156, 218, 225, 248, 282, 291-300
Zorrilla y Moral 7

THE THEATRE OF GARCIA LORCA

By Robert Lima

Out of the complexity of Twentieth Century Spain has emerged a most universal and unique creative talent—Federico García Lorca — whose reputation has justifiably risen, since the days before his tragic death, to epitomize the resurgence of Spanish drama in the modern idiom. García Lorca was, above all, the complete man of the theatre, his extensive participation therein ranging from actor, puppeteer and designer to director, producer and playwright. It was in his capacity as dramatist that Lorca mixed his myriad powers of poet, musician and artist, consistently and faithfully capturing the feeling of what it means to be a man living in contemporary society and particularly a Spaniard strapped to a strict spiritual and emotional traditionalism. Lorca grasps it with rare insight and telescopes this human condition in a drama that is charged with critical, passionate and moving expression. His drama is one of sheer theatricality.

Now, for the first time, there is a complete study of the theatre of García Lorca. Beginning with a comprehensive biographical chapter which serves as a cyclorama to the analysis of the plays, placing each within the scope of Lorca's growth, influences and psychology, Robert Lima

(Continued on back flap)